PRAISE FOR <u>KNOW-HOW</u>

"Uniquely Charan. Practical, insightful, application-oriented, and full of wisdom. Read it and then refer to it frequently to enrich your career. A real treasure."
—Larry Bossidy, retired chairman and CEO of Honeywell International
and coauthor of *Execution* and *Confronting Reality*

"*Know-How* is the distilled wisdom of one of our era's most insightful business minds. How do you achieve great business performance? Ram Charan knows how."
—Geoffrey Colvin, editor-at-large, *Fortune* magazine

"Ram Charan cuts through the fog and "mystique of the leader" with bold, fresh insights into the real substance of business leadership. What is truly pathbreaking is *Know-How*'s integration of the eight skills for running a business with the personal and psychological traits of the successful leader. It is the must-have book if you want to differentiate yourself from the pack."
—Bill Conaty, senior vice president, human resources, General Electric

"What Peter Drucker's *The Practice of Management* and *The Effective Executive* were to the 20th-century industrial age, Ram Charan's *Know-How* is to the 21st-century global digital knowledge worker age. Brilliant, immensely practical, and comprehensive—with almost self-evident prophetic wisdom. But, as we all know, what is common sense is seldom common practice."
—Stephen R. Covey, author of *The 7 Habits of Highly Effective People*
and *The 8th Habit*

"*Know-How* brings the complex subject of business leadership down-to-earth with practical advice on what you really need to know to run a business."
—Michael J. Critelli, chairman and CEO, Pitney Bowes

"*Know-How* puts to rest a lot of myths and false assumptions about the job of a leader. In a commonsense, practical way, it provides eight how-tos that are the foundation of leadership. *Know-How* is a breakthrough book for leaders and those who aspire to a leadership job."
—James M. Kilts, Centerview Partners, former chairman and CEO of Gillette

"If you believe (as I do) that 'leaders are made,' or more precisely, choose to lead and to develop their skills as leaders, then you will find Ram Charan's very practical book on the eight 'know-hows' that are the foundation for leadership performance and success a very worthwhile read."
—A. G. Lafley, chairman and CEO, Procter & Gamble

"Ram Charan has hit the nail on the head by constructively linking personal attributes and business success. His is an important message at an important time for business leaders."
—W. James McNerney Jr., chairman, president, and CEO, The Boeing Company

"This is the leadership book for the new generation. It's not about climbing to the top of the heap. It's about substance—becoming the kind of leader who makes the right decisions time and time again. If you want to make your business, yourself, and your world better, use this book as your guide."
—Ron Meyer, president and COO, Universal Studios

"Ram has an unparalleled track record of providing executives with compelling yet practical advice on how to succeed in tumultuous business environments. *Know-How* continues the tradition, defining in detail the performance factors that can give executives a competitive edge no matter how markets evolve."
—Ivan G. Seidenberg, chairman and CEO of Verizon

KNOW-HOW

The 8 Skills That
Separate People Who Perform
from Those Who Don't

RAM CHARAN

WITH
GERI WILLIGAN

CROWN
BUSINESS
NEW YORK

Copyright © 2007 by Ram Charan

All rights reserved.

Published in the United States by Crown Business, an imprint of the Crown Publishing Group, a division of Random House, Inc., New York.

www.crownpublishing.com

Crown Business is a trademark and the Rising Sun colophon is a registered trademark of Random House, Inc.

Library of Congress Cataloging-in-Publication Data
Charan, Ram.
Know-how : the 8 skills that separate people who perform from those who don't / Ram Charan.—1st ed.
1. Leadership.   2. Management.   3. Organizational change.
4. Succession.   I. Title.
HD57.7.C4737   2006
658.4'092—dc22   2006014255

ISBN: 978-0-307-34151-8

Printed in the United States of America

Design by Maria Elias
10 9 8 7 6 5 4 3 2

First Edition

Dedicated to the hearts and souls of the joint family of twelve siblings and cousins living under one roof for fifty years, whose personal sacrifices made my formal education possible.

CONTENTS

KNOW-HOW

KNOW-HOW

The Substance of Successful Leaders

Know-how is what separates leaders who perform—who deliver results—from those who don't. It is the hallmark of people who know what they are doing, those who build long-term intrinsic value and hit short-term targets.

What gets in the way of finding people who can perform is the *appearance* of leadership. All too often I see people being chosen for leadership jobs on the basis of superficial personal traits and characteristics, such as:

• *The seduction of raw intelligence*: "He's extremely bright, incisive, and very analytical. I just feel in my gut he can do the job."

- *A commanding presence and great communication skills*: "That presentation was awesome. How she ever boiled down all that data onto the PowerPoints is beyond me. She certainly had the committee in the palm of her hand. Mark my words, she's going to the top."
- *The power of a bold vision*: "What a picture he painted of where we are going, moving forward."
- *The notion of a born leader*: "The people in the unit love her. Such a morale builder and motivator!"

Certainly intelligence, self-confidence, presence, the ability to communicate, and having a vision are important. But being highly intelligent doesn't mean that a person has the knack for making good business judgments. How many times have you seen people confidently making decisions that turn out to be disastrous? How often have you heard a vision that turned out to be nothing more than rhetoric and hot air?

Personal attributes are just one small slice of the leadership pie, and their value is greatly diminished without know-how, the eight interrelated skills that bring leadership into the realm of profit and loss.

We need leaders who know what they are doing. Change is always with us, but its current magnitude, speed, and depth is unlike what most readers of this book have experienced in their lifetime. A Google can come from nowhere and grow into a multibillion-dollar business in a few short years, becoming one of the world's most highly valued companies. There are not only huge opportunities but also great pitfalls that can swallow up whole companies and industries. Think for a moment about the challenges Google has presented to companies in the advertising, broadcasting, and publishing industries, to name just a few.

World-class competitors can now emerge from anywhere—witness the wave of emerging-nation players that have clear advantages in their industries—thanks to mobility of talent, capital, and knowledge.

You will be constantly tested for your know-how to lead your business in the right direction. Will you be able to do the right things, make the right decisions, deliver results, and leave your business and the people in it better off than they were before?

- Can you **position your business** by finding the central idea that meets customer demands and makes money? And, as will increasingly be required, can you appropriately **reposition** it?
- Are you able **to pinpoint external change** by detecting patterns ahead of others and put your business on the offensive?
- Do you know how to lead **the social system of your business** by getting the right people together with the right behaviors to make better, faster decisions and achieve business results?
- Can you **judge people** by finding their best talents based on facts and observations and match them with a job?
- Are you **molding a team** by getting highly competent leaders to submerge their egos and coordinate seamlessly?
- Do you know how to **develop goals** by balancing what the business can become with what it can realistically achieve, not merely looking in the rear-view mirror and making incremental adjustments to what's been done before?
- Can you set **laser-sharp priorities** by defining the specific tasks that align resources, actions, and energy to accomplish the goals?
- Can you deal with forces beyond the market by creatively and positively responding to **societal pressures** you don't control but that significantly impact your business?

Command of these know-hows enables you to diagnose any situation and take appropriate action, lifting you out of your comfort zone of expertise by developing skills that prepare you to do what the situation requires, not just what you've traditionally been good at.

The know-hows do not, however, stand alone. There are a million things that can block human beings from making sound judgments and taking effective action. That's where personal traits, psychology, and emotions enter the leadership picture. But instead of trying to define and adopt the ideal set of personal traits, it's more useful to focus on a simple question: How do your personal psychology and cognitive abilities affect the way you cultivate and use the know-hows? For example, the know-how of detecting the patterns of external change might be affected by your ability to connect the dots and whether at heart you are an optimist or pessimist.

Know-How is about what you must both *do* and *be* to lead your business in what is shaping up to be the most challenging business environment in decades. It plants business leadership squarely on a foundation of profit and loss, capital utilization, resource allocation, productivity, and customer satisfaction while never losing sight of the fact that leaders are human beings.

Let me illustrate the difference between having know-how— the real substance of leadership—or not, using two situations I personally observed.

I've disguised the executives and the companies, but they are true stories that I witnessed. The stories center on two CEOs, Nick and Bill. Nick had all the traits commonly associated with leadership in abundance. He had an incredibly facile mind and high energy. He was highly articulate and decisive, and had the charm to make you feel like you're the only one in the room. He was a financial wizard and an inspirational leader. Bill had many of those traits too, but he also had the know-how to go with them. Their stories are very different.

NICK

The board of the company Nick joined was worried. The company had for many decades been number one in its industry in America, but ten years previously it had been eclipsed by a competitor that had grown by leaps and bounds and had displaced it as the industry leader by a wide margin. The company had been losing market share to its growing rival for two main reasons. One was customer dissatisfaction and defection. The second was operational problems resulting in higher costs and negative cash flow. The two previous CEOs had failed miserably. Now the board was trying again. The best headhunter in the business was on the case, armed with a meticulously prepared list of the criteria a candidate would have to meet. This time the board was determined to get it right.

When Nick interviewed for the job, the board's search committee recognized him as the company's savior. He was extremely quick on his feet and accomplished, and he had a commanding presence and was a great communicator. He had progressed swiftly through the ranks in his previous job, yet was humble and sincere. He had risen through finance and willingly admitted, when a board member asked, that it would be a stretch to learn operations and logistics, both of which were crucial to the business, and he promised to surround himself with top talent in those areas.

At age forty-four, Nick was energetic and fit. He also radiated an emotional maturity beyond his years. He was seen as a visionary, someone with the passion to revive the glory days of the company. He exuded confidence and was young enough to see the mission through to its conclusion. All the meticulous reference checking confirmed that his apparent strengths were real.

Wall Street was thrilled when the board announced Nick's appointment. The business press rushed to do glowing profiles. Employees emerged with new energy after every rousing speech Nick made. What a relief; here, at last, was the CEO who would restore the company's former luster.

True to his personality, Nick took hold of the company quickly and made some bold moves. He told the board, then publicly announced, that he intended to gain market share head-on from the company's biggest competitor. Within a few weeks he replaced the homegrown president with the head of one of this competitor's divisions, a reputed expert in operations and logistics. And he brought his longtime information technology consultant aboard to head the IT department and make radical changes to fix IT, an area in which the company's chief competitor excelled by a wide margin.

It was exciting at first, but it wasn't long before the accolades stopped. Nick's former IT consultant, now his vice president of IT, had built her career giving companies advice about what they needed to do. She had never actually done it. She had no skills in motivating a group of very bright and independent technology experts and the IT overhaul soon lagged badly behind schedule. She had to return to Nick several times over the course of a year to ask for increases in the IT budget.

Meanwhile, the new president had been building a personal fiefdom, hiring many of his former colleagues from the competitor. Together they set out on an ambitious effort to win discounts from suppliers by buying in large lots. The idea was to get prices down to win back market share. Of course, the big competitor quickly countered the new strategy by discounting prices in select merchandise at locations strategic to

Nick's. The price discounts hurt the competitor's profits a bit, but the competitor was so large that its targeted price cuts did not have a significant impact on its bottom line. It wasn't long before Nick noticed that merchandise was beginning to pile up in the retail outlets. Over time some of those products became outdated and had to be marked down drastically, far below what it had cost the company to purchase them. Worse, the large purchases and inventory buildup sapped much-needed cash.

The company's chief financial officer became increasingly concerned about the company's cash position. He warned Nick several times that the president's unchecked buying sprees were endangering the company's survival. Cash was dwindling at an alarming rate and unless that trend were reversed—and soon—the company would be in default of its loan covenants. As the CFO's warnings became increasingly shrill, Nick became increasingly irritated and finally told the CFO that he wasn't supporting the company's goals and would have to leave.

It's obvious, of course, where this is going. One day a key board member received a telephone call from the chairman of the company's lead bank. It was over. The banks would formally announce the next day that the company was in violation of its debt covenants. The board ordered Nick to fire the president and, after weeks of negotiations with its lenders, the company filed for bankruptcy protection. Nick was soon replaced, and the company continues to struggle today.

Once again, the board had botched it. They had been beguiled by *form* and didn't search for *substance*. The directors had focused too much on the candidate's personal traits, his intellectual prowess and emotional intelligence, his ability to inspire and motivate, and the health of his ego. They had neglected to probe deeply into Nick's skills in repositioning a company, his ability to judge people and to build an effective team of senior executives. All were in short supply and seriously compromised Nick's judgment and ability to get the job done.

Was Nick's abject failure his own fault? Not really. After all, he hadn't deceived anyone. In fact, he had demonstrated precisely the qualities that people admired and respected, fulfilling in every measure the criteria the board had given the headhunter.

I've seen this mistake repeated over and over again at several levels of organizations, from the choice of a Fortune 100 CEO to business unit managers, country managers of multinational companies, and high-level functional leaders, such as R&D and sales. Aspiring business leaders don't set out to do a lousy job, but it happens. Young people learn quickly what they have to do to be recognized: impress others with their intelligence, fast thinking, and commanding presence. Over time, they polish all the outward appearances of leadership and their superiors buy it lock, stock, and barrel. It seems incredible, but when it comes to business leadership, we don't consider the most important pieces of it: Does this person have the know-hows to succeed? Is he or she capable of developing them and driven to continue to hone them? The seeds of personality traits might be born, but know-hows are learned, developed through practice, and honed through experience. Leaders who are disciplined, determined, consistent, and persistent in developing these know-hows tend to be successful on a sustained basis. In that sense, leaders are made.

BILL

When the board of another company went outside to name Bill to the CEO's post, earnings had been flat for two years and investors were getting out of the stock. The board had reviewed many candidates. Bill, at age forty-five, was the youngest. But he also had the most diverse experience. He had repositioned three different businesses—in Switzerland, Mexico and the United States—in three different industries. What he lacked was experience in this company's basic technology.

As Bill studied how to reposition the company, he discovered that one of the company's three divisions produced a third of the revenues, but very little profit. More to the point, that division wasn't closely related to the company's core business. Bill assessed the various opportunities for making money in different market segments, then ditched the low-margin third of the business, focused resources on the remaining market segments, and started a new division with a new cutting-edge product. That was the easy part.

More important, however, Bill surveyed the changing environment for the industry. The bulk of the company's revenues came from just ten customers with operations around the globe. His company's technology originated in Germany and the products were manufactured mostly in the United States. But Bill saw that the center of decision making among his customers was moving toward Japan and Taiwan. Should he reposition the company to put the bulk of R&D and production in Asia? Who would run such operations? What about the language and cultural barriers? At best, such a fundamental change would be difficult. As Bill pondered what to do, he focused on the increasingly rapid evolution of products in the industry. Design times were getting shorter and shorter. Prices were being cut sooner and sooner. His designers and engineers in Europe and the United States were smart and efficient, but were paid several times more than designers and engineers in Taiwan. If he was going to be able to cut the price of new products in half just eighteen months after they were introduced, he had to get his costs down. That capped it. The company's center of gravity for decision making would move to Taiwan.

Bill's decisions fundamentally reshaped the entire company, and they were risky. Once in place, however, the wisdom of the moves was clear. The company could compete more aggressively in the chosen segments, be world competitive in cost and cost structure, give customers better value, and increase market share and earnings. Bill's confidence in his decisions wasn't just bravado; it was rooted in his know-how of positioning the business to make money. Bill's personality was a huge asset in the decision-making process. He is a good listener, willing to probe deeply, confident that if he asks the right questions he will come to the right answers.

Bill also had the know-how of judging people. The company already was multicultural, with operations in Germany and the United States and sales forces in Taiwan and Japan, when Bill joined. He had never met his team of direct reports before joining the company and had to decide who among them would be able to make the leap to Asia, who would be able to cut cycle times and reduce production costs.

Once he had chosen the people to make the changes, Bill had to ensure that they worked in close synchronization as a team despite multiple languages, cultures, disciplines, distance, and different time zones. To do that he set up a process of repetitive, simultaneous, and intensive communications through weekly international conference call joint problem-solving sessions, as well as getting together on a monthly basis. The process brought all of the relevant people together to talk about the latest issues at hand that required coordination and trade-offs, the actions to be taken and by whom, and the follow-through.

Behind it all, though, was Bill's know-how of seeing the changes in the external environment that would require his company to slash its development cycle times and be able to make money even when steadily cutting the price of new products in half over a period of just eighteen months. With his eyes firmly on those goals, he was able to carry out an effective repositioning of the company that quickly resulted in rapidly rising revenues and profits, and a stock price that climbed even during the difficult days in 2001 and 2002 when the entire industry was in a slump.

The difference between Nick and Bill boils down to one simple thing: Bill knew what he was doing, and Nick really didn't. In today's environment of lightning fast change and transparency, leaders who lack substance get discovered sooner, but the damage they do in the meantime can be greater. Missing an opportunity or failing to move on a threat can destroy a company, as can mistakes in judging people or organizational capabilities or even in setting goals.

Successful leaders learn, practice, hone, and refine the know-hows until they become natural. Mastery comes with lots of rounds of practice. Just as a superbly fit human being who hasn't practiced won't be as good at a sport as someone who practices diligently, leaders who do not practice these know-hows will be less effective than those who do. Business know-hows aren't taught in schools, and cultivating them isn't easy. But over time, with lots of development, the know-hows become automatic, instinctive, and superb, and judgment improves. You become a master in exercising them at the right time and in the right combination as each new situation presents itself, the way Michael Jordan knew how to position himself on the basketball court or Tiger Woods knows how to adjust his golf swing to accommodate the terrain. While it is unrealistic to expect every leader to become superb in every know-how, you need a basic understanding of each in order to know where your strengths and weaknesses lie and what kind of expertise you may need to support you.

LINKING KNOW-HOWS WITH THE WHOLE PERSON

There has long been a debate about whether the personal traits commonly associated with leadership are inherent or learned. That debate is beside the point. By the time you're age twenty-five or so and entering the workforce, your essential personality traits, psychological constructs, and patterns of thinking are pretty much set, regardless of whether or not you were born with them. But those things get you only so far. You can succeed or fail even if those things seem to match the profile of a leader. From that point on, your ability to succeed on a sustained basis depends on cultivating and practicing the requisite know-hows, while at the same time refining the personal traits you have. Know-hows reinforce personal traits, and personal traits reinforce know-hows. For instance, successfully detecting external change and repositioning a business will boost your confidence and perhaps make you more decisive next time. With greater confidence, you might become more open to contradictory views and thereby expand your cognitive bandwidth. A wider bandwidth will help you detect external trends. That's why it's so important to practice the know-hows through a series of deliberate, appropriately challenging job assignments, combined with self-reflection on your personal traits. That's how leaders are made.

Let me begin to show you how with the story of Liz, now a senior executive at a Fortune 500 firm. She had at an early point in her career been responsible for a P&L product line, reporting directly to the CEO of a small company. Early on she had impressed her boss with her numerical, diagnostic, and analytical skills. But Liz had gaps in her ability to position the business and find patterns in the external environment because she lacked the same passion to go out into the marketplace and meet with customers. After her boss pushed her to go on some sales calls, Liz was able to recognize what had been holding her back: a vague but very real fear that customers would react negatively to her youth and relative inexperience or ask questions she couldn't answer.

Liz was highly ambitious, indeed often in overdrive, but in her drive to achieve, she often made snap judgments of people. If one of her direct reports didn't deliver, she was ready to fire the person. Her behavior created an atmosphere of fear that clogged the flow of information, especially of bad news. Her boss, again acting as her mentor, showed her how to channel her drive to get to the root cause of the problem by asking probing questions. What were the factors underlying the poor performance? Was the person really at fault or had there been a shift in the marketplace? Perhaps the person in question was in the wrong job and his talents would be better used elsewhere in the business.

As her career progressed, she was given assignments that required her to do some repositioning, and as she wrestled with the challenge, her thinking broadened. She was able to see the total business picture of the product line and she became better at seeing patterns in the external environment. With each success, her self-confidence grew.

After a number of other challenging jobs in another, larger company over a ten-year period, Liz is now leading six different units at the Fortune 500 firm. Her early experiences not only improved the know-hows but also made her aware of the personal traits that were getting in her way, while she honed some traits that would work to her advantage.

Liz now has no fear about how people will react when she asks incisive questions of her business unit managers, who develop through her ability to probe. Her ability and willingness to drill to the specifics gives her more insight into the business and improves goal setting and repositioning. She is able to see and evaluate people's personal traits, for example, their appetite for risk taking to take advantage of new opportunities for growth. She tests their cognitive bandwidth—how well they are connecting the dots to detect breaks in the external landscape, what's their nose for repositioning the business, are they on the offensive or taking a defensive position.

Like all successful leaders, she is a continuous learner,

self-aware and able to reflect on her experiences and observations, thereby distilling what she has learned and converting ideas into action. With responsibility for six businesses, she has a huge number of opportunities for diverse observations through her continuous interaction with the teams of her six different businesses. Her judgment regarding people, positioning, and selection of goals has continually improved in perceptible ways and has set the foundation for becoming a successful CEO.

There are dozens of personal traits that can affect leadership and some, namely integrity and character, that are absolute. But in my years of experience I have observed that the ways leaders develop and deploy the eight know-hows are especially influenced by a handful of them: ambition, drive and tenacity, self-confidence, psychological openness, realism, and an insatiable appetite for learning.

These personal traits come out in many different ways. Do you stew over a decision alone or bring in trusted advisers for candid discussions? Do you allow yourself to be influenced by other people, changing your position in light of better analysis by a subordinate? Are you a procrastinator who wants more and more data—more certainty—before making a decision? Or are you impulsive, making a snap decision based on your gut instincts? Do you like to be liked? Your personality and psychology play an important role in how you interact with your business, whether you impose your will on the organization or seek a productive consensus that aligns the entire business with your goals.

Ambition—A desire to achieve something visible and noteworthy propels individual leaders and their companies to strive to reach their potential. Leaders need a healthy dose of it to push themselves and others. But ambition can be blind.

That's when you see leaders making flashy acquisitions that are financially unsound or setting attention-getting goals or taking on more priorities than the organization can handle out of a desire to do everything. Overambitiousness, combined with a lack of integrity, can lead to undesirable behavior and even corruption.

Drive and tenacity—Some leaders have an *inner motor* that pushes them to get to the heart of an issue and find solutions. They drill for specific answers and don't give up until they get them. Their *high energy* is infectious. They consistently drive their priorities through the organization. They search tenaciously for information they're missing and keep tweaking their mental models until they arrive at a positioning that works. But drive and tenacity can cause a leader to stick to a plan that isn't working or to outdated assumptions or an investment that is no longer promising.

Self-confidence—You have to be able to listen to your own inner voice and endure the lonely moments when an important decision falls on your shoulders. You have to be able to speak your mind and act decisively, knowing that you can withstand the consequences. It's not a matter of acting tough. It's having a tough inner core, or what some refer to as emotional fortitude. Underlying fears and insecurities can be just as detrimental to your know-hows as can excessive self-confidence in the form of narcissism or arrogance.

Some leaders have a *need to be liked.* They therefore tend to go easy on people. They have an especially hard time dismissing people who have been loyal to them. Such leaders often find their own progress slowed because they promote people for the wrong reasons, tolerate nonperformers, and allow the social system to corrode.

A *fear of response* is also common. Such leaders tend to avoid conflicts and find it hard to challenge people on their performance or point of view. They back off when they should be giving brutally honest feedback, and sometimes have a third party do that work for them.

Leaders with a *fear of failure* are often indecisive, defensive, and less likely to spot opportunities because they're risk averse. They find it hard to select goals for fear of choosing the wrong ones and wait too long to connect the dots in the external environment or to reposition the business.

Self-confidence also affects your *use or abuse of power*. Every leader has to use power from time to time in assigning tasks, allocating resources, selecting or promoting people, giving differentiated rewards, or redirecting dialogue. An excessive fear of failure or fear of response can make a leader uncomfortable using power, and not using power appropriately actually erodes it. Failure to deal with a recalcitrant direct report, for instance, diminishes the leader's power. On the other hand, narcissistic leaders tend to abuse power, using it irrationally or against the interests of the organization.

Psychological openness—the willingness to allow yourself to be influenced by other people and to share your ideas openly enhances the know-hows, while being psychologically closed can cause problems. Leaders who are psychologically open seek diverse opinions, so they see and hear more and factor a wider range of information into their decisions. Their openness permeates the social system, enhancing candor and communication. Those who are psychologically closed are secretive and afraid to test their ideas, often cloaking that fear under the guise of confidentiality. They're distant from their direct reports and have no one outside to bounce ideas off or to provide information that counters their own beliefs. In the new environment of complexity, being psychologically closed makes it particularly difficult to reposition the business because the leader lacks perspectives from diverse disciplines, functions, and cultures.

Realism—Realism is the mid-point between optimism and

pessimism, and the degree to which you tend toward one or the other has a particularly powerful effect on your use of the know-hows. Optimism can lead, for example, to ambitious goals that outstrip the company's ability to accomplish them, or can compromise your judgments of people: "I know his ego has no bounds, but I can coach him to become a team player." But pessimists don't want to hear ambitious plans or bold initiatives and can find all the flaws and risks in pursuing them when they do. They're likely to miss opportunities. A realist is open to whatever hand reality deals him. Only the realist wants to get unfiltered information that can be weighed, measured, evaluated, and tested to determine what step to take next. He spends time interacting with customers, employees, and suppliers, getting information and a "feel" from those constituencies about their thinking.

Appetite for learning—Know-hows improve with exposure to diverse situations with increasing levels of complexity, so an eagerness for new challenges is essential. Leaders who seek out new experiences and learn from them will build their know-hows faster than those who don't.

It is important to understand that these personal traits interact with one another and with the know-hows, for better or worse, and that in excess, they have a dark side. Overconfidence combined with excessive drive, for instance, can lead to narcissistic behavior, overcompetitiveness, and distrust of others. Combine those traits with being psychologically closed and overoptimistic and you are sure to shut down anyone hinting at bad news or suggesting that there are practical limitations to your plans.

It goes without saying that developing the know-hows requires innate intelligence. But the best leaders have distinct cognitive abilities that go beyond simply being bright. Their thinking encompasses a **wide range of altitudes** from the conceptual to the specific, they have a **broad cognitive bandwidth,** meaning they see things through a wide lens, and they are good at **reframing** issues and problems, looking at them from various points of view.

It's essential to be able to navigate a full range of altitudes, from the 50,000-foot level of conceptual thinking to the worm's eye view, probing the messy details of a situation. Early in your career you have to concentrate on the details of your job. As you rise you become more concerned with the big picture and high concepts. But your use of the know-hows is better when you're able to do both: think in terms of concepts but also drill to the specifics. You see this ability in leaders who ask *probing questions* that hit on exactly the right points or unearth the critical but unspoken assumptions, and in those who can *cut through complexity.* Many leaders love the world of big ideas but can't link them to the specifics of how they will be achieved or how they will make money. Their questions are broad and general rather than incisive. On the other hand, some leaders are so focused on the details that they miss the forest for the trees. Either extreme can be damaging.

A broad cognitive bandwidth allows you to take in a wide range of information and see things in their broader context. You can take in more complexity, and see the interconnections. You're more likely to pick up on trends outside your industry that affect the positioning of your business and create new growth opportunities, and you're better able to see the business and its social system *holistically,* rather than as separate functions, units, or individuals.

Continually reframing improves the know-hows by helping create a more accurate picture of a problem, person, or phenomenon and a wider range of alternatives. By reframing, you come up with different ways of defining problems and novel solutions to them, such as turning a problem employee into a star performer by reframing your view of the person and finding where her talents fit best. Reframing will help you understand how special interest groups see your business and anticipate how Wall Street might respond to your choice of goals.

The point of course is to become aware of whatever human characteristics are blocking you from perceiving things accurately, making sound judgments, or taking effective business actions. Dissolving the blockages and expanding your cognitive range are essential for the know-hows to improve.

THE HUMBLE ORIGINS OF KNOW-HOW

I started my business experience in my family's shoe shop in India. It was there that I learned in the most visceral way about the know-hows of making a business work. The most basic lesson was that if there was no cash in the till at the end of the day, there was no food on the table. Constant vigilance about cash aligns your mind to know what customers buy, why they prefer to buy from you, and what to do when things don't sell. All these elements became part of my business acumen, a simple nucleus of thinking and decision making.

After receiving a degree in engineering in India, I went to Australia looking for a job. I was working as an engineering assistant in the drafting section of one of Australia's biggest companies when I had a chance encounter with the top research-and-development executive in the company, who invited me into his office to talk about the company. I asked him an innocent question and he was kind enough to take the time to explain the answer. He knew I had an engineering degree, but didn't know about my earlier obsession with cash and moneymaking in a business. Although only twenty at the time, I had read the company's annual report, and I asked an innocent question. What struck me was that the cash the company generated was less than the amount it paid in dividends. I hesitated to ask about it at first, because it was a finance question being asked by a junior draftsman. However, he had put me at ease and said that I could ask anything I wanted about the business. I took him at his word and asked if the company was borrowing money to pay its shareholders a dividend. He seemed shocked and bolted from his chair and moved toward me with a look that said, "How dare you come to this conclusion!" Such a possibility had never occurred to him and he seemed so surprised at the question that I thought I had just lost my job. He was a scientist and didn't know the answer, but he was broad-minded enough to pick up the phone and call the chief financial officer to test my allegation. After a little hedging, the CFO confirmed that was the case.

That encounter opened the door to what became a four-hour session of questions and answers every two weeks for the next four years. Imagine the value of that kind of opportunity for a kid who grew up in a small town in India with lousy English skills and no real knowledge of Australia. His willingness to open up to me began to deepen my know-how of moneymaking in a large company and ultimately inspired me to leave engineering and go to the Harvard Business School. These conversations opened my eyes to the breadth, depth, and complexity of moneymaking in organizations and how it was similar to and different from my family's shoe shop. It also spurred my interest in finding the underlying reasons leaders succeed and fail. Education didn't seem to matter. One leader at this company had little formal education yet was succeeding handsomely, while another, a Baker Scholar from Harvard Business School, was failing. I'd hear people say things like "that man is a born leader" or "she's got great presence," but then the so-called born leaders would make colossal mistakes while seemingly unremarkable leaders knew what they were doing. Much of my career since has been a search for the know-how of success.

My modus operandi for the past forty-five years, which is to do research by observing events in real time as they unfold, grew out of my experience in Australia. While my research has involved hundreds of companies, what has been especially significant is the duration of those relationships, many lasting several years. At more than a dozen companies, I've had a front-row seat for over a decade, and for some, several decades. As an observer and facilitator of many key meetings and discussions at the executive level, I was able to track leaders' actions and decisions and watch their behaviors. The results often have a time lag, but because I was there for a long period, I could see the impact on the company's overall finances and health in both the short and long term, thereby avoiding the risk of being caught up in the excitement of the day or the leader's charisma. My close involvement over time allowed me to see whether these leaders left their organizations better off in ways numbers don't always capture.

By giving me the chance to see many businesses being shaped, experimented with, and tested, and then observing the outcomes, these companies became a live laboratory for understanding the cause and effect of leadership practices. In addition, many of these companies have gone through two or more changes of leadership, giving me further insight into the difference individual leaders make and adding depth to the understanding of cause and effect.

The research underlying *Know-How* has thus been dynamic. Conventional research, conducted through questionnaires or interviews, tends to be static and retrospective. Companies are viewed at one point in time. In a static framework, leaders do something that is remarkable or noteworthy once. But leading a business is an ongoing process in which leaders have to repeatedly make decisions and take actions over long periods of time under changing conditions. Research done after the fact gives interviewees the opportunity to rewrite history, if only inadvertently. Reconstructing events through the lenses of multiple participants can create a fuller picture of events but is impractical to do.

Leadership is a messy phenomenon because there are so many things that influence it. What I have been doing is looking at these messy situations with their many variables, canceling out the uncontrollable factors, and extracting the substantive differences between leaders who deliver and those who don't. From that, I've developed a framework that practitioners can use. This has been possible only because the companies and leaders have allowed me to be present and shared with me their views and perceptions, all built on trust. Those conditions have allowed me to see what really underlies a leader's success. My research has led to a more complete theory of leadership, one that identifies business know-hows and explains how they interact with a leader's personality traits, psychological orientation, and cognitive architecture.

During the course of my research, I looked at the usual financial and quantitative measures of success, but I also took into account the intangibles, such as whether the leader strengthened the organization, for instance, by building a leadership pipeline or new organizational capabilities. I discarded many of the conventional explanations of success that may have been statistically correlated but showed little, if any, cause and effect. That helped me see the underlying foundation of business success and resulted in the eight know-hows that are the heart of this book.

Let's start the journey to understand and develop the critical know-hows and become self-aware of how personal attributes can help or hurt the cultivation of them. You already have a sense of how fast and frequent change is. You are very likely to need the know-how of positioning and repositioning to keep the business on a solid footing in such a changing world. In learning it, you'll have a chance to see how personal attributes such as optimism or pessimism or overambition can influence your judgment about how to position and reposition the business. This is the subject of the next chapter.

2

THE FOUNDATION

Positioning and Repositioning
the Business to Make Money

The Product Launch: *"My vision for LaJolla Premier All-Natural Organic Nutritional Products for Pets is to provide our beloved animal companions with high-quality food that's on a par with what we humans eat. After all, aren't we all fellow-travelers in this life? Our strategy is based on a thorough analysis of the market and we are certain of success."*

The Results: *The dogs wouldn't eat the dog food.*

Positioning is the central idea of your business and the foundation for whether or not you are making money. The true test of your positioning is the real world. If people like what you have to offer and you can sell it at a profit, you'll make money. If they're confused about what your business provides, or they don't like it, you won't. In other words, if the dogs don't like the dog food, you lose.

But even if your positioning is on the money today, there's a good chance it won't be tomorrow. Positioning is not for eternity. The frequency, depth, and abruptness of change in the world today means that you will be frequently shaping and reshaping your business so that it fits with the ever-changing landscape in a way that delivers your moneymaking aspirations. In my judgment, over the course of a forty-year career most twenty-first-century leaders will have to reposition businesses four or more times. That means making basic decisions about what to add to the business and what to take out. It also means spotting new opportunities for profitable growth, resegmenting markets, and deciding which technologies to adopt. Repositioning is certainly on the agenda of many major companies as this book goes to press. Hedge funds and private equity are on the prowl for those who hesitate.

Knowing how to position and reposition a business is among the most demanding requirements of the twenty-first century leader. While all eight know-hows that make up this book are important, the know-how of positioning is first among equals. If you don't get it right, the foundation of the business eventually crumbles.

A STROLL THROUGH THE MALL

You can easily find clear examples of positioning in your everyday life. Maybe you're one of the millions of customers who visit Wal-Mart and Target each week. It's safe to say that most shoppers know why they go to one or the other retail giant. They go to Wal-Mart for low prices and to Target for good prices on items that are slightly more stylish. Customers, employees, investors, and the general public have a clear idea of what Wal-Mart and Target have to offer. Wal-Mart's positioning at its core is to give consumers a wide assortment of good-quality merchandise at the lowest possible prices. The crux of doing that is through continual improvement in the total cost of the product from the supplier to the consumer and passing the savings to the consumer. Starting from one store, Wal-Mart today has 6,198 stores worldwide, according to its 2005 annual report. In its roughly fifty-year history, it has tweaked the central idea underlying its positioning twice. The first was when it expanded geographically, moving from rural areas to metropolitan areas and taking on the then big guys—Kmart, Sears, and JCPenney. A second tweak became a major driver of growth: using its strengths in logistics, information technology, and buying power to move into groceries, and gaining a larger share of the customer wallet—in fact, becoming the largest grocer in the United States.

In contrast, Target has a different positioning for its business. It aims to be a cut above Wal-Mart, a little bit better in store appearance, better in customer satisfaction, better in quality and style of its merchandise. Although Target's prices are not rock bottom, they represent a good value for consumers. Observing the present demographic and consumer style change and looking into the future, it is interesting to speculate which of the two positionings is going to be relevant.

What a great positioning Wal-Mart has had for fifty years. Its success is far beyond its founder's wildest dreams; in fact, it is now one of the world's largest companies in terms of revenues. It's been very adaptable at the operational level: change a category here, a store there. But now there is a crack in the landscape. In the past five years, Wal-Mart's comp sales (year-over-year sales increase at stores open at least a year) have been sluggish; in fact, they've often been growing more slowly than the rate of Target's comp sales, and Wal-Mart's management seems to have traced it to a bigger problem. Income has been rising for many people, and with it, people have shown a preference for goods that are a little more stylish and of better quality than what Wal-Mart has to offer. Even if they are buying a lot of household items at Wal-Mart, they are going elsewhere—including to Target—for clothing and other fashion items. At the same time, Wal-Mart is under pressure to provide more employee benefits. That would increase costs, result in lower margins, and put the traditional moneymaking formula at risk.

Under the leadership of CEO Lee Scott, Wal-Mart has taken some dramatic steps to reposition the business, experimenting with new merchandising concepts to appeal to relatively higher-income consumers. This includes offering fine wines and making major moves into fashion. Wal-Mart has placed an eight-page advertising spread in *Vogue* magazine to show off its new clothing line; presented a fashion show in New York; opened an office a far cry from Bentonville, Arkansas, in Manhattan's Fashion District; and hired a very senior executive from Target for a top job at Wal-Mart. It also changed the emphasis from cramming as many items as possible onto a clothing rack to making the clothing more accessible and the displays more aesthetically appealing.

There is, however, a question. Does developing a new positioning of appealing to higher income consumers, along with the traditional ones, run the risk of confusing the image of the Wal-Mart brand? Further, even if Wal-Mart gets its judgments about customers right and finds a moneymaking formula that fits the new positioning, can it change the skills and the psychology of its 1.4 million employees?

No doubt the leaders of Target are watching Wal-Mart like hawks. If Wal-Mart successfully repositions, by definition Target's relative positioning will also be altered.

The challenge Wal-Mart faces is almost without parallel, with the exception of General Motors. Wal-Mart's stock price has long been in the doldrums. It is under attack from the media and special interest groups, and its business model is at risk. It will test the cognitive ability of Wal-Mart's leaders to deal with the complexity and drill down to a simple executable value proposition. The clarity and specificity of positioning of a company in the mind of the consumer, employees, and other constituencies is paramount.

Too often a shift in positioning (sometimes originating because of the change of company leadership) in a relatively stable environment can cause a permanent blurring of the company's value proposition in the eyes of customers. Take, for example, Sears. People once knew exactly what to expect from Sears—who it was competing against and how—but as the competition changed, its positioning got blurred. For more than two decades, Sears has had a kind of identity crisis, emphasizing and de-emphasizing various aspects of the business and leaving people confused about its changing value proposition.

When customers first began to defect in favor of discount retailers, several consecutive CEOs at Sears in quick succession tried one fix after the other. In the early 1980s, it diversified into financial services; then, in the early 1990s, it got rid of its financial services. For a while, it focused on its "soft lines" like apparel, then on its hard lines of appliances and tools. It sought shopping mall locations for its all-in-one stores, then created stand-alone stores for furniture and hardware. It shut down its hundred-year-old catalog business in 1995, then got back into the catalog business through its purchase of Lands' End in 2002. It emphasized its individual brands—Craftsman, DieHard, and Kenmore—and then the Sears brand. In a *Wall Street Journal* interview shortly after he took over as CEO in 2000, Alan Lacy acknowledged Sears's positioning dilemma, posing the question he was struggling to answer for consumers: "But why should I go to Sears versus Target?" It was the right question. It's the basic question you must always know how to answer: What are we offering customers, why is it better than the other options available to them, and how will we make money from it? It takes a leader with know-how to answer it with the kind of laser-sharp clarity and specificity that ensures the business will thrive.

The know-how of repositioning requires you to be on constant vigilance to detect early warning signals and interpret them correctly, whether they indicate a change is an aberration, an opportunity, or a threat. The early warning signals come, for example, when customers start going somewhere else—think of GM's shrinking market share. Stagnant sales at Sears while Wal-Mart and Target were booming was a clear warning for it to reexamine its positioning, just as falling revenues from advertising is an unmistakable red flag for newspapers and magazines today.

Another early warning signal is when one or more components of moneymaking has begun to decline or is not meeting expectations relative to your competitors. You have to examine the real cause and effect: Is it because of the economy? Is it because of internal inefficiency relative to the competition? Or is it time to reposition your business in the new external environment? For example, the gross margin in PCs in the late 1980s was 35 percent, but by the early 2000s it was more like 18 percent—a huge change in the foundation of moneymaking and an unmistakable signal to a company like IBM that external change was happening, that the PC industry's competitive advantage of vertical integration was disappearing and power was moving from hardware to software. Dell saw the opportunity. IBM saw it later, and its competitive positioning in PCs not only declined but never recovered. Once the dominant player, IBM sold its PC division to Lenovo of China.

WHEN THE LANDSCAPE BREAKS

When there is a break in the continuity of the external land-scape, as there has been in many industries, the know-how of positioning and repositioning becomes even more important. One recent example is the new technologies, particularly the search engines, that are threatening the very foundation of the newspaper business. You can see it for yourself when you stop at the newsstand on the way to work and pick up a copy of, say, the *New York Times* or the *Wall Street Journal*. One thing you've probably noticed is that these and other news-papers (and magazines) are a lot slimmer than they used to be because there are many fewer ads. For decades the positioning of companies in the newspaper business was stable and straightforward, and the way they made money came from a combination of newsstand sales, subscriptions, and advertis-ing. Then, suddenly, that stability was shattered.

The venture capital industry, whose full-time job it is to cause change, funded Google, which in turn has been able to do what was never before possible: measure the effectiveness of advertising. As traditional audiences for print and TV have taken to other outlets for information and entertainment, ad-vertisers have been needing channels to reach them. Google offered them not only a different option, but a far better one. Advertisers could reach people who might actually have an interest in their product by putting ads on Google's search re-sults pages for the key words that fit the product. By tracking how many people clicked to view the ad, Google gave adver-tisers a measure unavailable from traditional media: exactly how many people actually saw it. When Mercedes puts an ad in *Fortune* magazine, it can only estimate how many peo-ple really saw it, much less figure how many people bought a car because of it. Google removes the guesswork, provid-ing a breakthrough benefit for advertisers, and one they're willing to pay for. Google's distinctive place in the world—its positioning—and its moneymaking approach are clearly linked. In 2005, it took some $7 billion in revenue from the roughly $255 billion in total U.S. annual ad spending, and it's poised to win lots more.

While Google's success has many of us marveling, it has newspaper managements quaking in their boots because the break in the landscape is very deep. For the print media, the question isn't how fast revenues will grow, but how fast they will decline. And then what? The moneymaking formula for newspapers and magazines must change. Therefore, the leaders of these businesses don't have a choice. They must reposition. The issue is how quickly they can get their arms around the nature of the change, pinpoint its exact content, and not be psychologically blocked from judging the reality of it.

It's easy to see why people working in an industry for many years can develop psychological blockages and fail to see bigger trends. For example, a veteran newspaper leader who is overly optimistic and too self-confident will see the precipitous decline in one major source of revenue as an aberration, rationalizing that the business is just going through a flat period, pointing out that in some regions such as the Southwest ad revenue is still on the rise. Such overoptimism blocks out important factors such as the signal from a big advertiser like Procter & Gamble that the company will shift a significant portion of its ad budget away from TV and print to online. You first have to sort through conflicting signals and be psychologically open to search for and anticipate the changes. Then you must start connecting the dots to understand the depth and speed of change and begin using your know-how to reposition the business. Staying with the traditional moneymaking model could be disastrous for the entire company, because external forces have changed the game.

Major newspaper companies are struggling to find their way in the new environment. For example, the New York

Times Company, which also publishes the *Boston Globe* and the *International Herald Tribune,* has made forays into the Internet (it bought Web site About.com, which was and is losing money) and even TV (it bought half of a digital cable network now called Discovery Times), but some 95 percent of revenues still came from newspapers and their Internet offshoots in 2005. While the Times's flagship paper generated more than a billion dollars a year in ad revenue, from 2004 to 2005, costs of fuel, newsprint, and employee benefits grew faster than revenues. One Times executive quoted in the *New Yorker* said that "it's just a matter of time until we start losing money."*

For a newspaper—or any business, for that matter—positioning is figuring out what the new composition of revenues will be, from what sources, and what the new cost structure will be to continue to make money. When repositioning a business, you have to look at it in a different, usually broader context. How you look at it is conditioned by your cognitive bandwidth and your personality. Are you on the offensive or in a defensive mode? Are you looking at it as the same old game or is your game being subsumed by one that is bigger and radically different?

For example, to change the sources of revenues in the newspaper industry, it's critical to know how the consumption of this media will change—from what to what. How will the consumer seek news and information—by reading a newspaper, for example, or watching the continuous broadcast of news on an iPod or on a handset telephone? Will the consumer want a long story or the essence of the story in less than sixty seconds? Such external change is huge and fast, and therefore successful leaders in this business need the cognitive bandwidth to simultaneously see the problem from both fifty thousand feet and at the ground level, where the messy details

*Ken Auletta, "The Inheritance," *New Yorker,* December 19, 2005.

are hashed out. They will also need the appetite to experiment and take the risks required to develop alternatives to position the newspaper in light of new behaviors of consumers, who are fragmenting and creating new market segments. Some will read newspapers, some will use handsets, some will watch television. Some will, in fact, engage simultaneously in more than one form of media, for example in handheld devices, the computer and television. How do you make the content a newspaper gathers available to consumers in ways that make them prefer your content and at the same time make advertisers willing to use your content and its route to market? How fast and how many consumers can a newspaper aggregate to command the advertiser's dollars? What choice of alliance partners and what timing and sequence of pursuing them would put you on top? Successful leaders do this type of mental gymnastics. They use intuition, experience, and facts, iterating these multiple factors to arrive at viable alternative value positioning propositions.

Positioning is a fast-evolving game that changes as the players act and react to each other. Only time will tell which leaders in the newspaper industry will have the know-hows, cognitive bandwidth, and personality to go on the offensive, and which will remain on the defensive and at risk. If the leaders don't move in the right way or wait too long to do the repositioning, Wall Street and the hedge funds will force the move or eliminate their independence, as was the case with Knight Ridder. Against the wishes of its leadership, it was sold to a smaller company, McClatchy, that will presumably reposition the combined company for a new era.

THE MONEYMAKING IMPERATIVE

The patterns of change in the external world and the challenges they present can make your head swim. But no matter what, the acid test of your choice of how to position your business rests simply on whether it meets your moneymaking aspirations. You can get overwhelmed by financial mumbo-jumbo and exotic financial tools, but the heart of the matter is very simple. In its essence, to exist over time, every business—from the Fortune 500 to a small proprietorship in your local community—has to sell something, make a profit, have more cash coming in than is going out, and earn more than the cost of using other people's money (the bank's or shareholders') to be in business. The basic moneymaking elements of revenue growth, margin, velocity (use of capital per dollar of revenue), cash, and return on invested capital are universally the same for every business, of any size or type, anywhere in the world. The magnitude of each and how they connect with each other varies from business to business, company to company and from time to time. The mastery of each of these elements enables you to cut through the complexity of any business.*

Wal-Mart and General Motors have the same core elements or nucleus of moneymaking as, for example, Hastings Electric and Hardware, a store owned by Kenny and Bruce Aluisio serving a small, well-defined community in the New York City suburb of Hastings-on-Hudson, New York. But the corporate giants have, of course, immensely greater size and complexity, which makes it harder to see the relationships among the elements of moneymaking and their link with positioning. The Aluisio brothers have all the information they need to run their business right at their fingertips. They have no middle managers or business analysts to filter information and little in the way of complexity. Almost all of Hastings Electric's customers live within a one-mile radius of the store and many are repeat customers whom the brothers get to know personally. Every day, the Aluisios see how many people walk through the door, how long they stay, what they're

*See the appendix at the end of this chapter for explanations of these terms.

looking for, and what they buy, and they know intuitively that customers' buying behavior has a direct effect on the dollar value of their sales (revenue), the profitability of those sales (gross margin), and how long items sit on the shelf (velocity). They know instinctively that margin and velocity both affect their return on invested capital ($R = M \times V$) and that inventory affects cash: excess inventory ties up cash that might be needed to pay the bills. If the brothers sense that people aren't buying, they can adjust their merchandise or their prices or their store layout or try to negotiate with their small number of suppliers—whatever it takes to keep margin, velocity, revenue, cash, and return where they need to be. Price cuts can boost sales but might hurt margin and return.

The top leaders at Wal-Mart must perform the same balancing act, but at Wal-Mart, several thousand leaders, several layers of management, and several functional silos are involved. Information about customers comes from the thousands of retail outlets in diverse geographic locations. Decision making about the mix of products, how much of them to buy, and at what price to sell them is delegated to many different people. Complexity notwithstanding, leaders at Wal-Mart, as at Hastings Electric, have to understand what is happening with revenues, margin, velocity, cash, and return and how shifts in the external world might affect customers and therefore the core of moneymaking. They master the mental process to make connections between seemingly disparate factors until they arrive at an acceptable solution. It's more than a numbers game. Neither is it solely a linear, analytic process. Everything must somehow gel in their minds. The quality of a leader's cognitive ability to sort out so many elements of the complexity of the business, and connect them to the moneymaking formula, is what differentiates successful leaders.

Executives at big companies have to be as quick on their feet as small shopowners like the Aluisio brothers. When a new Home Depot store opened a few miles away in Yonkers, they fully anticipated it would cut into their business and have an affect on their moneymaking and therefore made a shift in their business mix to supply more specialized services, such as electrical work and heating and air-conditioning installation and repair.

WHEN THE NEED FOR POSITIONING
CHANGES FREQUENTLY

Blockbuster, Inc. shows the difficulty of maintaining the moneymaking imperative as the ground shifts underneath the business. The tremors of external change for Blockbuster were driven by Hollywood and changes in technologies. They have been frequent, and three CEOs of Blockbuster have not been able to find the right fit for it in this environment. Blockbuster was founded on the simple premise of buying videotapes of Hollywood movies and renting them to consumers. Blockbuster's positioning was right for those times. In the late 1980s, videocassette recorders were affordable and commonplace, and movie theaters had become the province of teens and young adults. Many adults and families simply preferred to watch movies in the comfort and privacy of their own homes. Blockbuster's positioning also was clearly linked with moneymaking: videotapes were purchased from distributors on credit, customers paid for movie rentals in cash, and margins were high. Blockbuster was a net cash generator, so much so that it attracted the attention of Viacom, which bought it and set it up as a separate division in 1994.

Then, in the mid-1990s, several seemingly small changes outside the walls of Blockbuster began affecting the company's comfortable positioning. For one thing, Hollywood started selling movies to the public at the same time they made them available to rental outlets. Consequently, many customers were buying instead of renting. Also, satellite dishes and cable services were providing a new channel, giving consumers video on demand.

Recognizing the shift in viewing habits, Blockbuster repositioned itself to emphasize retailing instead of renting. It made sense from the perspective of what customers wanted, but what about the link with moneymaking? Margins on video sales were much lower than on rentals, and the difference was soon felt. Revenue growth slowed and cash flow started to dry up as margins fell from 42 percent in 1994 to 28 percent in 1995. Blockbuster's fading promise was a drag on its parent Viacom, whose stock price took a hard turn south.

A new leader, Bill Fields, the second in command at Wal-Mart, was brought in with the hope that he had the know-how to revive Blockbuster. His idea for positioning was to establish Blockbuster as a bright and lively neighborhood center that sold a variety of entertainment goods and convenience items, mirroring what he was psychologically comfortable with. People would go to Blockbuster, he asserted, for the shopping and social experience. But they didn't. The central idea of Fields's new positioning fizzled out—he made the mistake of doing what he was comfortable with—and the moneymaking ability declined significantly.

The next CEO, John Antioco, repositioned Blockbuster again, going back to the central idea of renting videos but seeking creative ways to improve the moneymaking. He negotiated deals with the Hollywood studios (which were having their own positioning problems) whereby they would share the profits from video rentals in exchange for selling their movies to Blockbuster at reduced prices. That way, Blockbuster could have more copies of new releases on the shelf without making a huge investment. Antioco bought some time, but the positioning seemed doomed as changes in the outside world continued. Taking their place next to other technologies came DVDs, Web-based movie rentals, and downloads off the Internet. Low-priced DVD players accelerated the trend toward buying movies. In 2003, Antioco acknowledged the changing external landscape by announcing a major push toward selling movies. This repositioning pitted Blockbuster against the likes of Wal-Mart and Costco. Unfortunately, the repositioning didn't work and moneymaking declined.

Still searching, in 2004, as the external environment of Hollywood was changing yet again, Antioco launched an online rental service to compete with Netflix. The path to moneymaking still wasn't clear, and late that year Antioco told the *Wall Street Journal*, "We're taking Blockbuster from a place where you rent movies to a place where you can rent, buy or trade a movie or game, new or used, pay-by-the-day, pay-by-the-month, in-store or online." Hollywood was helping fend off the threat from video on demand out of self-interest: a good chunk of its revenues came from DVD sales, so it had reason to continue to release DVDs ahead of cable. Blockbuster benefited. Nonetheless, in the third quarter of 2005, margins, cash, and revenues were lower compared with the third quarter of the previous year. Cost cutting in the fourth quarter, especially in marketing, helped margins but hurt revenues.

In 2006, Hollywood continues to be under siege by forces inside and outside its traditional industry. Moves by Steve Jobs to collaborate with ABC, NBC, and some cable TV companies to make content available on portable devices will likely affect Blockbuster further. In January 2006, Disney relaunched MovieBeam, a satellite-based video-on-demand service that sends movies from the major Hollywood studios to TV sets at low cost and at the same time they are released on DVD, posing a direct threat to other video-on-demand services and to Netflix and Blockbuster. Actions like these are likely to have a negative impact on moneymaking and also make the future very uncertain.

The story of Blockbuster is the story of every business in

this way: positioning doesn't last forever. On the contrary, in today's world, it doesn't last long at all. The life of a valid positioning continues to shorten, and is likely to do so in the future. The essence of the know-how of positioning is to know when a change needs to be made, to determine the shape of the change, and to tightly link it with the fundamentals of moneymaking. In addition, the leader may need more: the psychological comfort to dismantle that which made him or her successful earlier.

You find many examples today of businesses at crossroads, pharmaceuticals being one. Within a given industry some leaders with the know-how of positioning and repositioning will move ahead of others. For example, Novartis under Daniel Vasella has been on the offensive, moving from strictly patented drugs to become the second-largest producer of generics and into vaccines to fit new external realities.

THE ONGOING BATTLE FOR POSITIONING

Different players in an industry will have radically different responses to change in their environment; some will be defensive, some will be on the offensive, and some will basically ignore the evidence that something is wrong. Moves by one player influence the moves of the others, creating huge complexity and uncertainty as competitive actions and reactions take place sometimes over several years. Even when you find a good positioning, more external change can make what you accomplish obsolete very soon, even before you've fully implemented it.

When leaders first sense that the foundation of their business is crumbling and they see no good fix, their inner fears and insecurities sometimes take over and stop them from seeking help to figure it out. Those are lonely moments, in which leaders are often emotionally blocked. It's not a stretch to think that leading players in the newspaper industry could be psychologically blocked from imagining how radically different the newspaper business might be in the twenty-first century. Even if you see the need—and a clear way—to reposition such a business, you have the internal organization to consider. Resistance will likely be high and will test your conviction, courage, and drive. If you feel you can't win the organization over, you might unconsciously let your tenacity flag. These are the moments when your leadership traits and the know-how of repositioning will be tested not once but many times.

The complexity and unpredictability of the real world make positioning the business to make money inherently risky. It is impossible to predict, for instance, all the competitive actions and reactions of various players. You have to be aware that in such an uncertain situation, there's a high likelihood that the behavior of some players may be totally irrational. That makes the task even more complex. For example, you could say that GM's zero-percent financing and employee-discount programs, driven by the logic of filling capacity, are irrational because they destroy the profitability of the industry and at the same time diminish the relative value of brands in the eyes of the consumers. The know-how is in thinking through the possibilities and second- and third-order consequences and the tenacity to get to a clear solution. Your cognitive bandwidth and drive for success are critical to conceiving these possibilities. To be a successful leader psychologically, you have to be open, receptive, and active in searching for the signs that the business is being shifted or needs to be. You need to be surrounded with people whose conversations with you help you wrestle with these issues in a brutally honest manner. Here self-awareness really matters: Are you willing to psychologically wallow in this part of the job and do you devote enough time to it? Are you passionate to develop and hone this know-how?

FROM FIFTY THOUSAND FEET TO FIFTY FEET

No one would ever question that Steve Jobs is a visionary. In the contemporary business world, being called a visionary is meant as a high compliment. But while visions of the future can be inspirational, you must also do the hard work of translating your vision into down-to-earth specificity. The know-how of positioning requires that you have a range of altitude to think expansively and conceptually about new opportunities in the landscape—but also to think specifically about the down-to-earth realities of customers, competition, and moneymaking. This is not an impossible combination in a human being. All leaders with superb positioning know-how have it.

Steve Jobs has had many successes and a few failures during his long career. Jobs has an unusual ability to imagine things that don't yet exist and win people over to his vision. The Macintosh brought life back to Apple and set the standard against which the rest are compared. Then, with Pixar in the movie-animation business, and most recently in the music industry, Jobs has shown he has a firm hold on the realities of the marketplace. His successful launch of the iPod was based on a combination of detecting a need, imagining a new way to satisfy that need, thinking through the specifics of what it would take to make it fly in the real world, and then repositioning the company.

Jobs had the idea to make money by giving people a way to download songs off the Internet legally so they could listen to them when they wanted, where they wanted, and in the combination they chose. It was a concept rooted in keen observation of the consumer. Jobs could see, for instance, that demand for downloading music was real, because people were already doing it through Web sites like Napster and

Grokster, and, obviously, the download software was available. But before Apple was to act on Jobs's concept, more information was required: Would the music companies accept a fee for individual songs? Would consumers pay for them? If so, how much? The answers would provide the specific information needed to decide whether the concept was a go or no-go.

Jobs's tenacity and courage drove him to find the answers. High-profile legal action against downloaders and Napster were making consumers more willing to pay for their music, while the loss of revenues to the Internet was making recording studios willing to discuss ways to participate in the online game. Jobs sought to pin down the price point that would satisfy the targeted customers and studios, as well as Apple's own need to make money. With the concept *and* specifics in hand, Apple launched the first iPod in 2001 and the iTunes Music Store in 2003. He altered the pattern of competition, even though it involved no new technology, with little fixed investment, therefore low risk. He became the first mover, capturing a large share very early, and redesigning the money-making for Apple. He thereby enhanced Apple's image and brand, attracting better people, which in turn created additional opportunities for Apple. By the end of 2005, Apple had sold an astonishing 42 million iPods and 850 million songs, and reshaped the entire music industry.*

Jobs is now taking the lead in getting broadcast television to follow in the music industry's footsteps. By joining ABC he has also altered the landscape for NBC and CBS and changed the moneymaking formula for the entire industry. Jobs has always been on the offensive.

*Steve Jobs, speech at Macworld, January 2006.

WILL THE DOGS EAT THE DOG FOOD?

In the shaping of a positioning and its fit with the external environment and moneymaking, there's always that question we posed at the beginning of the chapter: "Will the dogs eat the dog food?" Will, for example, the consumer buy and pay for the combined services of telecommunications, data, voice, and video content, and in sufficient volume to make money? Many such attempts to offer the combination of services were driven by Wall Street considerations, where investors were willing to take the risk and were granting high ratios that encouraged mergers among the print, entertainment (content), and distribution industries. The concept of convergence emerged, and it was considered a brilliant idea.

The idea that combining companies in related industries like entertainment, publishing, and mobile communications would result in better cash flow and returns had an intellectual appeal, especially in the late 1990s when the Internet was "changing everything." The assumption was that the merged companies could offer a fuller range of products and services, and that those combined offerings had greater value to customers than traditional one-off services. Therefore, there was money to be made, somehow. AOL/Time-Warner and Viacom were both seduced by the concept, and both discovered after the deals were done that the concept would not deliver. Customers saw no value in combining a cable service, a magazine, and a call on their cell phone, for instance, and were unwilling to pay more than for the individual services. The converged companies had no edge in competing against niche players, and the moneymaking didn't materialize. These companies were forced to do massive cost cutting and divest assets when the hoped-for synergies failed to generate the money needed to pay off the debt.

There's no denying that big ideas are emotionally exciting.

Leaders at the forefront in shaping them get huge recognition and lots of emotional perks. Other leaders don't want to miss the train. That's when you see whole industries going in the wrong direction. Often the leader's enthusiasm is contagious and sustains investors, at least temporarily. The tide turns, though, when the results fail to materialize, usually after a big time delay. Positioning always requires some educated guesswork, but you have to get emotion out of the way. Sometimes the potential for big money can skew your perception of what will happen if some of the judgments prove wrong or if something unexpected happens. The margins may be huge, but how long will they last? When can you actually collect the cash? And what happens if a competitor does something unexpected, like cutting the price? The cognitive ability to pinpoint the exact source of uncertainty and the magnitude and timing of risk and the psychological comfort to deal with the consequences if the risk comes to pass differentiates successful leaders.

The idea expressed in Malcolm Gladwell's *Blink: The Power of Thinking Without Thinking*—that your first instinctive reaction to a situation may be correct—is dangerous when it comes to the know-how of positioning. By definition change is new, requiring different thinking than before, almost always demanding solutions that are not part of prior experience. You can trust your instincts and gut only after prolonged iterations of the many factors involved. You may go through periods of anxiety and frustration when the issue is unresolved. It tests the leader's temperament to endure such prolonged periods of uncertainty.

Look, for example, at Microsoft in mid-2006. It is the number one brand with the number one share, but its leaders have been living for about six years with a lack of clarity about what its future new positioning will be. It has invested some $30 billion in research and development, but there is not yet a very clear definition of repositioning despite its forays into several different market segments. Microsoft is, of course, in no danger at the present. Its great positioning in the past has resulted in a huge hoard of cash in the bank and the continued generation of cash each month.

HOW A COMPANY THAT GAVE ADVICE TOOK ITS OWN MEDICINE

In 1997, the Franklin Quest Company, a provider of time-management seminars, bought the Covey Leadership Center, a provider of productivity-training products. The Covey Leadership Center was perhaps best known for its bestselling book *The 7 Habits of Highly Effective People,* by Stephen Covey. The new FranklinCovey became a powerhouse of personal-effectiveness products. The sales force sold training directly to human resource departments and training directors, who liked FranklinCovey's approach to making individuals more effective. FranklinCovey expanded the number of its retail stores and invested heavily in information technology to support them. The company also continued to expand through smaller acquisitions.

Meanwhile, the world outside of FranklinCovey was changing. The company's positioning got out of sync with customer-buying patterns. By 2000, symptoms of the mismatch were showing up in the numbers—high debt, shrinking cash flow, and negative earnings. Seeking answers, the board elected as CEO one of its outside directors, Bob Whitman, who had a track record in repositioning businesses.

As the new CEO, Whitman, with the help of his team, dug into the numbers and what was driving them. Revenues appeared to be holding steady, but they were being supported by acquisitions; the core business of training was actually in decline, and even sales of products like day planners sold through FranklinCovey stores were being hurt by desktop software, Palm Pilots, and look-alike products for sale at office superstores. Margins were slipping because overhead had been creeping up year by year.

Before formulating a new direction for the business, Whitman wanted the team to cast the net wide to learn as much as they could about how FranklinCovey was being perceived in the marketplace. With a completely open mind, he and the entire team personally visited with sixty-two corporate customers, mostly senior managers in companies FranklinCovey did business with and who made time to talk with them because of FranklinCovey's great reputation. Whitman learned a number of important facts from those meetings—for instance, that people loved FranklinCovey products. If that was so, Whitman asked, why are only five hundred people of your five thousand employees trained in them? The responses were revealing: decision making in the client companies had shifted. The people FranklinCovey thought they were selling to were no longer making the purchase decisions. In most organizations, line managers—not the HR departments and training directors FranklinCovey traditionally sold to—were now making their own decisions about the kind of training needed and line managers wanted something different from FranklinCovey's value proposition.

Line managers wanted more than individual effectiveness. Customers believed in it, but the connection between individual effectiveness and business results was hard to pin down. Line managers wanted a tool that would clearly and measurably improve business results. They wanted to know what specific outcome—say, improved sales productivity or customer loyalty—they might get as a result.

By the end of 2001, Whitman concluded that the moneymaking was faltering for one basic reason: the central idea of the business could not win in the changed market landscape. It was necessary to rethink the very fundamentals of the business. FranklinCovey had to redefine itself and exit every non-core business and activity, which in time generated enough cash to provide a "long runway" for the repositioning. The real change in money making would not come from a tighter cost structure but from revenue growth and improved margins based on a new value proposition.

All of that information and long discussions with the team led Whitman to a kind of hypothesis for how to reposition the business. It became clear that while FranklinCovey was telling people to work on the things that matter most to their employer, most people didn't know what the most important things were. Research and a survey they commissioned confirmed that to be true; when people were asked to name the most important goals for the company or their team, the answers were all over the place. That insight pointed the way forward. Whitman, by being psychologically open to new ideas, was able to conceive and shape a new positioning. FranklinCovey's dominant theme in the future would be helping organizations deliver "on their own great purposes"—that is, to execute their most important goals with excellence. In marketing this new theme, FranklinCovey proposed to help clients clarify those goals and then provide processes and tools to enable their achievement.

Would it work? Repositioning is not just a mental challenge, but also a psychological one; you need the confidence to move on it when success isn't guaranteed. Hard data from the market gave Whitman confidence that he was getting the real facts. If he and the team hadn't observed customers directly, Whitman might have bought the views of some within the company who said no one would buy "business results" services from a company known only for "personal effectiveness." He might not have known that senior people in many organizations were immediately interested in the proposed idea for a new value proposition, and would in fact help define it.

Confidence soared in spring 2002 as FranklinCovey piloted the new approach in several companies. Every Friday night, the experimental team was debriefed at headquarters, and it soon became clear that the new value proposition was directionally right. Their clients were seeing dramatic changes in business results.

Although this story is far from over, the new repositioning seems to be working, and the moneymaking is changing for the better. FranklinCovey lost $100 million in 2002 but made $20 million in 2005. Closing many retail stores hurt revenues, but the training-consulting business has grown 12 to 18 percent yearly for the past several years. As a result of closing, selling, or outsourcing twenty-one businesses and restructuring others, debt is down and cash is improving. The new product line has helped bolster some traditional lines, such as the personal-effectiveness training business. Whitman continues to lead his team to refine the value proposition and the offerings through regular upgrades based on rich feedback. Regular visits to client CEOs and business leaders provide a stream of new insights. Whitman himself made 234 of these personal visits by early 2006. Such closeness to the market will help him and his team detect early on any breaks in the external landscape and whether and when it will be time again to reposition the business.

Sometimes hard times teach valuable lessons. Whitman began to acquire the skill and the mind-set to be good at positioning in his first job after business school. He had joined a resort-development company, which just three years later went into bankruptcy. When the CEO and the CFO abruptly left, he found himself in charge of doing the workout. It was an agonizing part of his life, but it dawned on him one morning that he wasn't asking the right questions. He had been asking, "What costs can we cut?" He realized that a better question was "Where could we win?" It was an entirely different way of thinking about things, and answering the question about where they could win shed light on the way to move forward. His psychology also changed during that period. Having seen the most dire of consequences, he didn't ever want to kid himself about the facts of the situation. Neither did he want to fool himself into believing that things would get better on their own, nor to be unrealistically optimistic that things would somehow work out.

His learning was reinforced in his next job as CFO of real-estate company Trammell Crow, when the real-estate market suddenly collapsed. With the company carrying $16 billion in debt, $4 billion of which was in default, he needed to confront reality fast, before it ran out of cash. But Whitman also applied the same way of thinking: Where can we win? Where can we not win? He had seen that everything outside the core business tended not to make any money, and that there had to be the willingness to develop new capabilities where Trammell Crow could win.

The key elements of positioning know-how—the mentality to dissect which new or already existing market segments would contribute to moneymaking and which would detract, and the psychological inclination to confront reality sooner rather than later—got ingrained in him and reinforced from the early stages of his career.

Whitman's drive for success at FranklinCovey led him to search for the right sources of information that would form the foundation for the conception and shaping of the repositioning. His diverse experience of repositioning several times expanded his psychological openness and lessened the fear of failure and increased his self-confidence. Whitman did not become the prisoner of the sales force and did not fall victim to the need to be liked. His cognitive bandwidth, his acuity of observation to discover the disparity between what the customer liked but did not use in sufficient quantity, led him to search tenaciously for a new need, until the fog began to clear.

■　■　■

As you've read this chapter, undoubtedly examples have sprung to mind of other companies or industries that failed to reposition themselves appropriately or that succeeded in doing it right. Maybe you stopped to consider how the leaders' personal attributes influenced their judgment. As you reflect on the thought process behind positioning decisions, you'll probably notice that the alternatives that come to mind are heavily dependent on how well a leader can pinpoint the nature and timing of external change. Building the know-how to detect external change is the subject of the next chapter.

Early-warning signals that the positioning of your business may need to change to take advantage of emerging opportunities:

- Nascent industries emerge.

- Nontraditional competitors start to appear.

- The positioning of a key competitor changes.

- The rise of new customers.

- Consumption patterns are being influenced by affordable new offerings from new technologies (think iPod).

- Customers are defecting.

- Loss of market share in select key segments.

- Emergence of new business models and new management models.

- Pressure on profit margins.

- Unexpected decline in cash flow from operations.

- Decline in customer satisfaction.

These signals may initially be small in magnitude, proceed slowly, then result in either a sudden decline or rise in opportunities for your business. You need to continually search for these and other signals even if your business is making money, continually reevaluate the positioning of your business, and have the self-awareness to do what needs to be done, not just do what makes you psychologically comfortable.

APPENDIX

- Revenue growth is how much sales increase from year to year.
- Gross margin is the difference between what something costs you ("the cost of goods") and what you sell it for, as a percent of the selling price. If the cost of producing a compact disc is $4 and you sell it for $20, your gross margin is $16. In percentage terms, it is 80 percent. Subtract $10 for sales and marketing and other expenses from $16, and you're left with $6. That $6 is your margin—30 percent of sales.

Revenues	$20
Less cost of goods	$ 4
Gross margin	$16
Less sales & marketing expense	$10
Margin	$ 6

- Velocity (V) is how much revenue you generate for a dollar of capital invested. For example, if you have $1 million in invested capital, and revenue for the year is $10 million, your velocity is 10.
- Return on invested capital is how much money you're making for a dollar of capital you've invested, which is margin multiplied by velocity: M × V.

3

BEFORE THE POINT TIPS

Connecting the Dots by Pinpointing and Taking
Action on Emerging Patterns of External Change

Business has always had to contend with a changing world, but
the pace and abruptness of change is new to this generation of
business leaders. Your job as a leader is to deal with that change,
to get and stay ahead of the curve, ensuring that your business
is positioned to make money now and in the future. It takes
a special know-how to mentally process the complexity and
deal with the ambiguity to form a view of the patterns that are
emerging. It is this know-how of pinpointing external change
that allows you to make a sound judgment about where the
world is going and put your business on the offensive.

From World War II through the mid-1990s change in the
United States tended to be *relatively* linear, continuous, and
predictable. Now, however, abrupt, exponential change is the

norm—witness, for example, the sudden and steep rise of China, and subsequently India, resulting in a disruption in the traditional flows of trade and the supply and demand of commodities, like oil, in turn causing flux in political alignments. We are, as former Federal Reserve chairman Alan Greenspan put it, in "uncharted waters."

Many people continue to look backward for a reference point they can understand, but matches with previous patterns and cycles are nearly impossible to find. China is not Japan in the 1970s, nor is the Internet like jet transportation. Never before have macroeconomic trends had such fast and devastating impact on companies and whole industries. Traditional ways for making business and economic assessments neither correlate with nor explain the reality of what is actually happening in the world today as they have in the past. As Greenspan noted in congressional testimony on July 21, 2005, referring to the spread between long- and short-term interest rates, "such a pattern is clearly without precedent in our recent experience."

On the other hand, the opportunities have perhaps never been greater for those who are ahead of the curve and able to take action ahead of the competition. Google shaking up the media industry, FedEx expanding into Asian markets, and Apple with its iPod phenomena are just the tip of the iceberg.

Sorting through the complexities of the external world for opportunities does not simply mean engaging in traditional competitive analysis, looking through the lens of your industry as it is currently structured to predict what may emerge in the near future. Nor does it mean leaning heavily on experts for advice about the future. Economists, demographers, social scientists, and strategy consultants are among the many intelligent people with narrow expertise relevant to business. Many have impressive titles and high positions, or have received honors that boost their credibility. They express their point of view very passionately and convincingly; sometimes the media is taken in and enhances their reputation. But they speak through the lens of their narrow specialty and rarely understand a business well enough to detect all the factors that might be relevant to it. Few have the broad lens required of a business leader.

Only by looking out far over the horizon and taking into account developing trends that may not seem directly relevant now can you really do the kind of analysis necessary to prepare for rapid change and new opportunities. You have to look at your business from the outside in. Too many people spend their time observing the context of their business from the inside out, looking at events through a narrow company or industry lens that is framed by the past. You need to expand your view, observe from the outside in, and be psychologically open to the patterns you detect and their implications for your business.

You need to spread the net wide, then do the mental processing to identify the underlying patterns. You need an insatiable curiosity and interest in the world, and an intense drive to find out what you don't know. Then you need to find the patterns. Finding patterns is akin to solving a puzzle, so personality traits like tenacity and confidence are necessary to keep searching for the missing pieces. On the other hand, arrogance and insecurity are likely to interfere with this knowhow, causing you to filter out unwanted news and other points of view.

Some changes take place on a global scale. Consider the political and economic changes that were beginning to emerge in just the past few years. China and Russia formed an alliance supportive of the oil-rich Iranian regime in an effort to displace the European Union's influence in Iran. India and China together made overtures to dictatorial African regimes and began buying oil assets together in Africa. The king of Saudi Arabia visited China, whose voracious consumption of oil has helped double oil prices in a matter of a few years. With the substantial increase in funds in the hands of energy suppliers, what changes will result? What opportunities are there for infrastructure? Where will they invest money? The changes will create huge opportunities for some and threats for others.

The world is becoming such that you can't go into a holding pattern waiting for the external patterns to become clear. Some people are so cautious that they won't make a move until a pattern is well defined and validated by others who have already moved into the space. And some, on the other hand, will make daring moves even when the externals are completely foggy. Some are off and running with a few bits of data that reinforce their preconceived idea and ignore everything that contradicts it. The fruits, however, will belong to the realists, to those who can pick out key variables amid complexity, seeing how they might combine and getting a viewpoint about where the external landscape is going.

IVAN, THE PINPOINTER OF CHANGE

Anticipating and pinpointing changes in the external environment is hardly an academic exercise. The whole point is to use that forward-looking view of the outside world to ensure that the business can continue to make money. Detecting changes in the external environment and linking them with the positioning of your business is what I call business acumen. It's a skill that Ivan Seidenberg, the CEO of Verizon, has been developing since the early days of his career. He started at New York Telephone climbing poles to do maintenance and repair, but quickly made the jump to management. Through a series of diverse and increasingly complex jobs, he honed his ability to discern the pattern of change in the external environment. A post at NYNEX (the successor company to New York Telephone) as liaison with congressional staff, unions, and regulators in Washington, D.C., for instance, broadened his perspective of the telecom industry and helped him see issues from diverse perspectives. That ability to reframe an issue is directly applicable to seeing how wireless companies, regulators, Internet providers, technologists, cable companies, and the like see the world, a viewpoint that is crucial to navigating the frequently shifting storms in the telecom industry. In 2004, he made the boldest move of his career when he made the decision to invest $2 billion as the first installment to link fiber-optic cable to consumers' homes, an initial part of a much larger overall plan to tie Verizon's future to fiber optics.

By the time of this decision, Seidenberg had moved Verizon beyond wire lines, repositioning it as one of the largest wireless providers. Technology and consumer habits continued to evolve and broadband cable started to look important as content was becoming king. Seidenberg not only had the clarity to see broadband delivered through fiber-optic cable as an important new communication service consumers would want and be willing to pay for, but the courage to make the bet. It was a bold move that some, remembering the telecom bust in the earlier part of this decade, thought was too risky and likely to have a delayed effect on moneymaking. But Seidenberg believed that this pattern of customer demand for speed, bandwidth, and choice did, in fact, link directly with moneymaking. By making shifts in the composition of revenues and profits, he would keep the business viable both financially and in the marketplace.

Still, the stakes are immense. "This is a decision made in our business once every thirty years," said Paul Lacouture, head of Verizon's network business. "It totally changes our business." My observation is that in the future decisions of this magnitude will be more than "once-in-a-lifetime" events.

The know-how of pinpointing *and* taking action on changes in the external environment is one of the most important skills you must master in your job. Put yourself in Seidenberg's frame of mind for a minute and think about the cognitive, psychological, and personality traits that are necessary to root out the answers needed from among the information and the multiple complexities that would weigh on a crucial decision such as this one. What might become of fiber optics is just one piece of it. Many analysts have concluded that it will be years before the glut of fiber-optic cable can possibly become a profitable business. Others speculate that new uses will emerge to soak up that capacity, but nothing has yet emerged on a major scale that will make money. Meanwhile, technology and regulatory policy continue to change at a rapid pace, a potent and dangerous combination that nearly bankrupted British Telecom in 2000. The company invested billions of dollars to get licenses in Great Britain for a new technology that executives believed would put them ahead of competitors. But neither the market nor the technology materialized and the entire amount had to be written off, bringing the company to the edge of bankruptcy.

Seidenberg had to consider how the rapid evolution of five major technologies would affect Verizon's future. He knew, of course, about the rapid growth of wireless, one of Verizon's platforms. But what about the potential for Voice over Internet Protocol, or VoIP, represented by the growing popularity of Skype's offerings? And Rupert Murdoch, a savvy player in his own right, continued to push satellite communications and search engines. Finally, Google, Goldman Sachs, and the Hearst Corporation are investing in a start-up that offers high-speed Internet connections over the existing electric power system.

To complicate things further, there was the shifting sand

of legislation and regulatory decisions. In July 2005, the Texas legislature cleared the way for phone companies to apply for permission to offer TV on a statewide basis rather than seek permission from each municipality. That same month, Kevin Martin, the new chairman of the Federal Communications Commission (FCC) and a political appointee who almost certainly would be replaced in the next few years, was circulating plans to loosen rules so phone companies would no longer be forced to share their Internet connections with competitors like America Online, a sharp reversal of the Telecommunications Act of 1996, which forced local phone companies to give competitors access to their networks at wholesale prices.

How would it all play out? Seidenberg had to think through all those nonquantifiable factors, *sifting, sorting, and selecting* what information could help him decide what will prevail, in what conditions, with what timing, and with a sharp focus on changing consumer buying behavior. In addition he had to take into consideration competitors, emerging coalitions of rivals, and special interest groups.

People like Ivan Seidenberg develop mental processes and convictions that drive them to find solutions through iteration and reiteration of scenarios, reframing questions and looking at the same phenomena through a variety of lenses. They realize that the answers they seek are qualitative in nature and cannot be solved with a quantitative formula. The changes they are seeing are unprecedented in their scope and create unique opportunities and threats.

How change is perceived is very much a function of an individual's psychological construct. Some fear it, while others relish it. Confident leaders with an optimistic or realistic outlook almost always try to convert their perceptions into opportunity, even though in the short run what turns out to be an opportunity may be a threat. A broad cognitive bandwidth enables them to see the threat as part of a larger opportunity. In Seidenberg's case, that would mean dealing realistically with the decline of the wire-line business and the intense competition of wireless to see a much bigger pie, of which these two are but a slice. Seeing the total picture and taking realistic action is an underappreciated combination of cognitive bandwidth and know-how that few possess. For example, since the 1984 breakup of the Bell System, of the thirteen CEOs of major telecommunications companies, only two, Seidenberg and Edward Whitacre, have really "gotten it" and made the right moneymaking moves over a ten-year period.

One way to become effective in the know-how of seeing emerging patterns is to be an active listener who continually searches for what is new and different. Seidenberg has said that in every conversation he looks for ideas he has never heard before. The initial picture you draw may be fuzzy, but continuing to search for the nuggets will help create clarity. Your psychology, however, must be realistic. A pessimist will see only threats and hurdles, while an optimist may be led by ambition to reach a conclusion and take action too quickly, before the picture has become clear.

The mental exercise involved in this know-how requires that you recognize how you have obtained information in the past. Did you actively seek it out, or did you just let it come to you? You must also recognize that information is asymmetrical; that is, it may be only partial or distorted. You need to continue searching to fill the gaps until the light bulb goes on and the important things come into focus.

For Ivan Seidenberg, it's a foregone conclusion that his business is entering uncharted waters, with uncertain boundaries, unpredictable consolidations and demergers, unknown pricing structures, and myriad technologies. Each move by any player in the industry triggers actions and reactions by all the others, resulting in evolving new rules of the game and changes in the architecture of moneymaking, while technologies are evolving, governments are taking actions, and consumer preferences are shifting and in many cases are untested. This is the world Seidenberg is immersed in and must crystallize into a plausible picture of the landscape. He extracts useful insights and ideas from sophisticated quantitative analysis and combines them with his personal imagination and observations and tests them through the lenses of other people with whom he interacts.

Judgments, of course, may be wrong, and it takes psychological strength to live with the uncertainty and risks. Seidenberg has made destiny-determining decisions based on his personal assessment of events that are not entirely predictable based on traditional probabilistic risk assessments. If he's wrong, he will have to deal with the consequences. He also knows that the risk of not making such a decision could be higher than making it.

LOOKING OUTSIDE IN

The earlier you can detect changes, the more time you will have to generate and test hypotheses, mobilize resources, and, if necessary, reposition the business to achieve your moneymaking targets.

Looking beyond the usual boundaries of the business environment helps you detect changes early on. For instance, the political process has far more impact on business now than ever before, and it is essential that you know and understand the ramifications of legislation and regulations for your business and industry, as well as special interest groups that may have an impact on you.

As you continually practice looking from the outside in, you must develop the skill to figure out what kind of change it is. Is it cyclical—this, too, shall pass—and therefore not a fundamental shift? Or is the change structural and secular, something that won't go away and must eventually be dealt with? If you can perceive changes as opportunities, you'll be more likely to see things as they really are.

Consider the television networks, which have been steadily losing viewers for the past twenty years even as programming costs have been rising. ABC wound up selling a portion of its advertising inventory for the 2006 Super Bowl at the eleventh hour at roughly half price. Is that merely an inventory adjustment, or is it an important indicator of a radical change in the way advertisers use various media? Additionally, is it also an early warning indicator of a permanent decline in the sources of ABC's revenues?

You must begin early in your career to lay the groundwork to practice this know-how by searching for the jobs that will give you the experience in testing, building, and honing it. One example would be a position as a regional marketing manager of a retail chain like Home Depot or Lowe's. Looking from the outside in, you could learn not just the quantifiable data on demographic changes—growing numbers of Hispanics and retired people in a region, for example—but also how the societal, political, and economic milieu affects the qualitative lifestyles and composition of the population of the area. You could in that position understand cause and effect, seeing how the fit looks for the business regarding how many stores should be in the region, which ones to close, which new ones to create, and how to shift the mix of merchandise. In this type of job experience, you tend to become broader. Success in pinpointing how change affects your business can improve your self-confidence as your cognitive skills expand. The same will be true—and you will expand your scope—by seizing opportunities for jobs like country manager and global product manager.

Anyone can begin to hone this skill by simply reading the "What's News" column on the front page of the *Wall Street*

Journal each weekday morning. I don't mean just skimming it to get a quick dose of the previous day's news, I mean reading each item carefully and slowly and then thinking about what it means for your company and your industry. What is changing and for whom? Where is the opportunity in that change and for whom? It's a simple exercise that over time helps condition your brain to detect patterns from these observations and what they mean for various businesses and industries.

HOW TO DETECT THE POINTS BEFORE THEY TIP

People with extraordinary know-how for detecting patterns in the external environment fly at a higher imaginative altitude than others. They see things others miss, seek sources others don't, and piece things together in their own creative ways. As with all the know-hows, the skill gets better with practice, and you become more self-assured in acting on your assessments. Thus this know-how is a source of confidence for going on the offensive, to be distinguished from the bravado of those who make bold moves (and have an occasional lucky strike) without it and those who are paralyzed or continually on the defensive for lack of it. This is the know-how that differentiates a Seidenberg, an Andy Grove, a Jeff Immelt, or a Steve Jobs, all of whom have superb know-how for pinpointing patterns in the external environment. Such leaders have this theater running continuously in their unconscious mind; for them, the sorting, sifting, and selecting is well practiced, automatic, and of high quality. Some leaders make a lucky call and look like geniuses, but continual practice and conscious effort improve the know-how and the chances for success. It is part of what differentiates leaders who succeed from those who don't. They have the drive and consistent dedication of time and energy to get exposure to new ideas and new information.

Jeff Immelt, who is running General Electric, a global company with several distinct businesses, develops and hones this know-how through a process of meeting with customers in what he calls "dream sessions." He invites people from one customer industry at a time, usually CEOs and one or two of their associates, to the GE learning center at Crotonville, New York, for a one- or two-day session in which the conversations and presentations are geared toward what each of the participants visualize over a long period of time—up to ten years. They discuss the external trends, the root causes of those trends, how they might converge, in what fashion, and what the picture might be as seen from as many different angles as possible, including the customer's customers, suppliers, regulators, special interest groups, and trends in technology. By having that discussion, everyone learns what the different possible pictures of the future are. The major purpose is to see what are the drivers, what are the missing pieces of the picture, what has to happen, what would be the early warning signals. It broadens the mind and prepares it to detect something it has not detected before. It builds a relationship between Immelt and his customers and may even generate ideas for shaping the landscape.

At these sessions, Immelt gets concrete. Take, for example, the energy business. Everybody knows the energy game of the future is in huge flux. People are talking about the supply and demand of oil and natural gas and alternate sources like ethanol, as well as the increased dollar reserves of oil suppliers such as Russia and the Middle Eastern countries, all of which will have implications for business units like GE Energy that manufacture turbines, engines, and infrastructure products and services. Immelt might raise the question "If GE were to invest one billion dollars over the next ten years in research and development in this sector, where should it put its priorities, what technologies are likely to have a better chance of succeeding, and what actions might be initiated now to build the future several years out?" For people who have an affinity for this kind of exercise, it is exhilarating. One of the great benefits is that it gets you beyond the day-to-day focus on details, helping you parse out what an ambiguous future is going to look like.

Meetings like the dream sessions could, for example, discuss how GE might develop ideas for ways governments in countries around the world could standardize requirements for the technology that treats the emissions causing mean temperatures around the world to increase. Through standardization, the price of the technology could be brought down, resulting in a win-win: creating an opportunity for GE to grow and helping solve global warming, an important environmental issue.

What Immelt accomplishes through dream sessions with customers is build a huge reservoir of knowledge of the world business landscape. He also widens his lens and increases his self-confidence by clearing the blur of ambiguity.

It isn't necessary that you be a CEO to seek the big picture. While CEOs and business unit managers need to see the external patterns to position the business, other leaders need this know-how too, for instance, for HR to do talent planning, for operations to choose plant locations, and for R&D to find new sources of innovation.

BETWEEN A ROCK AND A HARD PLACE

Some people reading this book may think, "Well, these 'dream sessions' are fine for CEOs with large support staffs. But, for me, I've to get cracking and organize the shipment out to the Toyota plant in Tennessee or get the weekly accounts receivable report done." All true, but you still have to make time to parse out what the future will bring. Without the insight and knowledge of the type Immelt develops about

GE's businesses, you run the danger of being a victim of events, rather than a shaper of them. With early warning, you become better prepared psychologically when something goes wrong. When you don't know, when uncertainty reigns, the doubt that results can be paralyzing.

The other fear arises when a key assumption in a thought process—I call it a "hinge assumption" because if that hinge breaks, it all falls apart—is wrong and eventually creates a problem. Being aware of these two possibilities helps you prepare for dealing deal with them, by always searching for clues or evidence and having a backup plan.

Jim, an executive I've observed over the past several years, dillydallied as a changing world stared him in the face. He runs an automobile parts company that his father started years ago to supply General Motors. The story of Jim's company is an object lesson of someone in the middle of a perfect storm of external change. Jim is an excellent operator, very much in tune with GM's production schedules. His company is profitable, and he is a respected member of Detroit's close-knit automotive community. But like anyone in the auto industry, Jim has been well aware that GM is undergoing a crisis as it struggles to find a survival path.

As he watched GM's market share, cash generation, and profitability dwindle, particularly over the past five years, Jim began to worry about the future of both GM and his own company. At first it was just a nagging concern, and he accepted at face value reassurances from his contacts at GM that the big automaker would soon stem the market-share losses and meet its moneymaking targets. But the reassurances began to sound increasingly hollow as the market-share losses continued despite GM's costly offers of rebates and discounts that hurt its brand image and GM's buyers pressed him for and received continually lower prices. His fears mounted when GM's bond rating was cut to "junk" status in 2005, but he drew some solace from his friends among the automobile executives who kept talking about how the government would work out a way to relieve GM of some of the crippling health-care and pension costs that put the company at a competitive disadvantage. But the last time I talked to him, Jim admitted that he was now worrying constantly about the near-term future. There was talk about GM filing for bankruptcy, and Jim was afraid that GM might default on its agreement with his company. Deep down he has serious doubts about the ability of GM's management to turn the company around, certain it will be several years before it makes money again.

During the five years that Jim watched GM declining, he had thought about making some bold moves. A Japanese auto supply company had once offered to buy Jim's company, but the discussions fell apart when the Japanese firm refused to meet Jim's asking price. At another point, he joined an industry group on a trade mission to China, where he met the head of a Chinese manufacturing company who expressed an interest in setting up a partnership with an American firm like Jim's. But Jim decided not to pursue a deal after being told by others how difficult it is to do business in China, particularly getting partners to respect contract provisions. There may be other opportunities ahead for Jim to sell his company, diversify his product line and customer base, or otherwise change the future course of his company. The doubt that plagues Jim is psychological fear of the uncertainty of each of the alternatives that could reduce his dependence on GM. Where would the right customers be? Is the center of gravity of those customers going to shift to China? Why didn't I pursue Toyota, Honda, Nissan, and BMW when they built plants in the United States? Given the uncertain prices of energy and the power of energy suppliers over consumers, what effect will that have on the nature of vehicles customers prefer? Where will they be manufactured and what new technologies will they require? In that context, what must be my positioning to enable my business to continue to make money?

GOING ON THE OFFENSIVE

In my observation, people who create organic growth that is profitable and sustainable connect the dots sooner and are on the offensive. The greatest challenge today is finding new opportunities for profitable and sustainable growth in a complex and tough environment. To achieve an objective like this, you have to be psychologically comfortable to go beyond traditional thinking about an industry and sense what is happening on the outside, connect the dots, and discover what the new opportunities are.

Consider the product that redeemed a foundering Chrysler Corporation. As a product planner at Ford, Hal Sperlich was a key player on Lee Iaccoca's team and the force behind the design of the original Mustang, the inexpensive sporty car that struck a chord with young people all across America. At Ford and later at Chrysler, Sperlich had access to lots of statistics on demographics and the American auto market. Very little of that data was proprietary and everyone in the auto industry used it. But Sperlich combined those facts in a different way and detected an emerging pattern. He didn't use the term "soccer mom," but he intuitively understood a significant shift in the lifestyle of middle-class Americans. His insight led to the idea of a minivan, a vehicle with the spaciousness of a truck but the comfort and handling of car, great for carpooling and family travel, and a perfect fit for the emerging market segment.

Ford rejected the concept of the minivan, but Sperlich stuck with his conviction even as he was fired from Ford and joined Chrysler. A year later, when Iacocca, who also had been fired from Ford, landed at Chrysler as president, the company was on the verge of extinction, relying on an unprecedented $1.2 billion in government backed loans as a last-ditch effort to survive. Iacocca, looking for salvation, bought into Sperlich's assessment of the external trend. Chrysler introduced the minivan in 1983. It was an immediate hit, the right product at the right time. The minivan's high margins sustained Chrysler throughout the 1980s, even allowing the company to repay its bailout loans seven years ahead of time.

One enlightening contemporary example of using this know-how to go on the offensive is the aforementioned General Electric CEO Jeff Immelt. He saw that if GE's growth was to rise to 8 percent per annum from 5 percent, the source of that growth would have to change, and he and his team found a new source in emerging markets. Periodically rethinking what is happening to the external landscape is a requirement of the top job at GE, and Immelt, by his own estimate, spends some 20 percent of his time just thinking and reconceptualizing what is happening in the world.

By firsthand observation and accounts of those who know him, Immelt has the capacity to take in a huge amount of detail and sift, sort, and select it to make sense of it. He is a voracious reader and a "searching" listener. He seems to relish rather than be overwhelmed by the breadth of information that is important and relevant to a company as large and diverse as GE. He didn't step into his role with announcements about major changes to the business; rather, he let the inputs percolate, he "wallowed" in the information, testing ideas among his top team, his board, and his peers. Eventually he conceptualized a clear picture of the patterns of external change. Despite his own acknowledgments of the complexity of GE's world, which includes what he calls a "tsunami of regulations," volatility of currencies and stock markets, and uncertainties about oil prices and the behavior of foreign governments, he is now moving with great confidence to shape a path for his company consistent with the emerging external realities that will deliver earnings and cash. Immelt hit his targets in 2005 and appears to be on the right course to deliver through 2008.

Immelt has made it clear, for instance, that in the face of "rampant globalization," the greatest opportunity for growth is in emerging markets, and he expects that more than half of all GE employees will be outside the United States in five years. He sees opportunities in health care, transportation, security, financial services, energy, entertainment, and advanced materials and has reorganized the company to pursue them. Accepting the reality that society will no longer tolerate abuse of the environment, Immelt has built issues like water treatment and global warming into his ideas about how to grow the business. Alert to hot-button issues like executive compensation and corporate governance, he has made transparency and accountability part of GE's modus operandi for the future.

Immelt appears to be making bold bets on an unknown future. But his know-how in detecting external patterns helps him identify and therefore manage the risks. Some people might determine that emerging markets present high risks and avoid them. Immelt (and others like him) contends that if that's where the opportunity is, the risks must be managed. As a leader, he is therefore making the right internal changes, assigning the right resources, and going on the offensive to be sure his people identify the risks and develop the tools and management innovations to manage those risks. One of GE's core competencies is quantifying risks and managing those risks through dispersion in the capital markets. He has made organizational changes to put the very best experts from GE Capital into the newly created infrastructure business that will work in emerging markets.

While his positioning for GE is right, it was not being recognized by the investors to the extent it should be. But Immelt's inner security, no doubt reinforced by the quality of his thinking, allowed him to withstand skepticism and get the support of the board. His know-how and confidence have positioned GE well for sustained growth.

The challenges, then, are to keep your perceptual and psychological lenses open, to actively search for what you don't know or is not yet clear, to avoid relying too much on the past for indications of what might happen in the future, to absorb and digest complexity, and to shape or let the patterns emerge as they will, even if they present unpleasant realities.

Seven simple questions can help you sort through and detect patterns in the complex world around you.

1. **What is happening in the world today?** The most significant trends affecting business transcend company and industry. They cross borders and infuse all areas of civil society. Take India as one example. The Internet has made it easy for corporations to link operations in Manhattan and Mumbai, exposing villagers in India to Western brands such as Dell and Levi's.

    While India's rapidly growing boom in IT-related software and services is well known, many are also watching carefully as the government gradually opens up other sectors of the economy, such as retailing, to foreign investor participation. Executives at Wal-Mart, Tesco, and Carrefour are waiting for the day when the retail sector opens up.

    But will that day come? There are those in India who believe that the benefits of foreign investment have not accrued to poor or less-educated citizens. Thus, political forces are pressuring the Indian government to keep controls on the retail sector, to protect the livelihoods of family-owned mom-and-pop stores. This political pressure has weight: in 2005, the same forces effectively blocked the government's plans to divest a portion of its ownership in Bharat Heavy Electricals Limited (BHEL), India's successful manufacturer of power-generation and -transmission equipment. Thus, foreign participation in retail, despite the government's stated intention, is not a foregone conclusion.

As this example demonstrates, trends that may at first seem disparate are not unrelated; they must be considered in combination. You must learn to fill in the gaps among them, and to iterate this mental process until a complete picture comes into focus. And the way to do that is not only to consider the direct effects of change on an industry and a company, but also to rethink the changes through the lenses of other industries and other players.

2. **What part of my frame of reference has worked for me? What hasn't worked for me?** The construction of your own frame of reference based on previous experience is a large part of learning to detect changes in external patterns. You should constantly be asking yourself, "What has worked for me and what hasn't worked for me?" When you experience a failure in detecting a change—and you will—you need to reflect on why you missed it. Only through that kind of reflection can you update your frame of reference and make it more useful. It is against this frame of reference that we all make instinctive judgments and react to situations.

A rising young executive I know learned this lesson in his job as a unit manager. From 2000 to 2003, he kept predicting that the economy would slow sharply. For three years, he was wrong. As he looked back recently at the factors that led to those predictions, he found that he had missed two key points. First, he failed to predict that the Federal Reserve could or would take real interest rates down to an effective level of zero. Second, he incorrectly estimated the impact of the Bush administration's tax cuts.

He discovered that the Fed was totally out of his perceptual lens, and, as a consequence, he misinterpreted the effect of the tax cuts. He should have been watching what Alan Greenspan said and did. Greenspan had to choose among several conflicting goals: ensuring job growth, keeping the federal and trade deficits in check, and preventing speculative excesses in asset prices, namely, housing. He chose job growth at the expense of swelling federal and trade deficits and a speculative bubble in housing prices. With interest rates low, the tax cuts fueled additional consumption that in turn fed both the trade deficit and the rise in housing prices. Greenspan's successor at the Fed, Ben Bernanke, said recently that it would take ten years to reverse the trade deficit.

After his dismal experience in predicting the economy's course, the young executive has learned to pay attention to the Fed. When Ben Bernanke took over from Alan Greenspan early in 2006, he listened intently to everything he said and realized that his promises—to set a target for inflation, to avoid bursting the housing bubble, to keep the trade deficit from worsening, and to sustain confidence in the dollar—could not all be kept. He knew something would have to give, but he didn't yet know what it would be.

3. **What does it mean for anyone?** The newspaper industry, as mentioned in the previous chapter, is undergoing vast changes as a result of the Internet and Google. Newspaper executives are scrambling to cope with the new reality as they begin to see the implications of these changes. Disenchanted investors even forced Knight Ridder to seek a buyer. And what is to become of the writers who supply content for the print industry? Many of them have started to pursue online opportunities, whether on a blog of their own, an online magazine like *Slate,* or an online news service like the one Yahoo! is building. Will the best writers

want to write for staid newspapers and magazines in the future? The effect on human capital bears watching.

What might the government do? Google's Library Project initiative hopes to scan entire books from public and university libraries. Readers could then search books and access pages through the Internet. Five book publishers filed suit against Google over what they perceive as copyright infringement. Will the courts side with the print publishers or with innovative new media producers? Will Congress write new laws to update copyright protections? The government's response could change the moneymaking model of book publishing forever.

Venture capitalists could direct money toward companies that are developing newer technologies for media consumption, such as electronic books (e-books) and portable video players. Should those products catch on, it could place further stress on traditional media's approach to moneymaking. Indeed, venture capitalists and university scientists exist, in part, to create change. And when a trend sparks reactions from these change makers en masse, the ramifications for the old guard can accelerate and broaden in scope.

All of these potential responses matter. Leaders with well-honed business acumen keep looking at trends through different lenses and from the perspectives of other key players.

4. **What does it mean for us?** Once you have the big picture, you can begin to examine what it means for your own company's strategies. That's what Jeff Immelt did when he decided to meld several of GE's businesses into the infrastructure business to sell items such as energy equipment and services, railroad locomotives, and aircraft items, all necessary ingredients in rapidly growing economies. But he didn't stop there. He also took account of the evidence that much of the world is becoming more concerned about

the environment, particularly global warming. Based on those concerns, GE launched growth initiatives—for example, turbines, solar generators, and nuclear power plants—that are relevant to energy concerns. Discerning macroeconomic trends, Immelt put GE on a course to seize the new opportunities.

5. **What would have to happen?** For macroeconomic trends to create opportunities, certain things have to happen. Apple's invention of the iPod, for example, would have been considerably less successful had it not created iTunes, the online source of downloadable music. But there were, in turn, certain prerequisites for iTunes to become viable: consumers had to be willing to pay for rather than steal downloaded music; the major music studios had to see that they could sell their copyrighted music; and, finally, the price point had to be right. Not all situations are easy to control, however. Market forces—the price of a gallon of gasoline, for example—can be an essential ingredient that makes something like a hybrid car viable. A competitor's move may be what it takes to create opportunities. When Apple and Disney agreed to offer downloads of ABC television shows for the video version of iPod, NBC and CBS soon announced their own partnerships with DirecTV and Comcast.

6. **What do we have to do to play a role?** GE's decision to market its infrastructure products in emerging markets required it to reorganize those businesses in a way that recognized the difference between selling a power plant to an American utility and selling that same power plant to a foreign government. Governments are fragmented, have high turnover, and, in the emerging markets, often lack the requisite financing to make big investments. The reorganization not only brought the infrastructure businesses under one leader focused on marketing, selling, building, and installing infrastructure products, it also incorporated

some of the financing skills and risk management in GE Capital. Finally, it included a major change in who and where GE began to recruit to build its leadership pipeline. Today half of the highest level executive development class at GE's Crotonville center come from outside the United States.

7. **What do we do next?** That's the question Ivan Seidenberg answered at the beginning of this chapter. After assimilating and processing all the information he could find, Seidenberg decided to invest $2 billion to begin to replace the copper phone wires coming into homes with fiber-optic cable. The investment wouldn't generate revenues for months or even a year or two, and investors clearly weren't happy with the idea. But Seidenberg knew that his customers, employees, and related industry groups that would use the wires liked the idea, so he went ahead.

So far you've been very much immersed in looking at a business from the outside in, looking at positioning from an external viewpoint, and building the know-how to become better in your judgment and linking it to moneymaking. Your inner voice might be asking, "But can we execute the change?" To execute it, things have to change internally—the working of the organization, the behaviors in the organization, the social system of the organization, and the culture. Often leaders choose a positioning, unconsciously making the assumption that it will be very hard if not impossible to change how the organization works. The know-how of making the organization's social system deliver what you need it to is now a requisite for success. This is the subject of the next chapter.

Leaders who connect the dots:

- Have a methodology for anticipating and detecting breaks in the continuity of the external landscape.

- Imagine one or more pictures of the future and pinpoint the gaps that make the picture incomplete.

- Have a reliable, diverse social network—both inside and outside the business—people with different perspectives who help them see their business through a new lens.

- Talk to their network for ideas about how to close gaps that they identify.

- Have the personal imagination to construct patterns from emerging disparate trends, always searching for the missing links and missing ingredients.

- Are psychologically self-aware of potential bias on their part or that of people they associate with to be overly optimistic or pessimistic, thereby distorting a realistic perception of external trends.

- Connect patterns of change with the question of whether the positioning of the business could become irrelevant or obsolete.

4

HERDING CATS

Getting People to Work Together by Managing the
Social System of Your Business

Perhaps the biggest untapped opportunity for your success as
a leader is shaping the way people work together to deliver
the numbers. Your own performance depends on your ability
to get other people to commit to and deliver their common
goals. But as every leader knows, getting people to align their
efforts is a lot like herding cats. You can put a lot of energy
into it, and they still do as they damn well please.

Some astute business leaders have solved the mystery of
how to synchronize the human elements of their organization,
and by observing them over many years, I've distilled their
know-how in managing the social aspects of their companies
to deliver results. Based on my firsthand observations of
leaders—some famous, some not—who were especially good

at managing what I call the social system of their organizations, I created a hypothesis about what they were doing to synchronize people's efforts, and I then tested it with many companies and their leaders. It has held up, and I'm now confident in saying that understanding the social system of your business is the best way to get a handle on the otherwise mysterious subject of managing and changing how people work together to meet ever-changing business requirements.

Every company—from a big business to the smallest two-person shop—has a social system. You probably don't call it that, but that's the term I use to describe the various ways people come together to do their work. As they meet, they influence each other for better or worse. They develop relationships and feelings about each other. They share information and make necessary trade-offs and decisions. How they work together creates energy gains or energy drains and determines whether they deliver on the commitments they make to each other.

Managing the social system has two parts. You have to be able to determine what critical decisions and trade-offs must get made, and by whom, to accomplish your business goals. Then you use that insight to design disciplined, routine, regularly scheduled meetings—I call them operating mechanisms—to bring the right people together at the right frequency with the right information to make those decisions. That's one part of the know-how. The other part is to actively shape the behaviors that are displayed in making those decisions. In the course of those interactions, people may be hoarding information, going off on tangents, and not getting to the nub of the issues. They may also be driving individual agendas, not surfacing conflicts, and failing to reach clear resolutions. You have to shape the content of these discussions and ensure that the right behaviors are taking place in them and the output links to results. In short, you have to actively design and lead the social system of your business, which comprises all of the operating mechanisms, the connections among them, and what happens in them.

Whenever you see a company that is doing something consistently well—creating one good product after another, delivering on time day after day, or steadily driving down costs—you can be sure that there is an effective social system behind it.

A social system that is running well enables a business to execute ambitious strategies to enter new markets, gain market share, or improve profits. But the social system at many businesses is out of sync with what it ought to accomplish. Business results can fall short for a variety of reasons—because the positioning is obsolete, the goals were unrealistic, or the business was hit by something unanticipated in the external environment—but a leader with this know-how will always investigate the social system to see if it is the source of the problem and take specific steps to fix it.

Know-how in diagnosing, designing, and leading the social system is how some leaders are able to mobilize people to deliver results and transform an organization from, say, a bureaucracy to a well-oiled machine, as Jack Welch did as CEO of GE, or from an entrepreneurial culture to one that coordinates actions without sacrificing flexibility, as Bob Nardelli did as CEO of Home Depot. It provides the tools for actually getting things done, even in businesses where people have a self-defeating mind-set, saying to themselves and each other things such as "We can't innovate" or "We're too risk averse" or "We can't even make a decision."

All too often when trying to initiate change, people fall back on changing the organizational structure, replacing key people, and altering what is measured and rewarded. While these steps may be necessary, it's putting the cart before the horse.

You need to look at your business through the lens of the social system. Look at the interaction among people, the information flows, and the anatomy of decision making. You have to be able to map your operating mechanisms, ensure that each of them is geared around a business result, and diagnose how each of them is actually working. If new ones are required or existing ones are obsolete, it's your job to change them. And if the people are not having the right discussions in them or behaving in the right way, it's your job to correct those behaviors, using persuasion, power, and rewards, whether money, recognition, or promotion, as necessary.

That's how the social system changes—through your conscious actions in designing and redesigning the operating mechanisms and conducting the dialogue in a way that shapes people's behaviors. As you do this repetitively, with discipline, you change the quality and substance of business decisions, and because the behaviors that get shaped in the operating mechanisms carry over to people's everyday work, you sustain a change in how people work together. With this know-how, you accomplish the elusive goal of culture change and develop the ability to deliver on commitments and achieve business results.

As you practice this know-how, you'll develop a keen eye for pinpointing problems in the social system, and you'll have more confidence in your ability to change it. You will then make better choices about how to reposition a business because you know you can change the social system to make it happen. This know-how is a must for twenty-first-century leaders.

CARL AND HARRY

Here's a story of how one newly appointed leader diagnosed the social system of his new company and within months had begun to change it.

"Keep up the good work, and thanks for your time, folks," Harry, the new CEO, said just before the video screen went dark.

A few seconds later voices erupted over the speaker.

"We should have told corporate that operating profits for next quarter are going to be higher," said one voice.

"For God's sake, don't give those SOBs in New York any of that information," replied another voice, clearly Carl's, the division president. "They'll just use it to crank up the target."

Stunned by what they had heard over the open mike, the company's corporate staff officers sat silently in their New York conference room, waiting to see how Harry would respond. He didn't. It was past seven o'clock and he was already late for a dinner across town, so he quickly grabbed his notepad and left the room.

Harry, of course, was quietly furious about Carl's comment. But his immediate reaction had been to keep his feelings to himself. Later that evening, as he sat sipping a Scotch in his study and thinking about the incident, he was glad he had restrained himself. In the two months that Harry had been in charge of the company, Carl had made a positive impression. When Harry brought all the division presidents together in New York to discuss his core values, especially the the need for candor, Carl had bought into the program. And he was doing an excellent job of running his division, the company's biggest and most profitable. But Harry knew from this incident that something wasn't right, and he wanted to get to the bottom of it.

None of the staff who had overheard the conversation brought it up the next morning. But when Harry questioned them each separately that day, the response was uniform: "That's the way it is. The divisions hold back as much information as they can. We have to beg and plead to get anything from them." The CFO went further, saying, "Carl's always sandbagging us on operating profit—and it hurts my credibility on the Street. I don't see how we can keep him long term."

Harry was slowly but surely starting to see that it wasn't just Carl who was not being forthcoming with headquarters, and he surmised that quarterly operating reviews under his predecessor had been full of fear and intimidation. Interactions like that wouldn't produce the kind of information flow he would need to make decisions about where to focus and how to shift resources. He had to be able to find out what was really happening in the field so he could make the appropriate adjustments. The quarterly operating review was the right mechanism to accomplish that—the right people were coming together for the right reasons—but the behavior was all wrong. Having worked in two different companies where candor was the norm, Harry knew instinctively—and exactly—what the company was missing, and he had an idea about how to open things up to get the information he would need to get things working properly. He would start by arranging a private dinner with Carl in a quiet restaurant in downtown Houston.

Like the jungle telegraphs at most companies, this one was highly efficient, so Carl had found out about the open speaker and was nervous when Harry called. When the two men sat down to dinner, Harry could sense Carl's discomfort and tried to put him at ease with some small talk. Then he calmly and confidently put the issue squarely on the table.

"I suppose you already know that the squawk box was open, and I imagine you're pretty embarrassed and worried about it," Harry said. Carl waited solemnly for the hammer to fall.

"Look, Carl," Harry continued. "I'd like to put that behind us and figure out how we can work together better."

Carl's face flashed both surprise and relief as Harry went on to solicit his ideas about how to improve their working relationship and the flow of information. Responding to Harry's candor, Carl opened up a little. The previous CEO had been an erratic personality who trusted no one; he often assigned targets with no rationale behind them, then he and the CFO came down hard on people for not achieving them. The average tenure for a division president was a mere three years. Harry knew the former CEO had never had a line job in operations and had no background in finance, but apparently that didn't stop him from meddling in both. The way to survive and do what was best for the business, the divisions found, was to keep operating and financial information close to the vest. "We do what we have to to stay out of the crosshairs," Carl told Harry.

Harry had broken the ice, and for the first time in his fifteen years with the company, Carl felt liberated from the toxicity that had plagued every quarterly review, every budget review, and every talent review, caused by not knowing which way the former CEO was going to go and the fear of being embarrassed in front of peers. Anyone would be skeptical of a new CEO, but the dinner-table conversation and the manner in which the new CEO approached Carl made him think, "Maybe this company will change for the better and I can be part of it."

As Harry reflected on the situation during the return flight, he wondered how deep and widespread the toxicity was. He knew that at this point spontaneously firing someone like Carl or changing the organizational structure was not the right remedy. What he had to do was change the interactions, largely through the operating mechanisms of quarterly operating reviews, budgeting and goal-setting sessions, talent-planning discussions, and weekly cash flow video conferences. What was far more important was what information is exchanged, how much freedom is created for people to opine, what new information is brought from outside, how candor is valued by the leader, and the know-how of the leader to draw everybody in, surface conflicts, and get the group to be decisive without making poor compromises. Although he was still new in the job, he was starting to develop a pretty good idea of what needed to change and how to change it.

OPERATING MECHANISMS AS THE
BUILDING BLOCKS OF THE SOCIAL SYSTEM

The know-how of managing the social system involves your leadership in building operating mechanisms at critical intersections—the places where information must be exchanged, conflicts must be surfaced and resolved, and trade-offs and decisions must be made for specific business purposes. You need to enforce the right behaviors in them, then ensure that the output from one operating mechanism (say, the changes to strategy that come out of a strategy review) become integrated into others (such as talent reviews and budgeting sessions, where resources are allocated).

If this sounds self-evident, it is. People must share information and make trade-offs to meet commitments, but it doesn't happen automatically. It's your job as a leader to design and manage a social system with a well-oiled set of operating mechanisms. It takes time, effort, and—yes—leadership to make sure that the right people are coming together and discussions are properly focused and intellectually honest so the business makes better, faster decisions and can accomplish what it sets out to do. If you're not doing your job of managing the social system, chances are information flow is inadequate, differences don't get surfaced and resolved, decision making slows, and things that should happen either don't or take too long. Execution suffers.

You also have to establish and enforce what behaviors are acceptable and which are not. You do this through conducting dialogue. You have to be able to perceive when a person's behavior is going off the track and have the emotional fortitude to correct it face-to-face, often right there on the spot. Through dialogue, people can see what you, the leader, think is important. They learn, for example, when contradictory views are really welcome, whether conflicts are to be aired or suppressed, whether it's OK to sidetrack or dominate discussions, and whether decisions are based on facts or personal power. It is in the conduct of these sessions, guiding the dialogue and flow of information, in which leadership becomes a performing art.

Most companies' social systems are a mishmash of operating mechanisms that are poorly designed and disconnected from each other, and behavior in them is left to chance. That's why so many people live with the drudgery of pointless meetings with no real output, unresolved conflicts that fester below the surface, and inefficient, distorted flows of information (such as the CFO feeling sandbagged by Carl and the other divisional presidents because they weren't providing accurate information), all of which render even the most talented of individuals less effective than they could be.

One CEO actually created a map of the meetings he attended during a typical year. There were fifty-two weekly staff meetings, twelve monthly meetings about operating results, four quarterly business reviews to prepare for meetings with financial analysts and investors, a strategy meeting to prepare long-term plans, a succession of talent-planning meetings to review human assets, and a budget meeting to prepare quantifiable goals commitments and resource allocation for the following year. And those are just the ones regularly scheduled, totaling at least seventy. (You have to include in the total number many other meetings called ad hoc to deal with some current pressing issue as well as meetings to prepare for the meetings listed above.)

A large part of the energy, time, and psychological reserves of highly valued leaders is invested in all of these meetings. It, however, is the combination of these regularly scheduled meetings, or operating mechanisms, that determines what is going to be delivered in terms of business results.

There are four pertinent questions you need to ask about the operating mechanisms that make up your social system.

1. What is the purpose of the existing operating mechanisms and how do they and their linkages combine to help deliver results?
2. Which ones should be kept, eliminated, or combined?
3. Which require a total redesign and a new way to lead them?
4. Are there new operating mechanisms that should be installed?

You don't have to be a CEO or even have formal authority over people to operate effectively within your company's social system. You could, for example, be like the product manager who gets engineering, marketing, and manufacturing to have open, constructive debates about product features and price points. And you can create your own operating mechanism around the results you need to deliver.

It takes know-how to cut through the organized chaos that exists in most companies and zero in on the critical intersections. When, for instance, your business is deciding where to produce the new product critical to your goals for organic growth, you need to know the implications of outsourcing, building your own plant in various locations, doing a joint venture or contracting production to an existing manufacturer, and protecting intellectual property. Only by bringing together people from finance, manufacturing, and logistics to share what they know about these topics and ensuring that their discussions are open and intellectually honest can you arrive at the correct decision. While the challenges are greater as you move to higher organizational levels or larger businesses—especially when you move from a functional silo like marketing to being in charge of a P&L center—your success will depend on how well you've developed your know-how in managing the social system.

HOW TO KNOW WHAT OPERATING MECHANISMS YOU NEED

If you are going to do an effective job of leading your social system, you will have to design operating mechanisms around your most important business activities, such as serving new markets and achieving growth. Each operating mechanism must have a clear business purpose. With that purpose in mind, you have to determine who should be required to attend and how often they should meet. If you are not personally conducting the dialogue, you have to be sure you assign a leader who has the skill to shape both the content and behaviors. Sometimes the appropriate operating mechanism already exists, but it needs to be adjusted, because the content, behaviors, composition, or leadership is wrong. This is often true of quarterly operating reviews, strategy sessions, talent-review sessions, and budgeting sessions.

What follows are examples of how operating mechanisms can be created or modified to deliver specific business and behavioral results. They range from creating new sources of revenue by developing new products on an ongoing basis to changing the culture of an entire company.

Creating New Products for Sustained Revenue Growth

When Todd Bradley became CEO of palmOne (now Palm, Inc.) in 2003, the pioneer in handheld devices was withering, and speculation was that it wouldn't survive the squeeze between mobile devices and big PDAs. Palm had experienced explosive growth in the 1990s with its early products, but as the market evolved and the company didn't, new models began to accumulate in inventory, hurting revenues, cash, and the stock price. Bradley had no intention of letting Palm become the ham in the sandwich; he moved aggressively to lower costs by working on the supply chain. But the bigger problem was rooted in a product design process that was disconnected from the needs of many potential customers. The technologists had to learn to see their products through the eyes of the average consumer.

Palm had never had a problem coming up with ideas for new products and features, but the designers and engineers focused almost exclusively on the technologically sophisticated elites willing to pay for whatever the company created. They effectively ignored lots of other potential customers who wanted simpler technology at lower prices. Reaching them meant making exactly the right trade-offs for each market segment, a process that required close interaction among engineers, who knew what was technologically possible; operations experts, who knew what could be manufactured at a given cost; and marketing people, who understood customer needs and wants. To incorporate the different perspectives, Bradley created an operating mechanism consisting of six to twelve people from various functional areas. Each team was under the leadership of a product manager carefully chosen for the ability to see things from a cross-functional perspective and to manage group dynamics. The objective was to create a product that would appeal to market segments Palm had never tapped before. The teams were each given different target markets and price points. For example, one team was assigned the task of creating a mass-market device to be priced at $99, far below Palm's customary $399 and $499 products. It was up to the team to take the $99 price, factor in a reasonable margin, and work backward to arrive at what a successful product would look like at that price. The Zire personal organizer was the result.

Some Zire team members set out to learn about the potential new customer, while others began to examine possible low-cost sourcing and the designers began developing ideas. By interacting routinely (once a week) to review progress and resolve any issues, everyone on the team heard the same information at the same time. They developed a clear picture of the customer: someone who is busy, price conscious, wants to stay on top of things, and doesn't want to have to spend time learning how to use new technology. The common view of the customer guided the Zire's development. It would be an electronic organizer that would help nontechnical people keep track of family schedules from soccer practice to meetings at school, make it easy to look up information like phone numbers for the kids' doctors, and maybe keep a list of things to do. In short, it had to eliminate the piles of papers on the kitchen table and the Post-it notes on the refrigerator. It should appeal more to women, who typically manage the family calendars. Everyone agreed that it wasn't about technology; it was about making people's lives easier.

Basic functions of the device were straightforward, but others drew heated debate in the weekly meetings. Typically, engineers wanted lots of memory. But others reminded them that memory costs money and that the target customer wasn't going to use fancy memory-hungry applications. By allowing people to challenge each other's assumptions, the open forum made it hard for individuals to cling to a point of view others disagreed with and created a built-in control system that kept the development process moving forward.

In the continuing life of the operating mechanism, whenever the group's self-policing didn't work, Andrea Johnson, the product manager, skillfully redirected discussions by getting the group to focus on their common view of the customer. Since no one in the group officially reported to her, her skills in managing interactions and keeping the dialogue focused on the business result were all-important. What worked was keeping the group focused on the common goal and the composite image they had created of their target customer. "Remember, it's not for you," she'd remind the engineers, "it's for the least technical person in your family."

Providing a good display at low cost was a hot topic. Color display technology was expensive, but it wasn't clear if customers would accept a black-and-white display. Ultimately, the decision hinged on cost rather than consumer appeal, and the monochrome screen was selected. The operations group kept exploring options with different vendors, trying to figure out creative ways to do things differently to keep the cost down. Some team members thought the product needed back-lights, but a display that lit up would add another $50. The ultimate solution was to provide a lighted stylus and consider adding a lit display in a follow-on product.

While Johnson ran the regular meetings, Bradley reviewed the progress of the meetings with probing questions, ensuring that the right information was being used and the right trade-offs were being made. Through his questioning he was able to assess whether they had the right people in the room, the team was functioning well, conflicts were being surfaced, and the decisions were reflecting good compromises. The way such a dialogue flows, the way individuals respond to questions, influences the behavior of the team members. Often he would change some parameters of the situation and test their thinking by asking how the decision would be different under new conditions. He was particularly sensitive to whether one or two individuals, by virtue of their persuasive powers or ability to articulate, were dominating the decision-making process and if the resulting decision might be the wrong one. He would give feedback to the individuals as appropriate, sometimes right in the meeting, sometimes after the meeting. His mannerism of approval or lack of approval of the team's progress had considerable influence on their energy going forward. He preferred informal dialogue versus PowerPoint presentations. Often such discussions brought out creative new ideas, which provided further energy for the group.

Palm's designs became more customer oriented not because the CEO said they should, but because he got people reoriented through well-functioning operating mechanisms. He was careful in selecting the people in charge of them, and he tracked their progress and output with consistency and appropriate frequency. He worked backward from the desired business results—products that exactly met consumers' needs—to the business activities that drive them and the critical intersection of people and perspectives.

Many business decisions require information from diverse sources and consideration of multiple viewpoints. Operating mechanisms should bring those things together so trade-offs can be made. Organizational structures divide people and perspectives; operating mechanisms conducted effectively can bring the right people together to reconcile their points of view.

Removing the Roadblock to Growth

When David A. Smith, the CEO of PSS/World Medical, saw a way to grow the business, he also saw a potential roadblock to getting it to happen: conflict between the leaders of the two main business units, Gary Corless and Tony Oglesbee. Corless and Oglesbee had run their individual businesses very well, but now PSS was going into a growth mode, albeit with very tight margins, and the search was on to free up every dollar possible to fund the growth and go on the offensive. Oglesbee's Gulf South Medical Supply division and Corless's Physician Sales & Service business each had its own support services, including information technology, human resources, and global sourcing. It would make sense, the CEO decided, to combine those support functions into a single organization supporting both businesses.

Sharing support services is hardly a unique concept, but the argument for doing it at PSS was compelling. Neither Corless nor Oglesbee could refute it on its merits, but both were quite concerned about how their individual units would be affected. Corless and Oglesbee were held accountable for meeting specific revenue, margin, and cash goals, but how could they ensure performance if they didn't have control over some key elements of the business? Each of the two felt he had some leverage with his own support staffs: if he wasn't getting what he needed from IT or purchasing, somebody's bonus got cut, someone else didn't promoted, and occasionally someone got fired. If a separate unit provided the services, neither of the two executives would have the same clout. Worst of all, they figured competing against one another for attention and resources would change the healthy relationship between them.

The CEO knew that organizational titles and dictums wouldn't make the shared services approach succeed. He had to ensure that the human interactions between the two division heads and the new heads of HR, IT, and purchasing didn't undermine PSS's ability to grow and thrive. If choices were to be made, all the participants had to feel that their needs, constraints, and priorities were understood and that decisions were based on the interests of PSS overall. If one division leader felt the other was being treated better because of political clout or personal favors, resentment or outright hostility would creep in and someone would withdraw.

The CEO created operating mechanisms to bring the relevant people together to resolve the tensions and potential conflicts in an open forum. First, Corless, Oglesbee, and the newly appointed leaders of HR, IT, and purchasing met to discuss the priorities Corless and Oglesbee had for their individual businesses. Following that meeting, the support service leaders created one-year and three-year plans that reflected Corless and Oglesbee's needs. Because communication and decision making had to be ongoing, another routine mechanism was created, this one a monthly review Corless and Oglesbee would conduct with each of the support service leaders. Ideally, Corless and Oglesbee and people running the support services would talk to each other informally and often, but the monthly reviews established a time and place for Corless and Oglesbee to air concerns and keep the support services updated on their business needs. Pulling the competing interests into the light of day and making them transparent would reduce or totally eliminate the side decisions that often take place outside the formal networks and build commitment by removing suspicion and distrust.

Bringing the issues into the open repetitively twelve times a year, ensuring no side deals are made outside this mechanism, bringing conflicts to the surface, and learning how to make the trade-offs with facts and figures is what makes the shared-services arrangement sustainable. People are fast learners. Those who provide the shared services learn how to make the adjustments and trade-offs and, more important, how to inform the adversely affected division. Further reinforcing the mechanism, the two division leaders evaluate the service providers on an annual basis.

In any business, conflict is built in as functional silos, departments, and individuals compete for resources and for their point of view. Whenever a business is repositioned or priorities change, you have to think about where the conflicts might erupt to block progress and perhaps create operating mechanisms to get them resolved. Unresolved conflicts are a drag on decision making and action, because people withhold their commitment when they don't think their ideas have been vetted. You have to build into the design and leadership of the social system the means to draw conflicts to the surface and get them resolved. The leadership skill is to mold people's thinking to see the bigger picture beyond their narrow self-interest and to ensure intellectual honesty in the decision-making process.

Improving Judgment for Better Revenue Growth

Paul Charron became CEO of Liz Claiborne in 1995, when it was essentially a one-brand company and some on the outside felt it was declining. Charron was a highly seasoned business leader, but really had no sense of fashion. That made two strikes against him in the minds of those who think fashion is mysterious, an art, God's gift. Charron repositioned Liz Claiborne through a combination of acquisitions, involving about fifteen brands, and organic growth and focusing those brands around lifestyle. He also opened some retail stores. By broadening the business, through more brands, channels, geographies, and a better mix of products, Liz Claiborne outperformed the industry over a period of roughly ten years. But perhaps Charron's most significant accomplishment was the way he changed Liz Claiborne's social system to combine people's creativity with commerce and drive better business decisions.

Fashion, like many knowledge-worker businesses, depends heavily on creativity and the ability to perceive what's coming next better than the competition. Fashion people have the reputation of not being able to work together and not being overly concerned about whether their creations actually sell. Everyone knows that geniuses don't like to work in teams and artists don't like constraints. All of that may be true, but it's still a business. The competition for top-line growth is fierce, and if the wrong product is produced, unsold inventory piles up.

One of the shifts Charron made in the social system was to establish an operating mechanism to tap two things from his creative people: first, their personal perceptions of the market and trends in fashion; and second, their creativity about what will sell in their own area of expertise. Charron established weekly intelligence meetings to bring together marketers, designers, and merchants across the brands to discuss design, price points, and choices of garments in several customer segments. He specified what the meetings were expected to yield—in this case, a broader view and new ideas rather than decisions.

The meetings are purposely free of hierarchy. Anyone can share his or her perspectives on emerging trends or changing consumer tastes regardless of title or area of responsibility. If someone identifies an emerging trend, people discuss how it might affect other segments or brands. Charron ran the early meetings himself to be sure everyone felt free to participate without fear of ridicule or criticism. Using simple facilitative techniques—"Pat, I haven't heard from you yet"—he went out of his way to draw people out. At the same time, he ensured that the brand managers knew they weren't getting marching orders, just ideas, an important step in persuading them to lower their defenses. Repeatedly hearing about fashion through different lenses—jewelry versus apparel, for example—broadens people's thinking and helps them pick up trends that lead to profitable growth.

The purpose of the mechanism is to increase people's confidence in their judgment through discussion about what will sell, how much will sell, and why it will sell, allowing them to cross-check their perception of trends. The discipline of the mechanism is that it happens every week, at the same time, and is very informal. Because of the discipline, consistency, and frequency of these interactions, people get to know whose judgment they should trust, recalibrate their own, and increase their confidence.

Short, frequent, content-rich meetings can be highly effective in distributing fast-changing information and are especially useful for staying in touch with the outside world.

Tapping Intellectual Horsepower

Strategy presentations at Sherwin-Williams were like the Spanish Inquisition. As each division head was trotted up to make his pitch, it wasn't long, perhaps the third or fourth slide, before the torture began. Not only bosses, but also colleagues peppered them with questions, and all the time and effort that went into preparation became worthless as it degenerated into a seven-hour general discussion.

When Jack Breen took over as CEO, he wanted his divisions and the company as a whole to deliver the strongest performance they could and knew the division leaders would benefit from the best thinking of the group. He wanted to use the strategy sessions as a vehicle to tap everybody's intellectual capacity to improve performance, and to translate the outcome of the sessions into the actions that would be taken in the budget mechanism. He also sought to link the output with people's issues, so the sessions were real and action-oriented, and not just intellectual exercises.

In the first review, Breen told the division chief that he had one hour in which to make his full presentation, uninterrupted. Then he told the others in the room that they should each prepare three written questions about the division's strategy. Breen collected all the questions, read each to the entire group, and selected as the basis for the ensuing dialogue a few key ones that got to the heart of the issues facing the division. At the end of the session, he asked the division head what value-added he received from the session, and how it would help his performance.

The company's jungle telegraph began operating right away. In the subsequent strategy session the following week, Breen found executives coming prepared with to-the-point, tighter, more-focused presentations with penetrating questions from all the participants. The focus of meetings had shifted from a chaotic one-upping inquisition to a focused effort to add value and creativity. In just six weeks, Breen had completely shifted the content of the operating mechanism and the mental activity in the social system.

Nothing ignites people's fire like asking them to think. Especially in companies dominated by knowledge workers, engaging the intellect energizes the business and is a source of competitive advantage. The more transparency and simultaneity, the more people can think things through for themselves and help shape the outcome, the more engaged and therefore motivated they are. In turn, the easier it is to attract and retain great talent.

Securing Commitment for Execution

One diversified company was in the midst of difficult times in 2002 when Joyce, who had become CEO nine months earlier, was charged with getting the company on solid footing and setting a new direction to move forward.

The longtime balance between manufacturing and technology had tilted toward technology. Joyce worked with a core group of direct reports and an outside consulting firm and came up with plans to make some major shifts in the portfolio, develop a long-term plan for the technology business, and create a technical sales force that could flex up or flex down as the portfolio changed.

But coming up with a plan for the business was one thing. Getting the organization to move on it would be a formidable challenge, for two major reasons. First, the business problems of those recent years had caused the organization to lose focus and people to lose confidence in the company. In fact, a survey of employees showed that their belief and conviction that the company knew where it was going was at an all-time low. Second, many people in the U.S. technology business knew very little about their new leader. Although she had worked in many different functions and businesses, Joyce had spent only a year in the technology segment of the business, and that was in Asia. Why should people think she could solve the problems in the global technology business?

Joyce had gotten a lot of advice from people about how to energize the thirty-two-thousand-person organization, but one suggestion made particular sense: to define and start with a core group of leaders, make a real, personal connection with them, and let them carry the message to others. The exact number was a matter of debate. The malaise was so widespread that it had to be a large enough number to make a difference, but at the same time, it had to be small enough for Joyce to make a human connection. She didn't want to round people up in an auditorium and make pronouncements from a podium. She wanted to create an environment in which people were comfortable interacting with her and where she could foster a constructive dialogue.

The company historically had a meeting of 280 senior leaders each January, and this group perceived itself to be at the top of the organization. That seemed to be a logical group for Joyce to reach out to, but not all at once. She created Future Forums, where thirty-five members at a time would meet for two and a half days. The eight Future Forums would be spread out over the course of a year, with Joyce personally conducting each one. The Future Forums were designed for informality and interaction, with ample time for the CEO to explain the six elements of the strategy in a way that was digestible, understandable, and could easily translate to others. In addition, Joyce wanted to provide each leader with ample time to ask questions.

Following a dinner the first night, Joyce spent about forty-five minutes explaining the strategy to the group of thirty-five people taking time to tell them the thinking behind it, why she thought it was right, what she thought the next five years would look like, and what some of the challenges and opportunities would be. Then the participants broke into two groups, each of which had forty-five minutes of questions and answers with the CEO and a rotating member of the executive committee. The participants asked thoughtful, probing questions on every element of the strategy and the company's future direction. Joyce responded with her vision and beliefs and with absolute candor.

Joyce laid out the facts to show that the organization needed to change and that some parts of the strategy— investing in nanotechnology, investing in R&D growth, focusing on fewer application areas—would be easier to do. What wouldn't be quite so easy was redesigning the sales force and holding down expenses. She also braced them for the repercussions of increasing investment in R&D during a period of declining earnings. The company's historical reaction had always been to scale back R&D when earnings were down, and that's what Wall Street would be expecting. But Joyce saw that the future of the company depended on maintaining investment in R&D. Rather than cut it, she wanted to prepare people for the impact of sustaining that investment.

After only two of the sessions, it was evident that the operating mechanism was delivering the hoped-for benefit. Feedback was that the Future Forum had been a terrific experience, unlike anything the leaders had experienced at the company, and people were getting excited about what the company was doing. They were getting aligned. Other benefits also began to emerge. Joyce found that as the participants got energized, she did, too. The forums were giving her an emotional boost at a time when the company was under a lot of external pressure. And whereas she initially wondered how she could possibly carve out the time, she came to realize that it was the best possible use of her time. She got to know people in the Q&A sessions, and they got to know her.

There was one other unexpected benefit. The groups of thirty-five often included small teams of people who regularly worked together and they were given time to meet on their own. The clarity and specificity of the context and the experience of the forums got those team members rolling up their sleeves and working on problems in their own part of the business. More than half of the groups came out of those sessions with some kind of a breakthrough or with a new insight into some problem they were having.

As the forums continued and the participants carried their attitudes, behaviors, and understanding of the company's strategy back to their organizations, support for the changes fanned out and took hold. A 2005 company survey found that 99 percent of all key executives in the company said they knew and understood the strategy, and 91 percent of all people surveyed in the company at every level said they knew and understood the company strategy.

People are far more likely to buy into a change when they fully understand the reasons behind it. Operating mechanisms are a powerful way to win commitment by giving people a fuller picture of the business and its context. But you have to be willing to expose the reasoning behind your decisions and overcome your fear of the response and ensure that people really "get it."

Reinventing an Entire Social System

When you need different business results, you almost always have to tinker with the social system. Otherwise, people will do what they've always done and how they've always done it, and the output will be pretty much the same. It might be a matter of creating a new operating mechanism here or there or changing the composition or the nature of the dialogue in some of them, but sometimes a major overhaul is required. It's the rare leader who has the know-how and confidence to undertake it. Bob Nardelli is one of the exceptions. When he was appointed as CEO of Home Depot in 2000, he dove in headfirst to learn the business and soon determined that very different business results were needed. As successful as Home Depot had been in the past, the business was at risk of running out of cash and didn't have enough qualified leaders to open new stores at the fast pace employees and investors had become accustomed to. He had to reposition the company and establish a new set of goals and new priorities, and accomplishing all of that would require a very different way for people to work together.

Nardelli had to evaluate the existing operating mechanisms to see what was working and not working in each of them and what had to be done differently to achieve the new set of goals. He eliminated some that were unproductive and unrelated to the new goals, and created new ones to get the organization moving toward the goals. An expert in managing a social system, Nardelli ensured that each operating mechanism was focused on the right issues, had a clear purpose in terms of what decisions to focus on, made information transparent, and, most important, corrected individual behavior to be more collaborative, which was a radical departure from what was happening before. Nardelli in essence overhauled the entire social system.

When Nardelli resigned as president of General Electric's power systems business to become CEO of Home Depot, he took the reins of an energetic company that had experienced huge success. Fueled by the charismatic leadership of cofounders Bernie Marcus and Arthur Blank, Home Depot had grown from a single store in 1978 to eleven hundred stores and $40 billion in revenues by 2000. But by the time Nardelli arrived, there were problems lurking beneath the surface, and it would take more than passion, high energy, and entrepreneurial verve to solve them.

Nardelli worked tirelessly gathering the facts and analyzing every aspect of the business, and concluded that Home Depot's unrelenting emphasis solely on sales, sales, sales had detracted attention from nearly everything else, even profits and cash flow and the efficient management of inventory. What is more, by encouraging individual store managers to make their own purchasing decisions, the company had failed to take advantage of its scale in negotiating with suppliers, and, consequently, operating margins were not what they should be. Making matters worse, archrival Lowe's, with its spiffier stores and more-fashionable merchandise, was making heavy inroads, particularly among women shoppers.

The business challenge as Nardelli saw it was to improve operating margins, velocity (inventory turns), and cash, and to find a different trajectory of growth. Recognizing that the excessive emphasis on sales growth and opening too many new stores at the expense of margins and cash was not sustainable, Nardelli identified different ways the business could grow profitably: by improving the performance of existing and future stores in existing markets; extending the business by offering related services such as tool rental and home installation of Home Depot products; and expanding the market by serving new geographic areas and customer segments.

As he thought about the goals and the new direction for the business, he realized that he couldn't just set a goal and expect it to be delivered. He had to be sure the organization's social system was built for getting it done. Improving velocity, operating margins, and cash would require a different flow of information, a different approach to decision making, and different behaviors. Take velocity, for instance. It had always been the case at Home Depot that each store manager made his or her own purchasing decisions, based largely on the individual's judgment, and the bias was always to have as much merchandise as possible—even if it sat on the shelf for years—in hopes of being able to make another dollar in sales. Nardelli saw that to improve velocity, decisions about how much merchandise to order would have to be made differently, based on different information—data instead of judgment—and by different people. Similarly, margins could be improved by combining the stores' purchasing power and working out better deals with suppliers, which would mean different decisions, and different people making those decisions based on different criteria.

As the new positioning, goals, and priorities took shape, Nardelli recruited former GE colleague Dennis Donovan as head of human resources to help him overhaul the social system that would allow those things to get done. Together they determined where information had to come together, what decisions had to get made by whom, and who had to take the lead and act on decisions and therefore needed to buy into them. As they thought those things through, they decided to move the locus of decision making in purchasing from the stores to a centralized purchasing department, taking away the autonomy of store managers in this area. It was a huge change in behavior. They also designed a series of new operating mechanisms to synchronize various staff functions and divisions to move the company toward the new goals.

Defining the behaviors the company would need for the future—collaboration, candor, informality, accountability, and realism were at the top of the list—had begun the day Nardelli arrived. He had been demonstrating and reinforcing those behaviors in every formal and informal interaction he had with people, and they became part of the basis for selecting, promoting, and rewarding others. From day one, he asserted that things would be different by asking questions, making himself available, and sharing information to put people face-to-face with the facts about things like customer perceptions in order to shake them from their complacency.

In the first few months, Nardelli initiated an operating mechanism designed to keep him and the senior team informed about what was happening in the external world and in every part of the business so the senior leaders could better coordinate their efforts and so he could gauge progress toward the goals. This operating mechanism was a two-hour simultaneous dialogue by phone to take place every Monday morning among all the senior officers, some twenty to thirty people. Nardelli himself would lead the discussion. "Two hours every Monday? You've gotta be kidding me!" was not an uncommon response among those who had been at the company before Nardelli, but attendance was mandatory, and after a while people saw the value of the sessions. In the early going, Nardelli asked a lot of very specific questions about what was happening in each part of the business, so it was clear that he was interested and wanted to be involved and that candor was expected. At the same time, by responding readily to questions asked of him, he showed people that he was accessible and available and that he, too, would be honest and open. Under the previous leadership, discussions were focused on quarterly results, but Nardelli was asking what had happened the previous week and what the leaders were planning to do in the upcoming week, so the business was making adjustments in a much shorter time frame. In each subsequent meeting, he would ask whether the leaders had done what they said they were going to do, creating a sense of urgency and accountability to the group.

As those discussions occur repetitively (they continue today) with the same intense focus on goals and business performance and reinforcement of the same behaviors of candor, collaboration, and accountability, leaders adapt, or if they can't get on board, they fall by the wayside. More important, those who participate in this operating mechanism create a picture of the business as the CEO sees it and carry the message to other parts of the organization. Tom Taylor, a division president at the time, recalls how his participation allowed him to serve as a link between Nardelli and people in the field. When people questioned Nardelli's sincerity in the early months, he told them, "Look, I had the same reaction you do, but he really means what he says." Taylor also found himself and others behaving differently. "Bob didn't accept excuses real well, so when he held people accountable, other people around him started doing the same thing, and before you knew it, there was a revolution."

Leveraging the scale of the growing company while remaining fast and flexible would require superb coordination and communication, starting at the very top. Especially those who had been with the company before Nardelli arrived needed to buy into any change in direction and priorities and shifts in resources. To that end, Nardelli and his team designed what is probably the most significant operating mechanism at Home Depot: the Strategic Operating and Resource Planning process, or SOAR. Its purpose is to establish the strategic and operational priorities for the entire corporation through give-and-take with the top functional and division leaders. It includes Home Depot's entire senior leadership team, who gather in one room for a full eight days each August to generate one-year and three-year plans for where the company is going, complete with specific goals and targets.

The process actually starts long before the August meeting, when Nardelli sits with his strategic planning and finance executives to get them engaged in setting goals and targets for the coming three years and how much "stretch" should be built into them. The targets are then sent out to the various parts of the company so that functional and division heads can work from the bottom up to figure out how best to meet them. For example, Carl Liebert, as senior vice president of operations (he's now executive vice president of Home Depot Stores), would gather his team as well as the senior merchandisers and field leaders to solicit ideas about what he should do to meet his goals. Then he took his developing plan to Carol Tomé, chief financial officer, and Frank Blake, head of business development, to see if the ideas made sense from their perspective. Other leaders do the same thing in preparation.

Then, when the meeting convenes, everyone hears one another's plans simultaneously, and Nardelli takes the lead in pushing people to probe each other's ideas and look for alternatives. By asking questions such as "What would happen if housing formation declines?" or "How does your view change if interest rates go to ten percent?" he encourages the group to think critically and creatively about various proposals for projects and investments. Through the process, the group forms a common understanding of the pros and cons of each proposal, and the priorities emerge rather naturally. Holding the discussions over eight consecutive days in what some participants liken to a leadership boot camp ensures that the information is fresh in everyone's mind, and the decision making doesn't get diffused. The result is a common view of where the business is going and what each leader has to do to help get it there in the short term, the medium term, and the long term. People are committed and aligned. SOAR is not a budgeting session, but in the process of setting priorities, the group is forced to make trade-offs, which in turn dictate where resources will be spent, and the rationale for those shifts is transparent.

The simultaneity, transparency, and discipline imposed by Nardelli as the leader of the discussion, reinforced by the acquired behaviors of the group—no personal attacks are allowed—contribute to fast decision making that everyone supports. If, for instance, Frank Blake, executive vice president of business development and corporate operations, sees an opportunity for growth through more smaller-format stores, the group discusses if resources are best spent there, or whether other opportunities make more sense in the next few years. Having a cross section of people in the room creates balance and ensures decisions are doable. A field manager, for example, might respond to Blake's proposal with a word of caution: "That's a great idea, but let me tell you some of the practical obstacles to getting it to happen."

While SOAR coordinates strategy and operations at the top-most level, another operating mechanism—quarterly reviews—ensures that the actions at lower levels are connected to the overall priorities as the district managers report on issues and opportunities to their regional presidents, who participate in the SOAR session. As tends to happen in social systems, the leaders conducting these sessions often replicate the tone and behaviors of the operating mechanisms their bosses run. This has been the case at Home Depot. Like his Home Depot peers, J. Paul Raines, president of the Southern Division, conducts quarterly reviews of his division over two days, with about twenty-five people in the room, including the operations manager for the region, the merchandising managers, the heads of specialty sales, at-home service, HR, and loss presentation, as well as the district managers' direct reports. Reviews have become more data driven: discussions center on a predetermined set of metrics, usually common to the entire company, which cover a wide range of business issues, from gross margin and sales to service metrics and talent upgrades. Raines drills down into those that are of particular importance or that need emphasis, asking a lot of questions about specialty sales, for example, so everyone in the room picks up on their importance.

While some time is spent reflecting on the division's performance to date, the real thrust of the reviews is on coordinating various parts of the business, including merchandising, HR, finance, and operations, for what lies ahead, and, on learning from one another, sharing information and insights. The Houston district, for example, found that putting wireless doorbells on the storage sheds on display in the parking lot helped boost doorbell sales, a tactic that other district managers quickly adopted.

While the tone in the reviews is informal, the leaders keep a sharp focus on the business purpose. Before the review is concluded, it's clear what the forecast projections are for the next three to six months, and those projections are revisited at the opening of the next quarterly review, providing continuity and follow-through. Raines sums it up simply by saying, "People come out focused."

Human resources is linked to the rest of the business through another operating mechanism—an annual review conducted by Nardelli and Donovan in May or June each year. The two leaders go through each division, spending a full day with the division president and his or her head of HR. Using common metrics, performance screens, and ratings, they sit together to talk about leadership talent in that division. Having been through SOAR, the participants have a shared understanding of what kinds of talent the business needs. In some cases, decisions to promote or move people are made on the spot. After talking about the division's leadership, they move down a level to talk about the directors and district manager level.

As Nardelli selected leaders, he kept a keen eye on their know-how in managing a social system and their tendency to be psychologically open, willing to be influenced by others, and intellectually honest in keeping the group focused on the business purpose. One of the people Nardelli entrusted with the social system is Carl Liebert, whom he appointed as senior vice president of operations and charged with creating processes where none existed. Knowing that any process designed by industrial engineers in a lab would ultimately fail, Liebert designed his own operating mechanisms at the crucial intersections of people from different hierarchical levels, from the executive suite to the "associate" (sales) level. For instance, Liebert set up a team to create a better process for receiving night shipments. The team included some of the night crews who actually did the job of accepting shipments. But saying that they were on the same team wasn't enough; Liebert had to prove it. He won the trust of the people on the receiving dock by working side by side with them slinging boxes for a week, until, as Liebert says, they didn't think of him as the VP of operations anymore. Then the communication began to flow, free of any hierarchical filters, and those who were closest to the problems began suggesting ways to resolve them. The result was a straightforward and fast solution that everyone endorsed.

Liebert also worked with Tom Taylor, who started at

Home Depot in 1983 as a parking-lot attendant and went on to become executive vice president for merchandising and marketing, to create an operating mechanism called the Store Manager Council, designed to make initiatives easier to digest. At the time they created it, the council consisted of Taylor and Liebert and a rotating set of some twenty-one store managers, handpicked for their ability to collaborate, representing all the regions in the United States. The Store Manager Council is pressed into service to resolve specific business problems, such as absenteeism, accountability for people not showing up for work, or the will-call process in the store, in a way that is practical from the stores' perspective and therefore can be rolled out successfully. Like any good operating mechanism, this one provides lots of fringe benefits, one of which is the ability for the people at corporate to "see into" the organization. Through the Store Manager Council, Liebert spotted a store manager who seemed to have exceptional leadership talent, including, of course, the necessary skills and traits to manage the social system. Liebert watched the young person carefully, even going to the store to work side by side with him for a week, and accelerated the young man's career by bringing him to headquarters. Small moves like that is how the social system becomes self-perpetuating.

Nardelli and Donovan created many more operating mechanisms throughout the company, each with a specific business purpose, and they say they could not have transformed the company any other way. Since Nardelli took the reins of Home Depot, the company has enjoyed strong and profitable growth. Revenue nearly doubled to around $80 million by 2005, and earnings per share have more than doubled since 2000. He had the know-how to determine what the business had to do. Equally important, he knew how to build a social system that could do it.

As you've seen, the social system is a breakthrough in how to operationalize a change in culture and link it to the change in positioning. Linking positioning and the working of the organization is paramount for success As you rebuild the social system, you need to make superb judgments on people. How do you select them? How do you get them into the right jobs, jobs where they contribute and also develop their abilities to lead? Most people think judging people comes from gut reactions. My observation is that it is a very developable know-how. This is what I show in the next chapter.

Does Your Social System Pass the Test?

- The built-in conflicts that are part of every organization are being surfaced.

- These conflicts are resolved in a timely way by people committed to delivering results.

- Information flows horizontally across silos and is not hoarded or deliberately distorted.

- The right questions are raised so that you can look at your business from both "50,000 feet" (the big picture) and at ground level and conduct brutally honest dialogue.

- Operating mechanisms are designed so that they result in high quality, timely decisions and help deliver the aspired results.

- You know the points of intersection where operating mechanisms are needed for people to make trade-offs and share information.

- Appropriate and continuous improvements are made in the working of the operating mechanisms: creating new ones, combining some, eliminating others.

- Each operating mechanism is connected in an unfiltered way to sources of external information.

- Leaders have the psychological courage to confront reality and shape behavior of participants in line with the values of the business. The right behavior and values are reinforced and those who deviate are dealt with.

5

HOW LEADERS ARE MADE

Judging, Selecting, and Developing Leaders

A sure sign of the know-how of selecting and developing leaders is that you leave the organization stronger relative to the competition than it was before you took over. That was one of the great legacies Tim left behind when he retired from Jasper Digital, the technology company he had led for eighteen years and grew from a $100 million niche player to a $2 billion industry giant. People had often remarked on the winning combination of his business acumen and his sixth sense about people. To him, developing young leaders was personal, and his genuine interest had earned him a great deal of loyalty. What had earned him the most respect, though, was his ability to know where a person would flourish, what the person needed to develop more of, and how to bring out each individual leader's personal best.

When Tim retired, he didn't want to interfere with Lorraine, the new CEO, but she was eager to pick Tim's brain. During her six months leading Jasper, she had invited Tim and his wife to her house for dinner several times. She always had questions for him about key customers or a major strategic move she was considering. But there was something about sitting out on the patio under the stars that made her a little more philosophic than usual when she asked, "Tim, you had such a great career, but if you were to do it all over again, is there anything you would change? I'm not saying you *should* have any regrets, but do you?"

Tim didn't even push back in his chair. He had a ready answer. "Here's something I was thinking about just the other day. You know the name Joe Bailey?" Lorraine recognized him as the CEO of a Fortune 50 company whose star was rising.

"He's a fantastic leader—I knew it when he was running our sales operation out of Atlanta. And I didn't do the right things for him. I let a good leader get away."

"I didn't know he'd worked for Jasper," Lorraine remarked.

"He was in his twenties, just getting his feet on the ground, but I could see the drive in him, and the ability to soak up everything around him. People loved him—and so did I. He was a real diamond in the rough."

"But he got recruited?" Lorraine asked.

"This is where I made my mistake," Tim replied. "He was reporting to the head of the Southeast region, who did a good job, but he was at the end of his career and his best days were behind him. He was very comfortable with steady incremental improvement and delivering the numbers the way he always had. So this young guy, Joe, comes in there to work for him and is outshining everybody in the group—exceeding his sales goals, generating some really great ideas, answering all the questions in the presentations, and getting everybody around him energized—but his boss kept trying to poke holes in his balloon. You could see it in the meetings, in the body language. I had just been put in charge of marketing for North America, and I was trying to let the regional guys run their own show. So I didn't say anything, which left Joe stuck in a job where he clearly wasn't going to be allowed to do much. But I spotted him, Lorraine, just like I spotted you!"

"That reminds me of a question my husband asked me," Lorraine said. "And I had a hard time answering it, so let me ask you: What was it you saw in me when you pulled me out of that first finance job? I wasn't a Joe. In fact, you said I was too reserved."

"Not just one thing. I saw the way you pushed your bosses to think about how the business was positioned, and when we were talking about taking particular product lines to Europe or going into new segments, I could see your mind working on multiple levels: Does that fit with our customer base? What's the impact on our cost structure? Will the competition change pricing? That's not the way a financial analyst usually thinks.

"But that wasn't all," Tim continued. "I saw how you interacted with your peers. You didn't reject other people's ideas, which a lot of young people do when they're trying to get ahead. You were always searching for the right answers, no matter where they came from. So I learned from my mistakes and moved you into a job where you could break out of finance and test your ability to reposition and grow a business. I didn't want to see your perspective get narrowed by spending too many years in one function. That's when I moved you to Mexico, so you'd have a chance to run a complete business with P&L responsibility."

"I always wanted to get into general management, but I didn't think it would happen so soon," Lorraine said.

"You had the latent talent for it, so it made sense for the company to let you go that way and develop it. Then when you showed you could handle it, I separated Latin America from North America so you'd have a bigger pond. And all of that paid off when we started looking at China. We needed somebody like you who could navigate in an environment that was a lot more complex, not only from a business and cultural standpoint, but also in terms of dealing with the government."

"China was a real stretch for me," Lorraine said. "Regardless of what I told you at the time, I wasn't so sure I could handle it."

"I think we all agreed there was risk in it, but those early jobs got you prepared, and I'd done my research. I'd watched you enough to know that you were driven to learn what you didn't know, and I'd seen you expand your perspective when you moved from finance to general management and from Mexico to all of Latin America. I knew you were open to other people's ideas, so you'd find whatever expertise you were lacking. And, of course, that's what you did. I got credit for growing the business, but I couldn't have done it without leaders like you."

"That's why people admire you so much, Tim," Lorraine said. "You always saw things in people and got them on the right track. Putting Jamie in charge of marketing even though he didn't have the usual credentials was brilliant, and he continues to do really well there."

"But remember, I created the opportunities. People have to succeed on their own, and not everyone does."

"Well, I hope I can provide that same kind of development for my people."

"Spend time on it," Tim advised. "Spend a *lot* of time on it. You won't get this company to ten billion dollars without it."

If Tim sounds like a dream boss, maybe so, but it's a true story. And Tim is not alone in terms of his ability to spot and develop leadership talent. There are others who do precisely what Tim did with his younger leaders: go on the offensive and actively search for people with leadership potential and create opportunities that leverage their abilities, test them further, and allow them to grow. That's what Jack Welch did when he lifted a young Jim McNerney (now the CEO of Boeing) from vice president of marketing in GE's second-smallest business unit to be a general manager of a small P&L center in a different industry. He did an outstanding job, and one year later Welch appointed him executive vice president of GE Capital. Similarly, he boosted a young Dave Cote (now CEO of Honeywell) several levels, from his financial analyst position to general management. Richard Carrión, the CEO of Banco Popular, headquartered in San Juan, Puerto Rico, does the same for his leaders—taking one leader from a high-level staff job to a lower-level P&L job, for instance, to make him a better leader, and switching the jobs of the CFO and the person who was running the retail system to expand their capability and make the organization more flexible. Such leaders, including Jim Kilts of Gillette, A. G. Lafley of Procter & Gamble, Reuben Mark of Colgate-Palmolive, Bob Nardelli of Home Depot, and Richard Harrington of Thomson, do this as a routine, and—as in the case of Welch—probably make the careers of hundreds of people. It is a source of pride, and an enabler of their own success.

Your job as a leader is getting it done, not doing it yourself, however you decide what the "it" is. Your ability to deliver results depends on how well and how consistently you grow other leaders. But it takes know-how to judge people accurately, imagining what each person's potential could be. You then must take the initiative to provide opportunities for them to not only contribute to the organization, but also to be tested and hopefully expand. If they reach a limit—maybe because certain know-how's didn't develop properly or personality traits got in the way—you then deal with this issue as well.

The usual way of deploying other people's leadership talent is to start with a job opening and see who can fill it. But the know-how of selecting leaders and helping them reach their potential means focusing on people first, not jobs— actively searching for leadership talent throughout your organization, creating for those individuals career moves that test their ability to take on more complexity or learn new skills, and creating processes to do it on a disciplined, regular basis. You have to develop and improve your judgments on people, which means spending time and energy on it daily, weekly, monthly, not just during once-a-year talent reviews or succession-planning sessions. You have to create a view about the person's competence in the know-hows, but also look at him more broadly to see what makes him tick: what he loves to do, how he thinks, how he behaves around others. Then you can match the leader to a job in which that person will shine and strengthen business performance.

As you practice and improve your observational powers, you have to prevent your own psychological blockages from getting in the way of perceiving people accurately. You can't afford to lock into unrealistically positive or negative views of people, thinking "he can do no right" or "she can do no wrong," and discounting information to the contrary. People grow and change, and jobs continually evolve, so you have to be psychologically open to continuously update your judgments on people and their fit with the job. It's up to you to spot leadership talent, grow it, and build a pipeline of leaders.

SPOTTING LEADERSHIP TALENT

Most companies do some kind of talent or succession planning, but most of those processes are based on prescribed lists of leadership competences against which superiors, peers, and direct reports rate an individual leader. Then an outside expert comes in to sort out the data, compare the results to an extensive database of other leaders, and give the leader feedback as to where she falls percentagewise compared to others. But no matter how many competences are listed and how expertly the ratings are compiled, they don't seem to create an accurate picture of the person's God-given talents and abilities.

Human beings, it seems, are not so easily disassembled into a set of pixels. You know the process is flawed when it fails to release people's energy and true potential. The job of a leader is to see the person as a whole, over time, in a variety of situations, and work backward from what you observe to determine what that person's individual gifts really are. As you develop your skill in observing people's actions and behaviors and check your observations with other people's perceptions, you can get very close to the truth of the person. Judgments on people are always subjective, but judgments must be based on facts, and facts are gleaned through careful observation of people in their everyday business life. What is the pattern of their actions, decisions, and behaviors? When you find the pattern or common thread in a person, people agree that it's right. Even that individual will agree that yes, that's me. Only then should you decide whom to bet on.

Ivan Seidenberg has done an effective job of repositioning Verizon through a series of mergers in a fast-moving, complex environment, as we detailed earlier (see pages 56–59). One of the personal traits that has helped him do that is his ability to look at a situation from many different angles. He also has the ability to contain his ego, which makes him open to contradictory viewpoints and other people's ideas and also allowed him to accomplish mergers in which someone else became the CEO and he became the number two. Those traits were observable in him when he was in his thirties and was a Washington lobbyist with no major leadership responsibilities. I knew him then, and I remember the skill with which he could steer a discussion among peers and build on other people's ideas. It was a wise leader who saw his natural tendencies and gave him a job with P&L responsibility so he could test his mettle as a business leader. Seidenberg took on a major division that was losing money and turned it around, and his career went upward to increasing levels of scale, scope, and complexity from there. His personal edge in reframing got developed in subsequent jobs, where he also acquired and developed and further honed a number of know-hows, including detecting patterns in the external landscape, positioning, and dealing with external constituencies.

You improve your judgments on people by reflecting on your mistakes and becoming aware of your own psychological blockages. Even Jack Welch, legendary for his good instincts about people, had to work at it. In his autobiography, Welch describes some of his hiring mistakes early on, but by the end of his career, he was a master at selecting people, getting the best out of them, and rooting out those individuals who were in the wrong jobs. By his own admission, Welch in his younger days was often seduced by a person's appearance, speaking ability, or academic credentials. But over time, he began to cross-check his judgments by soliciting different viewpoints about key people, first from his good friend and vice chairman Larry Bossidy and from Bill Conaty, executive vice president of human resources. Conaty proved to be a keen judge of people, and Welch highly valued his opinion throughout his career. During a board meeting, when Welch was discussing succession candidates, he spontaneously invited Conaty to express his views on the candidates, knowing full well that Conaty's judgments were different from his own.

Welch invested a tremendous amount of time talking to and learning about his direct reports. He would extend discussions for hours just to be sure he was getting to know his people in depth. As searching out the truth about a person became a habit, Welch's judgment improved, and then the insights became instinctive and superb. One of Welch's great legacies is his design of processes for evaluating people, which institutionalized the practice of judging people based on substance and multiple perspectives.

Judgments have to be intellectually honest and balanced, but the focus should be on the positives. Everyone has wrinkles; leaders succeed despite them. You should first nail down the person's natural talents and tendencies, and then look for situations that will allow those things to develop and take off. If the negatives are really getting in the way of job performance or growth, you can give the person coaching to see if they can be corrected. Sometimes people have a blind side in a particular know-how—say, in dealing with external constituencies—or they have a bad habit, for example, of cutting people off before they finish their sentences. These things can often be corrected or compensated for. Expecting people to be perfect is unrealistic.

During a talent review with the board, Welch was heaping praise on an individual who had had one success after another. After a while, a director asked, "Jack, did you ever have a bad year?" Of course he had. "And did you learn a lot from it?" Welch immediately got the point: of course he had; people learn as much if not more from adversity as from success. People who've had setbacks shouldn't be discounted without probing into the specifics of the situation. Maybe they made dreadful decisions. Did they learn, or is there something that makes you think they'll repeat those mistakes? Evaluating people by numerical performance alone doesn't give you insights. Digging in will help you see the person more broadly and prevent you from overlooking people who learn from their mistakes or failed to deliver for reasons beyond their control—say, because of an unexpected move by a competitor in the eleventh hour.

POOLING OBSERVATIONS

When you are precise in your observations and take the time to connect multiple points of information about a person, you begin to zero in on the real stuff. The best judgments come when five or six people who know the person well sit together to compare their observations and ask questions of each other, drilling for specifics. If someone says, "She's smart," you have to follow with "Smart in what ways? And what makes you say that?" "He always has the answer before everyone else" shows a quick mind, but what about the depth of thinking? How often is he right, and when he isn't, does he admit it? Muster the evidence, probe beyond the generalities. This kind of process gives everyone a fuller, more-accurate picture of the individual's positives and negatives and under what circumstances these things tend to come out.

One CEO introduced a terrific process to get his senior team to share their views on up-and-coming leaders. At one session, he broke them into small groups to discuss one lower-level leader, one at a time. The groups were instructed to identify five things the person was very good at—no negatives were allowed, just the positives. The first one up for discussion was a young leader who had an outstanding trait: she had a way of rubbing people the wrong way by being direct and to the point in a company where being polite and non-confrontational was the norm. As the senior leaders made their lists, they had to keep correcting each other, because they kept using phrases like "too abrupt" and "too direct," clearly not positives. Even when the small discussion groups compared their findings, one of them couldn't help but blurt out that the person lacked tact.

But, eventually, the positives came out. This young leader could see the bigger picture across functional silos. She could break assignments down to manageable tasks and deliver on them. She was great at coaching people and sharing her knowledge. She knew how to make money. All of these observations were backed up with specific examples. What the group had converged on described the mind of a general manager. The CEO then raised the question, "If this is all true, why couldn't she be a general manager?" The group replied that she was too direct. "What if I put her in a company like GE, Intel, or Dell, where that kind of no-nonsense approach is valued?" the CEO posited. One participant who'd come from GE chimed in, "They'd love her!" The room burst into laughter. They had figured out the woman's gifts and also where those gifts would flourish. It was a complete portrait that would never have been painted using a standard list of competences. Being direct is a good thing, not bad, in a results-driven general manager.

Michigan-based DTE Energy Company uses a similar homegrown process that was initiated by Larry Steward, the vice president of human resources, in which the top team discusses the key leaders below them, laying out among their colleagues the observations they've made of those leaders, focusing on their know-hows, talent potential, and areas where they could benefit from further development. All the senior officers are asked to write down twenty or so specific things they know about the person, backed up with examples, and then those observations are shared among the group. In every case, the lists have lots of items in common, and these begin to form a profile of the person that everyone concurs with.

But unique observations are not ignored. If one person notices something the others don't, the group probes for further evidence one way or the other, and if nothing else, the observation creates awareness of something the leaders should watch for when they leave the room.

The multiple viewpoints and insistence on specific examples drive out personal biases and other psychological distortions. And the CEO, Tony Earley, who conducts the discussions, drives the dialogue to be brutally honest and specific as he pushes the group to find the common ground.

When Earley and Steward first introduced the process in 2002, it was an effort to get through discussions of eight officers in an eight-hour session, but as they've become accustomed to the process and have gotten to know the individuals better, they now discuss the specific talents and development needs of about fifteen individuals per session. They discuss the same people frequently, often seven or eight times in a year, which allows the leaders to test their views, look for further evidence that the person is one way or another, and let the profiles evolve.

Once the group has zeroed in on a person's natural talents, they try to think creatively about where those talents might be applied. Through these sessions, the group found, for instance, that one leader had considerable financial talent, was a good teacher, a good negotiator, and a strategic thinker. He was very smart, had great verbal communication skills, and understood the company holistically. He was relentless, persistent, and extremely creative. What was his next role? They weren't sure he would be the right person to put in front of Wall Street. But some of them had another idea: they thought he'd do a great job in front of another key stakeholder of the company. Why not put him in regulatory affairs, where he would interface with the State Public Service Commission and the public?

The move to regulatory affairs opened a whole new

career trajectory for the person, and he welcomed it. It also required him to grow in the job. Much-broader thinking involving qualitative issues, not just numbers, was needed since he lacked experience in regulatory affairs. The top team created a transition plan that included direct involvement in rate filings as well as coaching and mentoring from the existing leader. At the same time, he brought something to the job the company needed. DTE Energy Company was going to be filing a number of rate cases with the State Public Service Commission in the coming years, and they needed someone who would be creative and effective in making its case.

Prior to this process, leaders at DTE Energy Company were uncomfortable making people move within the organization, especially in taking risks by putting individuals in new and different roles. But pinpointing individuals' God-given talents and brainstorming about where those talents would flourish opened their eyes to a wider range of possibilities. The whole orientation has shifted from defending whether someone should be in a particular job to trying to see the person as a whole and finding a good fit between the individual and the job. During one session, an executive vice president started describing one of his direct reports and stopped himself in the middle of it: "Why am I defending him? That's not what this is about." He laughed at his own mistake, and the humor made the rest of the session more candid and informal.

Most companies have these kinds of sessions, but you get more out of them by focusing on fewer people in more depth, zeroing in on the positives, and drilling for specifics.

GETTING TO THE TRUTH OF A PERSON

Drilling is invaluable in figuring out who a leader really is and what she has to offer. When the longtime CEO of a $3 billion manufacturing company reached retirement age, the board had a clear view of what was required to take the company to the next level, and they were committed to finding the right person for the job. The company had been through a hellish ten years following a leveraged buyout that burdened it with heavy debt and little cash. The outgoing CEO had done a great job of streamlining the business, improving global sourcing, and reducing working capital. He had achieved double-digit margins and a revenue growth rate better than the industry. The person succeeding him would have to accelerate revenue growth, broaden its base, and build a bigger presence in emerging markets like China and India.

A headhunter strongly recommended Frank, a candidate who was just the right age, was based in Europe, had the pedigree of a top business school, and presented himself extremely well. He had been running a $10 billion division of a multinational and had been passed over to be the CEO. The headhunter had indicated that although the candidate wanted to move from being a divisional president to CEO, it might be difficult to attract him to a company that was roughly a third the size of his division.

Determined to pin down the specific talents and skills Frank and any other candidates possessed, the board's search committee dug in to gather facts about what the candidates had actually done and how they approached decisions. Interviews confirmed that Frank was very articulate and would likely do well with Wall Street. He was intelligent, charismatic, and likable. But what did he really do at his company? The headhunter had presented glowing reports about Frank but never mentioned any specific financial accomplishments Frank had made in his division, and results by division were not in the public domain. In one-on-one interviews, the board members kept pressing Frank for those results, and as they pieced together the information, they learned that in his entire seven-year term, his division's margins never exceeded 3 percent and his return on invested capital (ROIC) had never exceeded 6 percent. He claimed to have made innovative moves to streamline production and introduce innovative products, but market share under his leadership had also been flat or declined slightly. He seemed to know a lot about sourcing from emerging markets, but there were plenty of questions about his ability to position the business to make money and to drive discipline in operations. What credibility would this candidate bring to a company that already had margins in the double digits and a ROIC greater than 25 percent? To the headhunter's chagrin, the search committee of the board gave a pass on Frank.

Then came Mark, another candidate. He had taken his former company from a return of about 14 percent to 22 percent, had mastered Six Sigma, and had a measurable record of improving margins and velocity and delivering results, all essential qualities in a candidate. But the board wasn't entirely convinced that Mark was the one. There were trade-offs and unknowns. No one was sure that he could manage Wall Street, and there was some reservation about whether he could grow the company. They took a calculated risk, knowing that the strengths matched the most important criteria for the job and agreeing to watch the rest. Over the next four years, Mark delivered what was expected. The unknowns of dealing with Wall Street and growing the company went in Mark's favor. He was not flashy, but he turned out to be credible, and Wall Street loves performance. He was able to achieve steady, nonflamboyant growth, and the stock price tripled, all in a low-tech business.

One CEO was surprised when he got to the truth of a person who was aggressively pushing for a promotion from the number three job of executive vice president of the second largest P&L center of a multibillion-dollar company to the number two job of president and COO. The CEO, who was new to the company, had heard mostly good things about Lee, but drilled to learn more before making this most-important decision. The company didn't have very good processes for evaluating people, so the CEO started asking a lot of questions about Lee. The observations included the fact that Lee was high energy, tireless, and could inspire groups like no one else. He had been very successful in running manufacturing and was extraordinary in cost cutting. He was very decisive and in command. As the CEO himself observed in extended staff meetings, Lee loved being the center of attention. Lee, however, had no record of developing people. He was self-centered, very ambitious, and thought in terms of bold goals, but often without thinking through the underlying foundation. When he was given broader responsibilities, he seemed unable to run on multiple cylinders simultaneously. He didn't see the big picture and didn't anticipate second-order consequences.

With the observations and comments about Lee in hand, the CEO sat back and considered what it all meant. Lee's skills seemed to be very narrow, and he didn't seem to know how to build organizational capability or to develop other leaders. The CEO began to wonder how Lee had risen so far, and further questioning got to the truth: Lee had landed several promotions by putting pressure on his bosses—just as he was pushing the CEO—convincing them that he was indispensable, and his bosses had acquiesced. Unlike the others, this CEO didn't cave. He observed Lee and, based on the facts, didn't promote him; on the contrary, he moved him out of the job.

Group processes for pooling observations and opinions are tremendously important for getting to know people. But you have to have your own methodology to keep your mental data base refreshed, as does Patrick Wang, the CEO of Johnson Electric, a highly successful manufacturing company in

Hong Kong. For more than three years, he has kept running notes of the top people in the company. Every time he meets with his direct reports or has a discussion by phone, he records his observations of the person in multiple dimensions—what they're doing well, where they appear to need help, how their behavior is changing. He then continuously updates his judgments of each person and is completely open with the person about it. His ongoing calibration helps him detect and address problems with a person's performance or behavior much sooner and, in particular, has accelerated how quickly he addresses problems with execution. He explains, "Sometimes you feel the person is so good and so honest that it must be the circumstance. But when you've attributed problems to the circumstance many times in a row, you have to question your own judgment about the person."

Wang says people are receptive to the process for two reasons: first, because people know he's fair. It's an open book, so people see that Wang is valuing performance, as opposed to saying "This person is good because I say so." Also, they always know where they stand. When he has asked people to leave, there were no surprises and no bitterness, because the process by which he reached that conclusion had been completely open.

Jeff Immelt spends 30 to 40 percent of his time on coaching, training, and managing people at GE, and for people at the highest levels, he says, "Everything we do is a performance review of some sort. Every touch point becomes a way to talk about that set of people. I'm thinking about this group every day." Leaders with this know-how simply make the time because they grasp the importance.

DEVELOPING AND DEPLOYING LEADERS
IN THE RIGHT WAY

Helping people realize their potential as leaders means clearing a path for them to grow, but it also means identifying what they need to work on in the current job. This is where leadership gets very personal. There's no substitute for ongoing face-to-face dialogue with people about what's going well and what isn't. You can't let fear of their response undermine your know-how in helping leaders grow and improve.

Stuart, the CEO of a global manufacturing and services company, found a simple way to save Kate, who had the potential to be a great CFO but was having trouble adapting to the company's Midwestern culture. Kate was hired for her tremendous talent in finance, and she made contributions in her first year by surfacing important issues and having the tenacity to keep them on the table. But others on the executive team complained regularly that she was too gruff with her peers and too intimidating to the people below her. She just didn't seem to fit in. Stuart recognized the talent and contribution and decided to be frank with her about what she had to change. He even got her a coach, but he was careful in choosing one. He didn't want Kate to lose her edge; he wanted her to continue to raise tough issues and set a high standard, just to do so more constructively. Her coach was frank about what was at stake and made some specific suggestions. One of them was to emphasize the positives as well as the negatives in her subordinates' presentations. Instead of cutting people down in front others, signal what was good, then make specific suggestions about what to improve. And stop using four-letter words—that was an absolute. Within a couple of weeks, people noticed the difference. The company retained a high-caliber individual, and Kate herself is working hard to improve with encouragement from her colleagues, who see the change in behavior.

The 360 evaluations many companies use can be helpful, but you have to be thoughtful about how you use them. Don't try to cover everything; zero in on one or two things the person has to work on. For one leader, the 360 showed a low rating (less than 3 on a 5-point scale) in every item having to do with peer relationships. He was one of four internal candidates to succeed the CEO, and the low rating puzzled his boss. The CEO knew him to be a great performer who regularly delivered 70 percent of company profits, and he was a born learner who stayed at the top of his game. He was also a good conceptualizer. But obviously there was something going on when it came to working with colleagues. By persistently digging and asking pointed questions, his boss got to the nub of the problem. When he respected the other person, the guy was great. When he didn't, his disdain was very visible. This type of behavior was keeping him from reaching his potential. The CEO brought this pattern to the leader's attention, and he instantly agreed that it was true and promised to try to curb that behavior. This kind of reflection, whether you do it on your own or with the help of a mentor or coach, improves your judgment and is essential to mastering each of the know-hows.

NON-NEGOTIABLE CRITERIA

As you're moving leaders to new jobs, you have to know the person, but you also have to be sure you understand what each job really requires to succeed in it. Contrary to common belief, long lists of criteria don't clarify what's required. The opposite is true: lengthy lists indicate fuzzy thinking and are inherently too general to point to the person who has the best chance of succeeding in that job. Worse, when the criteria are too comprehensive, they eliminate people who may in fact be the best choice in favor of people who are so-so in many categories. The consequence is mediocrity for the organization and unhappiness for the person. You have to have a laser-sharp view of what is absolutely required for a person to do well in a job, and define the three or four non-negotiable criteria, things you cannot compromise on. After years of hiring people in the retail business, Ben Cammarata, the highly successful founder and CEO of the $15 billion off-price retail chain TJX, has had a high batting average over a thirty-year period recruiting, developing, and retaining leadership talent. His non-negotiable criteria are simple and clear. You must be street smart, have great people skills, and be intuitively good at merchandising—none of which, he believes, can be taught.

To get the organization to perform, you have to get the non-negotiable criteria of leadership jobs exactly right. IBM got the job criteria exactly right in the early 1990s when speculation was that Big Blue was doomed. Investors complained that IBM had missed many opportunities that outsiders thought they should pursue, such as migrating out of mainframes and into microprocessors and software. They didn't think CEO John Akers's plan to split the company into a federation of autonomous units would solve the problem. Prompted by dismal financial prospects and shareholder activists, the IBM board came to the difficult conclusion that the company needed a new CEO.

Because there was no clear successor to Akers, industry pundits went to town writing everything from hardheaded analysis to country-club gossip about who would be the next leader of IBM. Job criteria began to appear in print as reporters solicited the views of various management experts: IBM needed a leader with intelligence and emotional depth, a rebel mentality, and technology skills. "Must possess top-notch computer skills" a *New York Times* headline read in

January 1993. Two frequently cited contenders were John Sculley of Apple Computer and George Fisher of Motorola, both of whom had a technology background.

But the IBM board determined that what IBM needed more than anything else was a business person and change agent. The new leader had to have superb skill in being able to diagnose and get to the heart of what was causing the decline in margins, unacceptable cash flow, and flattening of revenues, and then be able to change the social system of the organization to fit the new reality. Experience in a technology company was less important. Those criteria ultimately pointed to Lou Gerstner, then CEO of RJR Nabisco. Gerstner wasn't a technology expert—RJR Nabisco was a prosaic food and tobacco company—but he was very good at diagnosing complex businesses and positioning them in ways that resonated with customers. He had led a dazzling turnaround as head of Travel Related Services at American Express, where he had not just cut costs but was able to deliver top-line double-digit growth for twelve consecutive years.

The board's choice proved to be brilliant. While many industry pundits had declared the mainframe dead, Gerstner did his own analysis, starting from the customers' viewpoint, and found that IBM's mainframe business had been stolen away by competitors. The market was there, but the competition had dramatically undercut IBM on price, while IBM's finance department had disallowed price cuts to preserve margins. IBM's higher prices had irritated customers and put the company in a downward spiral of shrinking market share, falling revenue, and tighter cash flow against the backdrop of high fixed costs.

Gerstner concluded that IBM's pricing structure needed a heavy infusion of reality. That meant cost had to be taken out of the company (about $7 billion), and he hired a cost-conscious CFO to take on the task, which included breaking the "no layoffs" taboo. But Gerstner wasn't just a cost cutter.

He brought services and software into the picture, enabling IBM to break its reliance on the hardware sector and leverage its strong customer relationships. From that decision, others followed: to make the shift, IBM needed new skills, a different organization structure, and a different mind-set. Gerstner worked it through and brought the company back to life. The board's drilling down to the right criteria and finding a leader with those specific strengths reshaped the destiny of the corporation. By setting the right non-negotiable criteria and refusing to be swayed by the pundits, the search committee of the IBM board saved a jewel of American business.

When Richard E. Whitmer, the CEO of Blue Cross Blue Shield of Michigan, announced his plans to retire by 2006, the company was in good financial shape, but it faced huge uncertainty about how the health-care landscape would evolve over the next several years. The ability to reposition the business in the context of incredibly high and rising health-care costs, the emergence of national competitors, and the uncertain roles of federal and state governments became non-negotiable criteria for a new CEO. Choosing a CEO for this business is generally highly political, because the organization's board reflects multiple constituencies, including state government, representatives of local businesses, individuals, hospitals, and medical groups. The board also includes small groups and large ones, such as autos and unions. Some of these constituencies are by nature highly political and at odds with each other.

The board members were not experts in health care, but they invested substantial time speaking with many experts who helped clarify the trends and issues Blue Cross could face in the future. It led to clarity about the non-negotiable criteria, particularly the ability to reposition the business as conditions change and to bring multiple constituencies to the table.

The board was able to depoliticize the decision and reach unanimity. One person, Daniel J. Loepp, stood out as best meeting the non-negotiable criteria. He had demonstrated the ability to move decisively in the face of constant shifts among various players, various legislative positions, and consumer and societal demands. He could find a path despite the complexity and ambiguity, and was psychologically open to collaborating with different external players such as health-care providers, unions, and other interest groups.

THE POWER TO SHAPE DESTINIES

While you have to be sure that leaders meet the non-negotiable criteria, you can't focus only on the requirements of the job and lose sight of developing people. You have to actively search for and maybe even create jobs to stretch people and be willing to make creative moves that may seem risky but that can have a big payoff. Richard Carrión, CEO of Banco Popular, does this routinely. When he hired Carlos Vázquez, he put him in charge of risk management, a very unpopular staff job because you're the thorn in everybody's side. Vázquez was very successful in the job, but Carrión thought he could do more. To broaden his skills, Carrión moved Vázquez to a line job, where he would go from leading a handful of people to one with full P&L responsibility leading hundreds of people. Vázquez performed well in the new job, and the experience as a line manager prepared him for a wider range of options. In another case, Carrión switched David Chafey, now the head of the Puerto Rican bank, from the finance side of the business to the retail side. Chafey had come up through the banking side of the business, went to work for an investment bank, and returned as CFO. He was, in Carrión's words, "very much in the CFO mold." Knowing that Chafey had ambition, and believing that he would be a better leader if he had a broader view of the business and also that he would make the transition well, Carrión moved him into a job as head of retail systems. Carrión also saw in Roberto Herencia the same type of leadership ability. He cleared the path for him to flower by putting him in charge of Banco Popular North America, ensuring that he would run it without interference. Carrión explains the general approach: "Whenever we identify someone we want to nurture by putting him or her in a line job, we look for the first opportunity that comes up, and we put that person's name on the list, along with maybe the names of two or three others."

If you're compromising a bit and putting a leader in a job who does not meet all the non-negotiable criteria—maybe because you want to see if the person can develop them—you have to decide what kind of support you will provide, and you also have to be prepared to reverse your decision if the hoped-for growth doesn't happen. Selecting leaders is not risk free, but paying attention to whether the person is making the transition lets you address problems quickly.

The president of a technology company was in the job for less than a year when he took a chance by placing a famous researcher in a business leadership role. He did it because he believed the expert was one of those rare people who is half technologist/inventor/academic and half true businessperson. He saw that the researcher was extremely bright, had a ton of curiosity, was a change agent, and had an interest in business. But the president was also aware of the risk, and from the beginning, he was very explicit about what success would look like.

It was all about getting things done with other people and being able to make trade-offs. He himself was clear about what he was watching for, and he made the researcher aware as well. "A researcher of his stature walks in and has the whole lab at his command," the president explained. "But that wouldn't work for a business leader, so I explained at the outset what behaviors from his background could become derailers." The researcher was told that at the end of the year, he would be held accountable for the relationships with the heads of marketing and finance. The president said to think of those relationships on a scale from 1 to 10 where a 1 means you're not at all connected, a 10 means you're totally connected, and 5 is the worst place to be because it means you're not totally agreeing or disagreeing, so the honesty probably isn't coming out.

Throughout the year, the president frequently pulled the researcher aside and said, "One to ten, where are you?" Sometimes the researcher would send an e-mail saying, "Half a point achieved," and the president knew just what it meant. The point is that it became a kind of shorthand, and both the president and the researcher knew what he was working on. It became part of their ongoing conversation and provided a means for gauging whether the researcher was indeed growing into the job.

You make better judgments about people, find more creative ways to deploy and develop their talents, and make a greater human impact when you take a sincere personal interest in each leader's development. Leaders with this know-how look for those informal opportunities to get to know people better and to provide coaching. When, for instance, Carrión flew from San Juan to Philadelphia for an operating review, he asked one of his younger leaders to fly with him on both legs of the trip so they could talk. "That gave me a chance to bounce ideas off him and test him," Carrión says. "You see the talent, and quite frankly, you see the gaps, so you're in a better position to gauge how well that person will do in a particular job."

Ian Cook, president and chief operating officer of Colgate-Palmolive and a great developer of people, had a particularly poignant experience that drove home the importance of those one-on-one conversations. When he was running Colgate's business in Mexico, a young female executive, Christina, who was working in Colgate's Dominican business, was murdered, and he had to deliver the news to her parents, who, of course, were devastated. They were first-generation Mexicans living in the United States, the father had built his own tortilla chip business, and the daughter had gone to Harvard. She was truly their pride and joy. Christina was single at the time, so Cook and his wife had made a point of inviting her from time to time to the country club or to their house for a barbecue.

As Cook got to know her parents after Christina's death, he found out that they could recount every conversation he had had with Christina. They also knew all about Cook's wife and children, even though they'd never met them. His personal connection with Christina had obviously made an impact on her, and she had told her parents everything. As Cook says, "If your interest in the person is sincere, it goes a long way." Cook, by the way, has remained in contact with Christina's parents ever since.

DEALING WITH MISMATCHES IN A CONSTRUCTIVE WAY

Selecting a person for a job is always something of a bet. Honing your skills in judging people cuts the risk, but it's impossible to know for sure that the person will grow into and with the job and that his or her shortfalls (everyone has some) won't get in the way. People problems are never straightforward, but ignoring them causes setbacks for the organization and to your own progress as a leader.

It was 3:00 a.m. when Phillip found himself replaying a conversation he'd had with Dan, one of three division managers reporting to him and the thorn in his side.

"Just trust us techies," Dan had said. "This is West Coast stuff. . . . You don't really want to hear about Z-stacks and ion beams, do you Phillip?"

After eleven months as his boss, Phillip still couldn't get a straight answer out of Dan. Dan's division had been established as an entrepreneurial venture to develop a specific new product in the optics-technology field, a market with major potential. If they could develop a viable commercial product before the Koreans or the Japanese, the return on the initial $500 million investment would be huge. Yet every time Dan and Phillip talked, Dan was quick to say progress was being made, but also that they weren't "there" yet. Phillip walked away every time with the same fogginess about what the technical issues were, how they would be resolved, and by when. It was impossible for him to make accurate projections about when the division would stop consuming money and start generating it. Corporate was becoming impatient and increasingly concerned that the competition would beat them. Dan was unfazed. The previous July, when Phillip pressed him on timelines and targets, Dan asked for additional funding and groused about the company's low tolerance for risk.

Now, as the annual review approached, Phillip's frustration with Dan was reaching the boiling point. But the thought of replacing him was unsettling. Phillip wasn't a technology expert—his bosses didn't think he had to be. He was picked for his stellar record of exercising financial control, inspiring people, and delivering results. Without a technical background, how could he be sure to find the right person to replace Dan? He couldn't afford to make a mistake and lose any time. And, of course, Phillip would have to break the bad news to his predecessor and current boss, the very person who had hired Dan. His boss had considered it a coup to lure such an experienced technologist to an old East Coast company like theirs, and he was thrilled when Dan recruited a whole cadre of techies from his former employer, some of whom would probably follow Dan out the door.

The next day Phillip did some clear thinking about the whole history. He realized he'd fallen short in pressing Dan to be specific and setting milestones that Dan could be measured against. But as he assembled in his mind every piece of information he had about Dan—previous conversations, results Dan had or had not delivered, decisions Dan had made, things Dan had said to him or other people—a clear pattern emerged. Dan didn't like to be pinned down and avoided it at every opportunity. He used technology as a kind of smoke-screen to shield himself from accountability. And he made it virtually impossible for Phillip to communicate directly with the people in his department by doing things like answering questions for them following their presentations. Their loyalty to Dan was evident in their constant deferral to him and their reluctance to talk to Phillip and others in the company, even the marketing people who would eventually have to sell the product. When Phillip dug into the HR file, he found that Dan's résumé listed some impressive companies, but that he had never been in a job for more than three years and always left before results had materialized.

The pattern of behavior was so consistent and unmistakable that Phillip had to conclude that Dan was not the right person to lead the division, his technical brilliance notwithstanding. When he told his boss, the response was not what he expected: Phillip's boss wholeheartedly supported the decision to replace Dan, but he made it clear that Phillip had been too slow to act. The company had lost precious time and money. It was a black mark against Phillip's leadership that took several years to erase.

Phillip should have made sure the absolute requirements of key jobs were being met regardless of who had done the hiring and dug into the cause and effect when his instincts were first aroused. It didn't matter if others argued. Dan's job was key given the high stakes of a half-billion-dollar investment, the chance to take the lead in a growth market, and the serious hit to corporate earnings if the project failed to deliver in the prescribed time frame. Dan had not demonstrated his ability to convert technology into marketable products, to accept input from people in a variety of functions, and to break a project into specific milestones. Phillip should have gathered the information necessary to make a sound judgment about Dan at the first inkling of trouble, but his insecurity held him back, even as Dan got in the way of the team, the social system, and business results.

People often have temporary periods of disappointments, so you don't want to remove a person from a job too soon if there are things you can do to get the person on track. But many business problems are the result of letting things slide, ignoring the fact that the job is evolving while the person isn't, or vice versa, or that the decision to put the person in the job was wrong in the first place. Instead of dealing with the issue, you harbor resentment toward the person, maybe even avoid him or her, until the frustration boils over and you ask the person to leave. There are all kinds of psychological reasons for avoiding such situations, whether it's fear of the person's response, or a sense of loyalty, or your need to be liked. When one leader was put in charge of a division, she knew right away that two of the direct reports she inherited were not up to the work that lay ahead, but she also knew everyone in the division would be scrutinizing her every move and didn't want to be seen as a butcher. She wrestled with the issue for several months before finally concluding that her leadership would be short-lived if she continued to rely on them.

Familiarity is no substitute for careful thought about how the leader you handpicked for a job is really faring. While there's an advantage in knowing someone well, familiarity can lead to sloppy thinking about how a person is progressing. When John was given the chance to turn around a much larger division than the one he had been running, he attacked the job enthusiastically and correctly diagnosed that logistics was key to bringing the division back to health. For help in that area, John knew immediately where to turn: Kurt, his right-hand man in the old job. Kurt had been a great performer, plus he had been a consultant to freight companies early in his career. John offered Kurt the job, and he gladly accepted.

In the months that followed, whenever John's boss asked how Kurt was doing, John was quick to respond, "He's doing great." In fact, he was not. The logistics problems were mounting, and everyone but John could see it. Even the CEO's frequent questioning didn't open John's eyes. By the end of the first year, inventories had gone up, not down, the division missed its financial targets, and customers were incensed about late deliveries. The CEO didn't want to undermine John's leadership, so over the course of the year he kept trying to persuade John to confront the fact that Kurt was not doing the job that needed to be done. John wasn't completely oblivious to Kurt's shortcomings, but he kept telling himself that he could coach Kurt to make him successful. Deep down, he was blocked by his insecurity, which made him much more comfortable with Kurt than with the prospect of bringing in someone he didn't know.

Finally, the CEO's patience wore thin. When he saw that John was not taking any action to deal with Kurt, the CEO told John that he was losing confidence in him and that he had forty-eight hours to come up with a new plan. John finally replaced Kurt and hired someone else.

Sometimes a feeling of indebtedness gets in the way. Randy, the CEO of a technology company, struggled to reconcile conflicting views about his CFO. He had recruited the financial chief shortly after taking charge and felt beholden to her for sorting out the myriad accounting problems, imposing discipline in financial reporting, and working with him as a partner in making productivity improvements that doubled the company's stock price and won kudos from Wall Street. Once the accounting problems had been resolved, however, the financial challenges changed. The company wanted to expand through a series of acquisitions, which required analyzing the financial implications of potential deals. Along the way, the CFO brought a major acquisition to the CEO's desk, insisting that it was a great opportunity and a great price. Randy was swayed by the CFO's enthusiasm, but something gnawed at him. The offer the CFO had proposed was a bargain-basement price. Why would the target company, which was not in distress, accept it? The whole thing seemed foolhardy. The CFO didn't give up until the CEO shut down the deal. Then a few months later, the CFO proposed another deal, and again, the analysis seemed naive and incomplete. How would the deal affect cash flow and shareholder value? Randy did not pursue the second acquisition proposal, or a third, because they made no economic sense.

Even as Randy rejected the CFO's proposals, he stood by his direct report. Then something happened that spurred Randy to fine-tune his judgment: a securities analyst began to delve into the company's cash flow and discovered a problem. The CFO dismissed the analyst's warnings and assured her boss that cash flow was fine. Yet within months, the company was in a cash crunch. Now the CEO's ongoing commitment to the CFO began to unwind. He realized that his emotional bond had prevented him from seeing that while the CFO was a great accountant, she was not prepared to do the job that currently needed doing. It took emotional courage to face the reality that he had to ask her to leave. As painful as it was, Randy faced up to it and set out to find a replacement, ensuring the company would not lose the ground it had gained.

THE PROBLEM IS INCOMPATIBILITY, NOT INCOMPETENCE

When a mismatch becomes evident and someone is failing in a job, it is important not to jump to conclusions. When you first sense a problem, you have to get to the root cause. Maybe the person has a psychological blockage, a know-how that's missing, or bad chemistry with a key person in another function. Sometimes the fault lies with a boss who fails to provide direction.

You should use your insights into people to help them find their "pew"—the lane in which their talents flourish and their personal growth accelerates. Use your imagination to help them find terrific matches elsewhere.

One leader had successfully led a small business unit and, as a reward and a further test, was sent to Paris and put in charge of the European region. Nearly two years into the job, he was frustrated and floundering badly. He was determined to fix the many complex problems his predecessor left, but it wasn't going well. Meanwhile, he and his family, who didn't speak a word of French, were miserable in their Parisian post, and relations between him and his boss had become strained. The man was not taking hold of his job as head of Europe, and the boss couldn't risk keeping him in it any longer. When it came to marketing, however, this leader was a natural, with considerable talent and experience. The boss saw his affinity for marketing, did some networking with others in the company, and worked out a solution: to offer him a position as vice president of marketing in a major division. The new job used all his talents. It was a great fit that allowed him to finish his career and retire at the age of sixty-five.

At an East Coast energy company, the person in charge of strategic planning was not cutting the mustard because his plans were consistently too conceptual and unrealistic, nor did he have the temperament to deal with the political issues associated with being a regulated utility. This posed a dilemma for his bosses, who had come to value his tremendous knowledge of the business, ability to cut through complex financial data, and communications skills. When the higher-ups got together to discuss the situation, they came up with the idea to put him in investor relations. His natural gifts were the stuff investor relations is made of: the ability to make sense of complex business situations and quantitative data and to communicate and persuade others. It was an unusual but inspired career move, and it worked beautifully for the person and the company.

Sometimes, and often in smaller companies, finding a job that matches the person's talents is not an option. That's when you have to make it clear to the person that his future lies elsewhere. You have to know when and how to de-select people. I use the term "de-select" instead of "fire" to make a distinction in attitude. Leaders with this know-how understand that every human being has inherent value and that errors will be made in trying to deploy a person's talents. When the person must go, it's your obligation to ease the transition and preserve the person's dignity. People accept such realities when the communication has been honest and the intentions are constructive and sincere.

BUILDING A PIPELINE OF LEADERS

The most successful leaders leave a legacy by establishing a pipeline of leaders that is better than what they inherited and, in addition, becomes the standard against which the rest are compared.

Most sizable companies have some kind of talent-planning process, but the specifics of those processes vary greatly. They are often out of tune with current and future business needs, tend to focus too much on absolute personality traits, and aren't geared to unearth the specifics of a person's know-hows and behavior. You should be sure that the criteria for spotting leaders are consistent with how you're positioning the business and that the processes for assessing people have enough rigor in them to get to the truth about a person's performance and potential.

When GE's Jeff Immelt determined that delivering different numbers would require GE to develop strong capabilities in technology and marketing, he made sure the pipeline of up-and-coming leaders emphasized these criteria. Prior to 2000, the emphasis in GE had been on delivering performance largely through productivity improvements, requiring fierce operational discipline and expertise in techniques like Six Sigma. When Immelt set the company's sights on going from 5 percent to 8 percent organic growth, he realized that the drive for capital-efficient, profitable top-line growth would require leaders who understood how to combine technology and marketing to differentiate the business from the customers' perspective. GE revised its criteria for leadership to include the following:

- Can create an external focus that defines success in market terms.

- Is a clear thinker who can simplify strategy into specific actions, make decisions, and communicate priorities.
- Has the imagination and courage to take risks on people and ideas.
- Energizes teams through inclusiveness and connection with people.
- Develops expertise in a function or domain, using depth as a source of confidence to drive change.

Sometimes a particular layer of leadership or a specific job is so essential, or pivotal, to the success of the business that it warrants your attention. For a company that is seeking a higher rate of growth from emerging markets, for example, a pivotal job is the person in charge of recruiting, training, placing, and retaining leaders in jobs for fast development in India, China, Brazil, and eastern Europe. If, for example, you promote twenty vice presidents, you might want to ensure that at least five are from those countries.

For a retailer such as Home Depot, store-manager jobs might be pivotal, since this is where all the good ideas and good intentions get translated into specific actions that affect the customer experience.

Pramod Bhasin, the CEO of Genpact, the Indian company that provides information services to global giants such as Wachovia and GE, identified a pivotal layer of three hundred managers. He was getting the company geared up to deliver on multiple contracts for millions of dollars worth of services, knowing that if it couldn't deliver on its contractual commitments, the financial penalties would be devastating. The ability to meet these commitments would require doubling the number of employees from twenty-five thousand people to fifty thousand in a few short years. The way Genpact works is that it sends teams of roughly fifteen knowledge workers to take up residence with client companies for years at a time.

Those workers have to be able to understand the client's needs and deliver on time and within cost. Customer satisfaction is in their hands—but also in the hands of the managers they report to. Bhasin determined that the three hundred or so team leaders who hire and direct the knowledge workers on the client sites was pivotal, because that was where all the broad directives were translated into building the specific teams for specific clients. Although that layer was a few steps removed from the CEO (the managers reported to a vice president), the CEO took a personal interest in defining the nonnegotiable criteria and ensuring good hiring, development, and retention practices.

Criteria alone don't ensure the right set of leaders. You have to work with others to develop the processes for calibrating and developing people, and you have to revisit them often to test whether they're working the way they should, just as you would for any other business activity. You can, for instance, sample the kinds of leaders that are being identified at lower levels by getting to know some of them. Leaders who are great developers of other leaders sense what is coming through the pipeline of leaders. They make a point of visiting with leaders at lower levels in small groups, spending maybe two hours with, say, ten people, during which time they engage them with questions to see how they think and what their overall ability is. Immelt goes to GE's executive learning center at Crotonville, New York, some twelve to fifteen times a year, where he participates in class discussions and spends time afterward talking to people more informally. He can sense from those interactions the overall caliber and even the DNA, or dominant psychology and criteria, of the leaders in the room.

Money spent on training and development alone does not ensure a pipeline of leaders who are able to take the business in the direction you set. Companies like Unilever, Xerox, all the U.S. automotive companies, and until recently IBM fell short in developing leaders despite spending tons of money on it, while GE, P&G, Colgate, and some lesser-known companies like Sherwin-Williams have done a terrific job of growing leaders. Their leadership-development processes are linked to the need to deliver business results and are highly disciplined and rigorous. The senior leaders see leadership development as a tool for business success and get personally involved in it.

At Colgate, leaders are evaluated in their first year of employment, so job assignments can be tailored from the start. Each subsidiary identifies its own high-potentials and submits that list to local general managers, who add and subtract names and then hand the list off to the division heads. These lists wend their way up the chain to the very top of the organization: the Colgate-Palmolive Human Resource (CPHR) committee, composed of Colgate's CEO, president, COO, senior VP of HR, and senior leader candidates up for the top job. Once a year, the CPHR committee meets to modify and consolidate the lists into a single master list and dispatches it back down the ranks. Those who make the cut are deployed in one of three tracks. The first track, local talent, is for relatively junior staff who might become the direct reports of a general manager. A second track is for leaders who are more advanced; they are designated as regional talent, and given, for example, a significant position in Asia. The most elevated track—global talent—is the reservoir from which the most senior jobs are filled.

The idea is to be sure the high-potentials receive assignments that stretch their abilities and expand their knowledge, exposing them to a variety of markets, cultures, consumers, and business circumstances, in tune with Colgate's evolving leadership requirements. To be sure that goal is being met, the CPHR committee itself designs career paths for general managers and higher-level leaders. And they form a connection with young leaders through programs such as "visibility programs," in which high-potentials from all over the world gather at Colgate's New York headquarters for weeklong sessions, during which they meet with every senior leader in the company. Even the board gets involved in leadership development early, tracking the progress of not just one or two people but the top two hundred leaders through frequent reviews and discussion.

Colgate is one of the few companies that excels in using the social system to produce the leaders of the future, who come from all parts of the globe. They are global in their orientation, thereby enabling Colgate to outcompete, in the category that is the mainstay of its business, competitors that are several times larger and that have the advantage of scale and scope.

Your know-how in judging, selecting, and developing leaders doesn't automatically improve just because you hire and fire a lot of people. You have to reflect on your accuracy in crystallizing what a person is good at it, what his or her potential is, and what he or she needs to improve. How good is your judgment compared with the judgments other leaders make on the same individual? You also have to reflect on whether the individuals turn out to have the potential you saw in them. When you repeatedly practice making judgments on people *and* reflect on why you missed in some cases, you're on your way to becoming a master of this know-how.

To complete the set of tools for shifting the social system and developing personal judgment on people, you have to build a team of people around you at the highest levels. You know the age-old adage that a leader is only as good as the people around him. Especially in this environment, no one can win without a high performing team. In business, getting high level, successful, often big ego people to work together has been problematic. Don't think it can't be done. The next chapter shows how.

How to spot the future leaders of your business:

- They consistently deliver ambitious results.

- They continuously demonstrate growth, adaptability, and learning better and faster than their excellently performing peers.

- They seize the opportunity for challenging, bigger assignments, thereby expanding capability and capacity and improving judgment.

- They have the ability to think through the business and take leaps of imagination to grow the business.

- They are driven to take things to the next level.

- Their powers of observation are very acute, forming judgments of people by focusing on their decisions, behaviors, and actions, rather than relying on initial reactions and gut instincts; they can mentally detect and construct the "DNA" of a person.

- They come to the point succinctly, are clear thinkers, and have the courage to state a point-of-view even though listeners may react adversely.

- They ask incisive questions that open minds and incite the imagination.

- They perceptively judge their own direct reports, have the courage to give them honest feedback so the direct reports grow; they dig into cause and effect if a direct report is failing.

- They know the non-negotiable criteria of the job of their direct reports and match the job with the person; if there is a mismatch they deal with it promptly.

- They are able to spot talent and see the "God's gift" of other individuals.

6

UNITY WITHOUT UNIFORMITY

Molding a Team of Leaders

You've taken the time and made the effort to spot, recruit, develop, and get in place a group of smart and talented people who are your direct reports. That's crucial. But the bigger challenge is molding these high-energy, high-powered, high-ego people into a working team of leaders who synchronize their efforts and propel the business forward.

Individual team members naturally focus on their own functional specialties and have their own personal ambitions, but those differences often cause them to pull in different directions, especially considering the inherent tensions that exist between various silos of the business. As the leader, you have to get your direct reports to submerge their egos, aggression, and personal agendas so they're pulling together. You can't mediate every dispute, ensure that every trade-off is properly made, or that information is flowing as it should on a daily basis, but if you use the know-how of molding a team, your direct reports will do those things as a matter of course, and the business will perform better.

The centerpiece of this know-how is getting your team to understand, focus on, and commit to the total business. You have to help them create a common granular picture of the business in its external context as you see it. That way, they'll know how their respective areas fit together, and they'll have both the motivation and information they need to keep their efforts aligned. You have to mold people's behavior as well. Too often, talented and ambitious people have a single-minded focus, little aware of what their colleagues in other silos are doing, at worst deeply suspicious of them. Resources and information are hoarded, and communication is sporadic and formalistic. You're the one who tolerates or challenges narrow self-interest, big egos, and dominant personalities.

Most of the work of molding a team happens in group settings, which may require that you change the way you lead. You can't just work with your direct reports one to one, setting their budgets and goals in private and coaching them individually as you shift your attention from one part of the business to another. You have to help the group create a picture of the total business and correct any divisive behaviors in the presence of the team, so you need the emotional strength to direct and stand up to powerful individuals on whom you depend.

Many leaders think molding a team isn't worth the effort, but they're missing a tremendous opportunity to differentiate themselves and build the business. The more people can see the total anatomy of the business, the intersections of its moving parts, and the broader context in which it operates, the better job they do. When they all see the same facts, discuss their own observations and thoughts, and come to understand the interconnectedness of their functions and skills, they're able to raise the bar, setting higher goals and achieving them faster. They can pinpoint changes in the external environment faster and more precisely, and they can better communicate to their own people the positioning, goals, and priorities of the business. They help each other grow. An effective team becomes not only a powerful competitive advantage, it also becomes a source of satisfaction that is a great device to retain the best people.

Mark Fields, now president of the Americas at Ford Motor Company, used his know-how of molding a team to revive Japan's Mazda Motor Corporation, in a foreign culture, no less. Mazda, in which Ford holds a 33 percent stake, had invested heavily to expand in the early 1990s in an effort to compete with Toyota, Honda, and Nissan, its bigger rivals. But that effort failed, and Fields inherited a company with $15 billion in revenue and a staggering $7 billion of debt. At the same time, the failure to catch Toyota, Honda, and Nissan had left Mazda dispirited and basically aimless. The products weren't distinctive and the brand was unfocused. In short, it was a company on the brink not only financially, but also from the standpoints of brand and morale.

The team that Fields inherited was one in name only. "I would call it a collection of individuals as opposed to a group aligned around business issues and a plan to address those issues," he recalls. Just as important, Fields was in a totally different culture, one that even his extensive experience in Argentina couldn't prepare him for. Styles of thinking, communicating, and even behaving were alien. Fortunately, Fields had nine months as the company's sales and marketing director to become familiar with all those issues before taking the reins. The challenge when he took over was to position the company to survive.

Japan is a consensus-building culture, and Fields set out to ensure that the management team understood the business issues and the reality as well as he did so they could develop a plan together that would allow Mazda to survive and, ultimately, to thrive.

"I came in with the very clear point of view," he says, "and I needed to figure out the process that was going to allow the management team to see the business from my level. In Japan, you rise through your function, and even when you become a functional head, you never see the business from the CEO's level. Yet seeing it from that perspective really determines whether the business succeeds or fails."

Fields discovered early in the process that Japanese companies in almost any industry compete against one another mostly in terms of operational effectiveness. Product lines are often very similar and the competitive advantage goes to the company with the best quality and greatest cost efficiency. Fields, however, determined that Mazda would position itself as a "different" kind of car company. Certainly, it would offer good quality and be cost effective, but the products would be different from those of Toyota and Honda—very distinctive in design and a bit quirky in performance and handling.

"I wanted to bring us back to our roots, the things that we did well, and that was creating vehicles that had a different product approach than the others. That meant we would have to pick the spots in which we wanted to compete."

That decision set off a process of getting every manager on the same page, understanding clearly Mazda's new positioning.

"The main thing I had to do to bring them there was show them the reality and show them very clearly what were the benefits if we made these changes to the business versus what were the consequences of not," Fields says. "The reason that was so important is because in the past, the truth or the reality was never really driven home to all of them in the organization. If the manufacturing person produced the number of units that he was supposed to produce, then the company should have profits. Or if the head of purchasing achieved his objectives for the year, his assumption was that Mazda would be in good shape. The business was never put together for them so that they could see how each of their pieces added up to a corporate whole."

Fields took pains early in the process to avoid being seen as the foreigner who was going to be telling the Japanese managers what they had to do. In early sessions, he brought in two Japanese experts, one a business-school professor and the other a financial analyst, to explain their views of Mazda's situation and what might be done to correct it.

Fields had also witnessed during his time as sales and marketing manager the typical Japanese reluctance to speak out in meetings. "I was flabbergasted, because in the first few top-management meetings I sat through there was not one comment about the presentations. Now I know I don't have all of the answers, but collectively as an organization we do. Therefore, we needed to drive a culture in which people could speak their minds, and that's doubly challenging in Japan because of the culture."

At first many of his direct reports came to Fields individually for one-on-one meetings. He would listen to their concerns, and then he would encourage them to bring up those concerns at the next meeting. "I told them it isn't a question of weakness that you have concerns, it's a question of maturity and leadership to be able to put the issues on the table in front of the rest of your colleagues and then let us wrestle with that so we can come up with the best solution for the company."

To help overcome that reluctance to speak out, he began during meetings to break up his group of direct reports into smaller groups of three or four.

"After we went through an overview of what the issue under discussion would be, the small groups would spend a couple of hours together discussing it and coming up with some solutions. Then we'd reconvene in the big group to hear their thoughts and recommendations. Slowly but surely, we got to the point in the top-management meetings in which we actually had active debates about them. To me that was one of the small indicators that I could look at and say we're making progress."

The process took about six months, during which the team held several off-site meetings of a day or more in addition to the normal corporate meetings. What emerged from that process was a management team that had what Fields labels "unity without uniformity." The management team understood clearly the situation and, more important, what they were going to do about it so that each director could articulate to their own teams what the new positioning was all about.

Fields says there were two gut-wrenching decisions that really brought the management team together as a team of leaders. One was the decision to close one of the company's main plants in Hiroshima. Mazda is based in Hiroshima and is the city's largest employer. The issue was not only economic but societal. In the Japanese culture, closing a plant is a decision with huge emotional implications. Nevertheless, the team studying Mazda's capacity situation came back and said the plant would have to be closed. The second was the decision that the company simply had too many people and would have to reduce its workforce by 20 percent.

"Those two decisions were extremely difficult for the team to get to," Fields says, "but I would say it was a participatory process. There was a lot of give-and-take. In the end the final solution was not a democratic one, but when the decision was made, people rallied around it, and we walked out of the room as a team as opposed to walking out of the room as a set of individuals who then second-guess the decision."

With the management team committed to the new positioning and key priorities, they brought in every one of the company's twelve thousand salaried employees for two-day sessions to explain the decision and the rationale behind it in a condensed form. Fields knew that it would take some time to build a consensus throughout the organization, but he also knew that once the social system reached that consensus, it could execute very rapidly and very well.

The result was a five-year business plan, called the Millennium Plan, that mapped out quarter by quarter the company's very clear objectives so that each functional head who reported to Fields, and the organizations that reported to them, understood the reality and the objectives the company was aiming for. To reinforce the urgency underlying the plan, Fields began announcing financial and market results every six months rather than just annually, as did other companies.

Once the positioning was clear to everyone and the execution had begun, Fields established operating mechanisms to ensure that everyone kept their eye on the ball. All his direct reports would meet at the beginning of the year to share one another's objectives, something few companies do. It's a tedious, time-consuming process, but it's the differentiating factor in building teams since it creates transparency between the intersections of the moving parts of the business.

"The car business isn't a sequential sausage machine," Fields says. "One function has great impacts on others back and forth during the year. The intersections of manufacturing and engineering directly affect our ability to drive revenue and sales in the marketing and sales arena. It also affects our purchasing in terms of what we expect of our suppliers, not only in cost reductions and quality improvements, but also in consistency."

The annual sessions in which objectives were shared were followed by quarterly gatherings of the team to analyze performance quarter over quarter and year over year. The chief financial officer would send each member a detailed report on quarterly performance, and Fields would ask each member of the team to be prepared to discuss their insights into the results of the entire business, not just their own function. The repetitive nature of the process and team members jointly drilling down into the results of the entire business is what molds the team. It develops the sense of a team delivering not just their own functional results, but the overall business's results. It drives change in the social system.

In retrospect, Fields estimates he spent at least a third of his time building the team and in the process replaced only one person. "I viewed it as reframing their mind-set," he says. "The way I saw it, that was going to be the single biggest factor in either success or failure."

It takes blood, sweat, and tears to build a team, but the return on the effort is huge. Fields took a group of people, most of whom were older than him, earned their respect, and then took them to a new level as a team that can make their company survive and grow. He got them on the same page, discussed the business issues until every member of the team had a total understanding of all the key components of the financial picture, and led them to a decision about what had to be done.

Mark Fields's experience demonstrates the principles involved to mold a team of leaders:

1. Share numbers, reasoning, and results to shape a common view of the business and its context.
2. Have the psychological courage to confront behaviors that harm the team's effectiveness.
3. Anticipate, surface, and resolve conflicts.
4. Pick the right people.
5. Provide prompt feedback and coaching.
6. Recognize and avoid derailers.

SHAPE A COMMON VIEW
OF THE TOTAL BUSINESS

A team of leaders starts being molded when everyone is on the same page. It begins to happen when every member of the team masters the basics of the business: its markets, market segmentation, customers, and buying behaviors; the nature of the competition; and what drives or inhibits the ability to make money. In short, the entire team needs to know what you know. That might be self-evident, but in traditional one-on-one top-level relationships the leader, whether consciously or not, usually does not share the full picture of the business with all his direct reports. But even when you share information with the team, it takes an enormous effort and sustained repetition to get every member of the team to arrive at the same point. At first team members will see and hear what you are saying through the lens of their job specialty and select only what seems to apply to them. Learning curves differ, and it will take longer for some team members to get up to speed than for others.

The key is to develop an internal team dialogue in which each member contributes to the discussion that shapes the team's common view of the business—its challenges and opportunities and the resources available. Getting on the same page tests the cognitive bandwidth of not only each member of the team, but of the team as a whole. Once drawn, however, the common picture channels the team's energy and, more important, provides a reference point for future dialogue as team members influence and are influenced by their colleagues. The stage is set for collaboration.

A group chairman at a medical company has sixteen direct reports. They are high-energy, self-driven people, but work in an environment in which they know they are dependent on other people. "Leaders learn over time that leading is not a matter of being independent," says the chairman. "When you bring people as talented as they are and get them interacting and working together effectively, you get teams that are able to do what an average team couldn't."

This leader expects each of his five business units to have two major initiatives under way at any given time. Monthly meetings are the forum in which the leaders of the units give him formal status reports. "The purpose of the meetings is to have an intense power zone where we get aligned on a monthly basis," he says. "We exchange e-mail or talk to each other at other meetings in between, but this is the forum where we power each other up and get aligned on issues. The conversation is filled with questions like 'And how do you feel about that?' I try to get them to talk about their insecurities. I expect those leaders to bring me their 'reds,' not their 'yellows' and 'greens.' I want to hear what you're working on that's a challenge. What's at risk, and what do you need help from me on? So those conversations become not just indicators of risk but also conversations about performance and accountability. The goal is to get them to put it on the table and to admit where they're feeling psychologically weak, because it's my job as a leader to power them up. And a lot of times it's just a matter of a conversation."

Having all the right people and great processes isn't enough. You also have to have the right behaviors. The group chairman and his team have articulated the behaviors that will give them an edge. He says, "As a management team, we have thirteen behaviors for working together and strive to use them consistently. This is what makes breakthrough teams work, and we're going to become a breakthrough team. We're moving toward rating each other on them every quarter, and I reinforce those behaviors by being an active participant in meetings, because that's where words on a piece of paper come to life."

CONFRONT BEHAVIORS THAT HARM
THE TEAM'S EFFECTIVENESS

Leaders often avoid conflict, hoping that a problem with one of their direct reports' behavior will somehow resolve itself. They seldom do. When I observed George he was two years into his tenure as CEO of a company in a fast-paced industry heavily dependent upon technology. He was having a lot of trouble molding his team of direct reports. He was searching for a new CFO after firing the previous one for failure to comply with Sarbanes-Oxley and his HR director was new. But his real problem lay with his vice president of sales, who had been with the company just six months.

Doug, the vice president of sales, had come with great credentials and very positive reference checks. But none of his references had talked about his tendency to throw temper tantrums at high-level meetings, lecturing his peers about what he perceived as their many failings. They also hadn't mentioned his lack of analytical abilities. Already the director of R&D had warned George that he and his team were tired of Doug's abuse and simply couldn't work with him. With a new product on target to launch in just six months, R&D desperately needed strong input from sales but couldn't get Doug to cooperate. And after the company had missed its sales targets for three consecutive months, the only explanation George could get out of Doug was that "external factors" were to blame. Doug's presentation to the board the month before had been very slick, but when it was over George still couldn't pinpoint the cause and effect of the missed sales targets. He was afraid that he might be in for a hard time from some of the directors at the next board meeting.

George had resolved more than once to bring Doug to task for these problems, but each time the two met in George's office he had decided to back off, instead urging

Doug to get a coach or take other steps to improve his relationships with other departments and to look more deeply into the sales misses. Doug readily agreed, but nothing ever happened as a result of those meetings. George's dilemma—either to confront Doug or to simply fire him—is a common one for leaders who are uncomfortable with conflict. The hard truth is that if you want to mold a team of leaders you must have the inner courage when an individual's behavior is destroying the team to confront that person head on and say it isn't acceptable and has to change.

ANTICIPATE, SURFACE, AND RESOLVE CONFLICTS

Organizational structure divides people. It results in inherent conflicts that can take several forms, some more corrosive than others. Task conflicts—who will do what—and process conflicts—how do we get this done—are among the most common and easily resolved. Conflicts over resource allocation are less common, but more corrosive since resources are, by their nature, limited. Priorities and goals change, resulting in someone being given more resources, necessarily at the expense of someone else. Any one of these conflicts, if not resolved, can culminate in personal conflicts, the most corrosive of all.

Two people in conflict usually can take the same information, massage it differently, and make plausible arguments why each of their positions is the correct one. You can, of course, handle such disputes by simply decreeing a decision. But the value of a team and your ability to lead it is that a decision can be reached that allows everyone to voice an opinion, debate the merits, and the right choice emerges. Handled like this, conflicts are powerful team-building tools because people recognize that the group makes better decisions than individuals and no one person has all the information.

Surfacing such conflicts begins with the agenda you set out and the early team dialogue. But people can be reluctant to offer opinions or comments in a group setting where they may be challenged or, worse, ridiculed. Those who do speak out can become committed too early to a position and be unwilling or unable to retreat. As the leader, you have to be sure that an overly competitive team member doesn't exploit another's vulnerability when discussing problems or concerns.

Once an issue has been adequately framed in early group discussions, it often is useful to divide the team into groups of two or three, pose a few relevant questions, and have the small groups go off to formulate alternative answers. The social dynamics change radically within such small groups. The fear of being challenged evaporates, informality sets in, and individuals gain confidence. When the small teams return to the group, the architecture of the group discussion has changed. Mental attitudes have been realigned beyond each individual's narrow spectrum, the pros and cons are articulated and discussed honestly, and the group is able to consider second- and third-order consequences of a given action. Often a commitment to finding a solution develops. If a clear alternative does not emerge as the consensus of the group, the leader can always call the shot and ask for commitment.

Dinesh Paliwal, head of the $12 billion automation division of ABB, inherited a business that hadn't made money for years. It was on the rocky road to bankruptcy because it was too slow and indecisive. One reason was its culture of polite restraint. People didn't express their honest feelings. They agreed to things in meetings, then dragged their feet on decisions they didn't think were right. Moving faster would take commitment, and commitment would come, Paliwal believed, by getting the relevant information and opinions on the table and deciding as a group what path to take. But to do that Paliwal knew he would have to increase the level of candor so that the issues could be resolved head-on.

In a meeting of the top leaders in his group early in his tenure, Paliwal sensed that one executive was unhappy about the direction certain projects were going, though he was reserved to say so. Paliwal mustered his courage and called on the man anyway. There followed an awkward sixty seconds or so of silence as Paliwal and the embarrassed and angry executive stared at one another. In a nice way, Paliwal urged the man to speak his mind, and finally he did. Much to the man's apparent relief, none of his colleagues were angry about his position or ridiculed him. In any case, Paliwal was prepared to redirect them if they had. Instead, the man's statements triggered a deeper discussion and another look at the assumptions that brought some clarity to problems that might be encountered along the way. Moreover, the individual got a fuller explanation than he'd heard before about why the projects were so important to the business. Through consistency and leadership of the dialogue, Paliwal conveyed to the team that it was safe to express contradictory viewpoints and share information. As the business became more decisive, the division's profitability and moneymaking gradually improved.

PICK THE RIGHT PEOPLE

It goes without saying that building a team means having the right people on it. As the foundation, you must have people with obvious qualities such as technical competence, decisiveness, the ability to deliver on commitments, the respect of other members of the team, and the skills to lead subordinates. Perhaps as important are receptiveness to new ideas and the willingness to work horizontally with others, submerging ego and personal agenda to make trade-offs that are best for the entire organization.

You may have the best expert possible in a particular field, but if his or her ego cannot be submerged to work with the team, you have to decide what is more important to you: the person's expertise or the working of the team.

It takes time and effort to find, recruit, and keep the right people, as Dave Cote discovered when he succeeded Larry Bossidy as CEO of Honeywell International. When he took the job, he knew that the CFO planned to leave. While intent on creating the best possible team of direct reports, his search to replace the CFO took almost a year, creating some concern among both his subordinates and his board of directors. But he ultimately found in David Anderson precisely the mix of financial skills and collegial attitude that ensured the CFO would play a critical role on Honeywell's management team.

One of the biggest problems team leaders face is maintaining the continuity of the team. Once the right people are in place on your team, how do you keep them there in the face of their own ambitions and solicitations from other companies? David Novak, CEO of Yum! Brands, which includes KFC, Taco Bell, and Pizza Hut, says his company's considerable research into why people leave found that money is seldom the motivator. "It's difficult for most people in whatever position they're in to make a quantum leap in terms of money by moving," says Novak. "We found they leave for two reasons: they don't like their boss and they don't feel appreciated."

Teaching managers to be "coaches" rather than "bosses"—asking questions rather than just telling someone what to do—can go a long way toward solving the first problem, and embedded processes that recognize peoples' contributions can help with the second problem, he says.

Nevertheless, there will be departures, and with the departure of a team member comes the necessity to integrate a new member into the team. Newly promoted or brought in from outside, the new team member might be intimidated by the apparent closeness of relationships among the existing team members. You will need to use facilitative skills to bring the new member into the team dialogue. Breaking up the team into small groups to work on problems helps the new member develop confidence and trust in his teammates and helps others be receptive to the inputs.

PROVIDE PROMPT FEEDBACK AND COACHING

Keep a mental inventory of the skills and methods for getting things done for each member of your team. One team member may be too blunt in arguing a point with others, another may be too shy to participate in debate, and yet another may have a habit of holding back information essential to reaching a good decision. All these impediments to effective teamwork must be clearly identified to the individual, and he or she must be counseled in overcoming them. Feedback is most effective when given in written form and given frequently, but you must realize that human beings typically can change only one or two behaviors at a time.

"Most people don't like to give feedback, but they have to look at it from the proper perspective," says David Novak. "Feedback says you're committed to someone's development. Higher performers want to know how to get better, and the only way they'll get better is to get coaching and feedback."

Some team members will need more coaching and feedback than others. It won't take long for you to observe who in the group are the energy drainers and who are the energy generators. Drainers are prone to useless philosophizing, which can lead down sidetracks, or focus on a minute aspect of an issue, drilling down to the nth degree. They tend to put other team members on the defensive by the nature of their questions, and they keep coming up with problems without offering any solutions. It is critical to the team's success that you act decisively to end such behaviors in the group setting and later give feedback to the person in a private setting. Confrontation of such behavior displayed in a group setting can be tremendously valuable for the message it sends everyone about what will and won't be tolerated and about your resolve and integrity.

Jack Welch was known for the intensity of his constructive feedback on individuals in front of groups, and the transparency helped him build a remarkable team of direct reports and a cadre of exemplary managers.

It requires inner security and courage to be able to bring a high-ego individual who is performing well but disrupts the team in line so that the team as a whole benefits. The trick is how to do that without unduly bruising the person's ego, but at the same time showing the other team members that you are willing and able to exercise the leadership necessary to build the team. The leaders I have personally seen do it well earn huge respect, even from those who need to be shaped up.

People with this know-how are very direct and to the point. When they give feedback to their direct reports, there is no mistake about whether that person understands the feedback. It's an essential part of team building to remind the team members of the core values they have agreed upon and the behaviors that are to be followed, and to reinforce those values and behaviors when necessary.

David Novak routinely identifies members of his team of direct reports as well as their direct reports who might benefit from coaching. "Sometimes people don't have the interpersonal skills to motivate and inspire teams," he says. "They don't see themselves as they really are. We'll get a professional coach to follow them around for a few days and act as their mirror, telling them what he saw and how it affects people."

In addition to the routine formal reviews, Novak also

does his own coaching and teaches managers throughout Yum! to do "spontaneous coaching," offering advice on the spot. "You don't want to wait until a cataclysmic event," he cautions. "People should be getting better every day, so we should be coaching them every day."

What if a powerful and ambitious direct report rejects criticism and threatens to leave the company? Many refrain from giving their most valuable subordinates direct and unvarnished feedback for fear of losing them. This is a serious weakness in a leader.

In addition to helping each member of the team become better at making the team more effective through feedback and coaching, the leader needs to link improvement in the individual's team behavior to tangible rewards and recognition. Most leaders at higher levels give tangible rewards to the financial performance of the individual with little, if any, weight given to their team behavior.

RECOGNIZE AND AVOID DERAILERS

To mold a team, you have to watch out for the following pitfalls:

Last In, First Out. Let's say that you and your team discuss promoting Bill Smith to vice president of software development. There seems to be agreement and the meeting breaks up. Then the CFO, who tends not to voice controversial points about people at meetings, walks into your office and tells you that Bill really doesn't understand the financial implications of developing software products. He convinces you that at such a critical point in time Bill is likely to be the wrong choice. Meanwhile, the executive VP of technology calls Bill and says, "It's a go, the job is yours." The next day you tell the executive VP of your decision, and he starts wondering what the hell is going on. Who snuck in to see you last night?

Falling Prisoner to the Team. Joe likes to be liked. When he meets with his team, they come prepared to discuss the agenda items and advance the specific viewpoint of their function. Joe, in the name of empowerment, lets the dialogue evolve. The team then develops a predictable consensus solution, but deep down Joe doesn't believe it's what really should be done, thinking, "I know it can work but we can do a lot better." Instead of raising the bar, he settles.

Kitchen Cabinet. Sally has a team of ten direct reports, but Susan, her finance person, and Fred, in charge of human resources, are her confidants. Sally is on the road 60 percent of the time and is always short of time. Her psychological comfort with Fred and Susan is deep. She has known them for a long time and they're very loyal to her. Her communication and interaction with the other members of the team largely is through Fred and Susan. This continuing pattern of behavior disempowers those in the "second circle."

Fear of Giving Feedback. The single biggest reason for teams not performing effectively is the psychology of the leader. It often lies in a profound discomfort and even fear of giving the candid feedback that helps mold direct reports into a team. When it comes to taking business risks such as bold moves to gain market share, the image projected is that of the fierce competitor willing to push himself and others hard. But place the leader in the role of critiquing a direct report whose behavior is impairing the team's effectiveness and a fear response kicks in that leaves him or her indecisive. Perhaps surprisingly, that fear arises from insecurity. Many business leaders have a deep longing for loyalty from their subordinates and will go to great lengths to encourage it, including withholding criticism.

"What if the person doesn't accept my criticism and leaves the company?" they'll wonder. "What if the person I'm critiquing is really smart and articulate and argues with me, refusing to accept my counseling?" If they choose to provide feedback at all, such leaders often fall back on their human resources executive to deliver the critique. While that may work on one level—the person usually gets the message—it does nothing at a higher level to build the respect for the leader that's so necessary for the team to function well.

The same psychological barriers arise not just in one-on-one relations between the leader and his direct reports, but also in team interactions involving conflict. As stated earlier, one of the most powerful advantages of teamwork is the team's ability to identify and bring to the surface conflicts that must be resolved, such as which executive gets a choice assignment or a bigger budget at the expense of another. If such conflicts are not brought into the open and resolved, they fester and eventually create debilitating personality conflicts. Yet for many reasons leaders are reluctant to deal openly with such conflicts. They may want to avoid embarrassing anyone or creating a win-or-lose situation for someone. In the worst cases, the leader may simply lack the intellectual horsepower or emotional fortitude to withstand the powerful arguments that talented subordinates can make in the presence of the group. Some are really uncomfortable exercising power. Whatever the cause, the result is the same: a lost opportunity and the loss of the team's respect.

The Decision Is Final . . . Not Really. Two months ago you and your team decided to approve using people from three different areas to develop the new digital product. Everyone was in agreement and the meeting broke up. Now the issue has come up again because no one from software development has been assigned due to the freeze in head count. In this situation, commitments everyone thought were made were not delivered because people were allowed to drag their feet and bring the so-called final decision up again and again.

A MASTER TEAM BUILDER

Roberto Herencia, a vice president at Banco Popular who was tapped to build the bank's North American business, had both the know-how and personal traits to build a team of direct reports. Great teamwork has allowed Banco Popular North America to compete against much bigger banking rivals such as Citigroup, Bank One, and Bank of America. His example provides important lessons about the personal characteristics needed to mold a team of leaders: the sheer willpower and tenacity to stay with it; the judicious and explicit use of power; the enormous role played by persuasion; and the discipline to do it repetitively.

When Herencia took on the leadership of Banco Popular North America, his task was to build the business through acquisitions of small banks, integrate them, and then grow organically, primarily in the Hispanic markets of New Jersey, Chicago, and California. The only way to differentiate an up-and-coming player from the big guys and grow profitably, Herencia thought, was to come up with good ideas that could be executed faster and with a greater degree of customer service. Growing profitably would require the ultimate in collaboration among his direct reports; they had to operate efficiently and effectively and to integrate mergers quickly. Creating a team required that each direct report clearly internalize the goals and priorities of every other team member and make interdependence an integral part of the way they did their work. These points were reiterated, stressed, and practiced in the team's monthly meetings. Everyone knew the numbers and objectives that had to be delivered by every other team member.

Banking has an inherent tension between the lending side,

which is driven to make loans, which result in revenues and margin growth, and the credit side of the business, which has to ensure creditworthiness and control risk. Herencia would need to build a team that could keep those tensions in proper balance as the bank grew, with a focus on getting the overall business to perform. In short, building the business meant building a solid team at the top.

Building the team started with careful selection of team members. People had to be highly talented, of course, but equally important was how well they related to and empathized with others. Herencia made collaboration a non-negotiable criterion. In some cases, he knew the talents, skills, and behaviors of some people he had worked with before, but he also kept an eye open to spot new talent. When, for instance, his secretary asked him to watch a videotape of a presentation she had made in a communications class she was taking at night, Herencia was impressed by the perceptive remarks the teacher had made. He subsequently interviewed the teacher and found that she had not only the ability to help others improve their communication skills, but also a natural bent toward collaboration. Herencia ended up hiring her for a newly created position: facilitator of communications.

Herencia articulated the kinds of behaviors he would expect from his direct reports, and more important, modeled those behaviors in group meetings, during which the team "practiced" collaboration by tackling real-life business issues, such as how to improve talent management or how to reach their financial and service goals. His own behavior conveyed the fact that it was important to be a good listener, to be fair and respectful, to continually raise the bar, to be honest and candid, and to be willing to submerge one's ego for the welfare of the team. He demonstrated, for instance, the importance of candor and his own willingness to overcome his ego by not becoming offended when someone had an opinion that differed from his own and by not overreacting to bad news, especially by not lashing out against the person who delivered it.

When someone's behavior oversteps the bounds, whether inside or outside a meeting, Herencia doesn't hesitate to address the issue directly and with as much transparency as the situation allows. A case in point was when he discovered that one of his organization's leaders was openly challenging the bank's strategy and execution and as a result was stirring up controversy and confusion among the ranks. Knowing how quickly rumors and miscommunication can erode candor and collaboration, Herencia acted fast to stem the problem. Having just returned from a business trip, he reached out to the individual and requested an emergency meeting on a weekend evening.

"We went at it," Herencia recalls. "I told him what I had heard and asked him if it was accurate. He basically said, 'Yes,' and I told him that I saw it as a very serious offense to the team and the spirit that we had been building because it broke all kinds of communication channels."

Herencia listened nondefensively and then calmly reiterated the strategy and the rationale behind it and put a stake in the ground that this was the direction. He said he needed to know if the leader was committed to pull it forward or push it backward.

Herencia had no fear of the executive's response to confronting him swiftly and directly, as allowing the behavior to continue would erode the company culture and damage the team spirit. He also used it as a teaching point for his entire team. Herencia used it in a group meeting to launch a discussion of how the team could improve communication and conflict resolution by stepping in and talking to colleagues directly. They didn't have to funnel everything through the president.

Herencia also uses self-evaluation to build the team by having his direct reports periodically reflect on their performance as a group, usually at off-site meetings three or four times a year. What are some examples of where collaboration worked well to resolve an issue, and what could they be doing better? During one team self-analysis, the group concluded that the smooth integration of a much-larger organization that it had acquired in Southern Florida was an example of teamwork at its best.

But besides celebrating victories, the team also identified certain behaviors that it needed to improve. Among them was the need to do more coaching and mentoring at lower levels in the bank. In other words, there was an opportunity to improve their own leadership of the teams reporting to them. Another was sharing the best practices among the five geographical divisions that stretch from South Florida to Southern California. But perhaps most challenging was the recognition that they had to do better as a team to deal with conflict, as the incident with the executive who was challenging bank strategy had shown.

Recognizing the importance of interpersonal relationships among individual team members, Herencia creates exercises aimed at improving them. One such technique is to pose thought-provoking questions during monthly team meetings to get people more intellectually engaged and talking on a more personal level. Usually over dinner, Herencia raises a question, sometimes unrelated to the business at hand, to stimulate conversation, such as "How do you define excellence and how do you commit to it?" or "What is your dream?" He asks each of his direct reports to ask that same question of their direct reports right down the line, so within a few weeks the entire organization is talking about and debating the question, helping build teams at all levels.

Improving the group dynamics of the team is a complement to, not a substitute for, a one-on-one relationship between Herencia and individual team members. While the team of direct reports have to work well together, Herencia also spends individual time with each direct report, providing coaching and counseling, sometimes on business issues and sometimes on behavior, such as "You know, I think you need to be more engaged in our meetings." And while he tries to let people know that they are special and valued, he is also aware discussions behind closed doors can raise suspicions and questions about being treated equitably. Ever conscious of the effect on the overall team, Herencia tries to push as many subjects as possible into the open—for instance, by encouraging the person to bring a good idea to the team and not just to the president.

Herencia is the first to admit that his selection has not been 100 percent right. Several times he's had to deal with team members who couldn't adopt the appropriate behaviors, and he's learned to address the problem quickly. In one case, he hired a leader with outstanding credentials and terrific references. The bank really needed the person's functional expertise, but Herencia kept noticing that the individual's ego was such that he constantly advocated for his functional area and couldn't seem to see how his function fit into the overall picture. After what Herencia now describes as a too-long period of coaching and consideration, he asked the individual to leave.

Few leaders devote the time Herencia does to building a team of direct reports, perhaps because they don't recognize the value. Herencia figures he may have devoted 20 to 25 percent his time to the team-building process in the early stages. As time has passed and the team has matured, he finds himself devoting even more—perhaps as much as 50 percent. "It's becoming a bigger piece of my time," Herencia says, "because it's becoming more clear to me every day that this has real value and is what we need to do."

Everything we've covered so far—positioning and repositioning, the external landscape, linking the two with moneymaking, changing the social system, improving your personal ability to judge leaders and building a leading team—needs to be translated into results. The first and most critical step in execution is choosing the right goals. This is where the buck starts. Many leaders are conceptual, high-level thinkers, but they fail in choosing the right mix of goals. It matters. Goals align people's energy. How to choose the right goals is a special knowhow, which is the subject of the next chapter.

Nine Questions to Ask Yourself

1. Many people espouse the merits of building a high-performing team but actually prefer to deal with people one-on-one. Be intellectually honest. Are you really willing to invest your emotional energy and time to mold your direct reports into a high-performing team?

2. Are you psychologically uncomfortable dealing with your direct reports as a team rather than one on one? Can you overcome your discomfort?

3. Do you have the confidence and temperament to confront one of your direct report's behavior when it is not conducive to the team, even if that person is a high performer and/or a strong personality?

4. Have you articulated and communicated the expected team behaviors and got your team to commit to them? Do you reinforce them consistently? Are they linked to rewards?

5. Do you include as the basis for selecting and evaluating your direct reports not only competence and performance in their particular area, but also their

unmistakable willingness to make the team more effective even if their area is adversely affected, their ability to contain their ego, and their cognitive bandwidth to see the total picture?

6. Do you build openness, trust, and intellectual honesty among your direct reports by ensuring that conflicts are surfaced and resolved without making poor compromises, giving feedback and coaching on team behavior, and pushing as many critical issues as possible into the group setting?

7. Do you encourage your direct reports to communicate and make trade-offs directly, rather than having to go through you as the leader?

8. How well has each of your direct reports internalized the total business as you see it? Are you willing to help create for your direct reports the same total picture of the business that you have?

9. On a scale of 1 to 7, where 7 is the highest, how would you rate your direct reports' ability to function as a high-performing team? What will sustain the high-performance functioning?

7

THE BUCK STARTS WITH YOU

Determining and Setting the Right Goals

Goals are the destination you want to take your business to. Once stated clearly and communicated to the organization, goals align people's energy, and when they're linked to rewards, as they usually are, they have a powerful effect on people's behavior. Goals set the tone for decisions and actions that follow and greatly influence the business results that get delivered.

Many leaders think setting goals is simple and straightforward, but in fact, selecting the *right set of goals* is the ultimate juggling act. The goals have to be of the right type and magnitude to be both achievable as well as motivational. They have to be acceptable to investors, most of whom care more about the short term, but also ensure that the business can make money in the long term. Because the pursuit of one goal necessarily affects the others—achieving short-term gains in market share from promotional deep discounts, for instance, can have an adverse effect on operating margin and cash flow—the individual goals have to be balanced with one another. And above all, the goals must reflect the opportunities in the external world, while taking into account the existing and potential ability of the organization to pursue them.

If you can't take all that in and mentally process it with a heavy dose of self-confidence, your goals will almost certainly be too modest or too aggressive or internally contradictory. In fact, the best way to judge the quality of any leader's goals is by the quality and rigor of thinking that underlies them. How else would you know whether a goal of 8 percent organic revenue growth, which Jeff Immelt announced as one of GE's goals in 2003, makes sense?

Soon after Immelt took the helm as CEO of General Electric in 2001, the stock price dropped. There were several factors involved, including the September 11 terrorist attack and the resulting downturn in general business activity. GE had had a beautiful run of consistent earnings growth under Jack Welch's leadership, but now many security analysts were concluding that many of its businesses were facing slow growth in their industries. GE would therefore be an efficient machine for churning out cash and earnings per share, but wouldn't be much of a growth engine.

The market bubble had burst, the economy was in a post-9/11 slump, and investors were weary of overblown promises about revenue growth and synergies that never quite materialized in many companies. Instead, they wanted to see organic growth in the high single digits, which for a $130 billion behemoth like GE just didn't seem possible. Sure, GE could continue to generate cash and earnings for the foreseeable future, but expectations for revenue growth were a humble 5 percent.

But Immelt wasn't about to let investors' expectations decide where GE was headed and what its goals should be. He didn't look backward at where GE had been and what it had been producing and accept modest growth. He looked forward at how the entire business landscape was changing, and he identified opportunities for GE to grow at roughly twice the rate of world GDP, roughly 8 percent beginning around 2005. Eight percent growth on a $130 billion base is a whopping $10 billion in new revenues annually, the equivalent of creating a new Fortune 500 company every year. It wasn't blind ambition or wide-eyed optimism that was driving GE's aggressive sounding goals. It was Immelt's know-how in reasoning out where he believed the organization could go, and how it would get there.

Immelt used his extraordinarily wide cognitive bandwidth to see GE in the context of the global economy. Shortly after the beginning of the twenty-first century, total world GDP was $40 trillion and growing at a rate of 4 percent, or $1.6 trillion, per year on average. More important, though, the bulk of that expansion was expected to come from emerging markets, particularly China, India, Russia, Eastern Europe, and Brazil. As Immelt and his team did the market and geographic segmentation, he pondered what those markets would need as they tried to develop. The answer would be the expanding need for health care, entertainment, and security, plus basic services, things like transportation, energy, and clean water. GE was already in the business of providing aircraft engines, locomotives, wind turbines, and coal and nuclear power plants. Why couldn't it supply those and other infrastructure-related products and services to help nations grow? Clearly, the opportunity for GE was huge.

As Immelt set his sights on top-line growth, he knew it was just part of the puzzle. What would GE have to do to take advantage of that opportunity, and what resources would be required? Some things were clear: the company would have to intensify its research efforts and use of technology, build or acquire new capabilities in areas such as water purification, expand its presence in places like China, and build relationships with the foreign governments that would buy its infrastructure products. Others weren't so specific: GE would have to become as good at innovation, technology, and marketing as it was at productivity improvement, managing operations and cost. All of that would take hundreds of millions of dollars. But for a variety of reasons, GE's robust balance sheet and triple-A credit rating couldn't be sacrificed, and the dividend was sacred. That meant the resources for growth would have to come largely from improved operating efficiency and from better margins, which in turn would mean products and services would have to be differentiated, perhaps through the use of technology. And all of these things would have to occur in the context of what was at the time a tough economy.

Immelt factored in all those realities, and defined not only the revenue opportunity one, two and three years out, but also the other important measures that would keep the organization balanced and moving forward. He brought his set of goals to the GE board at a landmark board retreat in 2003 and to shareholders soon thereafter.

He predicted that 60 percent of GE's revenue growth would come from emerging markets in coming years, and he expected annual 8 percent organic revenue growth within the next three years. In addition to pursuing 8 percent organic revenue growth, GE would maintain its AAA credit rating, produce a return on invested capital of 20 percent and an operating margin of 20 percent, and generate cash flow equal to or more than earnings. His personal long-term incentive is totally tied to those kinds of measures, plus the relative performance of GE's stock price against the S&P 500 Index over a five-year period.

With the goals came the essential outline of actions about how they will be achieved:

1. Defining the criteria for growth leaders of the future and thus incorporating the criteria in the talent planning and succession process, the operating mechanism that GE calls Session C.

2. Investing in technology, opening labs in China and India, and refurbishing the existing GE research labs.

3. Making shifts in the social system by creating a new operating mechanism called the Commercial Council and changing the reviews of growth projects. Immelt has eighty projects of $100 million or more on his dashboard and he personally reviews ten a month.

4. Changing the portfolio of businesses: taking out some businesses like reinsurance; expanding some businesses such as entertainment by buying Vivendi Universal; broadening the scope of medical systems by acquiring Amersham; and entering new areas of growth like water purification. The end result is a transformation of the positioning of GE in the new global context with particular attention to becoming the leader, for example, in the infrastructure market space.

Built into Immelt's set of goals was the idea that revenue growth would be funded by cash generated from operations. Some of GE's businesses, for example consumer and industrial products, would be cash generators fueling the businesses identified as growth engines, including health care, infrastructure, and entertainment. Immelt expected the company to generate $60 billion cash from operating activities in 2005–2007, and that was after investing $15 billion in technology, $10 billion in media programming, and $12 billion in marketing and information technology, as well as funding the growth of financial services.

Accomplishing the ambitious goals a few years out would require breaking the long-standing tradition of annual double-digit growth in earnings per share for a year or two. That was a trade-off Immelt had the courage to make. He tried to win over analysts and investors, but GE's stock price clearly signaled that many investors didn't like the short-term hit and considered the growth goals he was setting too good to be true. He held to his conviction amidst the many raised eyebrows, and won over important constituencies—the board, analysts, and employees. In his letter to shareholders in the 2004 annual report, he thanked investors for being patient and allowing him to pursue the right goals.

By the fall of 2005, what might have sounded like a pipe dream had become a reality. When GE announced its results for the third quarter of 2005, the company had achieved what it set out to: 8 percent organic revenue growth, while building the capability of the organization and keeping the cash increasingly flowing, the balance sheet strong, and earnings once again growing in the double digits.

Immelt demonstrated the four key points you need to focus on when setting goals. First, he was looking down the runway to see what opportunities lay ahead for GE. Second, he took into account the organization's capabilities—now and in the future—to achieve the goals. Third, he understood the relationships among the goals and ensured they could be achieved simultaneously. Finally, he skillfully kept his long-term goals in balance with short-term goals.

Unlike many leaders who set grandiose goals and implore others to achieve them, Immelt established aggressive goals only after he assessed how the organization might go after them. The granularity of the thinking makes all the difference. The goals were realistic at every stage, and realism eventually earns credibility, just as surely as unfulfilled promises destroy it.

There's a know-how to setting the right goals, in the right combination, with the right time frame, and at the right level.

You can't set goals by looking in the rearview mirror at what was accomplished last year and adjust this year's numbers accordingly, and you can't go by what is being projected for the industry or the economy overall. Goals should reflect the opportunities that lie ahead and what is possible *for your business* as it goes forward. You have to choose more than one goal to keep the organization in balance, and the goals don't all have to be financial and quantitative. There will always be tailwinds and headwinds that will help you reach the goals faster or slow you down, but the goals must be clearly defined with specific time frames at the start. Then you must be willing to adjust them as the world changes and the opportunities and organizational capabilities expand or contract.

While choosing only one goal distorts the business, choosing multiple goals poses its own mental challenge. You have to dig deep to be sure the goals are internally consistent. I was in a meeting one day with the CEO of a Fortune 500 company when some outside consultants made a presentation. Using an impressive array of statistical correlations, the consultants urged the CEO to shoot for 12 percent top line growth, a measure that would propel his company into the much-desired top quartile of Fortune 500 companies. The CEO listened politely, asked a few questions and then thanked the consultants for their presentation. After they had gone, he turned to me and said somewhat wistfully, "It certainly would be nice to have twelve percent growth." But then he added, "That isn't really achievable. My margin is 2 percent and it takes fifty cents of investment to gain an extra dollar of revenue. Such a goal of top line growth is unrealistic and inconsistent with how money is made in this business." In a matter of minutes he had cut through the carefully presented argument for 12 percent growth in light of the realities of his business.

THE POWER OF GOALS

Let there be no doubt that selecting the right goals is important. Goals matter. When Rick Wagoner took the reins of General Motors in 2000 he faced a real dilemma. GM's North American market share, the bellwether by which the automotive industry measures success, had been slipping for several years, the victim of intense competitive pressure, particularly from Toyota and Honda. Cash generation and operating margins were shrinking and the auto giant's vast array of factories was running far below capacity. If Wagoner wasn't careful, he would go down in history as the CEO under which GM lost its place as the world's largest auto maker. Everyone knew Wagoner had to turn this behemoth around. But how?

Since one of the time-honored measures of success in the automotive business is market share in the United States, Wagoner set a bold goal: Stop the erosion in market share, then reverse it. GM would battle its way back from a 27.8 percent market share to 30 percent. Its beleaguered employees and shareholders applauded the announcements even as they wondered how Wagoner would accomplish this goal.

Then reality intruded on the grand plans. In 2001 GM's market share edged up while cash generation and operating margins slipped. The next year, all those measures were down. And the next. By 2005 GM clearly was in serious trouble. It lost nearly $5 billion in North America in the first nine months of that year as it struggled to prop up sales with heavy discounts. That year the once unimaginable came to pass: GM's bond rating was downgraded to junk status. Knowledgeable people began talking seriously about the possibility that GM would file for bankruptcy to escape the onerous provisions of its labor contract and pension obligations. Wagoner's bold goal to regain lost market share became instead a struggle for survival.

What went wrong?

In choosing as his main goal to restore the luster of 30 percent overall market share, Wagoner was overoptimistic and set an unattainable goal. Gaining market share sounded like a perfectly plausible goal, especially in an industry obsessed with that particular measure. But a closer look at GM and its major competitors, Toyota and Honda, reveals how extraordinarily difficult, if not impossible, it would be to achieve that goal.

Toyota and Honda have several major competitive operating advantages over GM. The two Japanese companies are masters of short cycle times, able to design and bring to production new models showcasing the best of automotive technology faster than GM. As a result, the offerings from Honda and Toyota are fresher, incorporating the design features and technology that consumers want. Further, both Toyota and Honda have far fewer models in the global market so that the costs of redesigning any model can be applied to more unit sales per model. Given their legendary quality and knack for giving consumers precisely what they prefer, both companies earn superior margins on most of their vehicles. Toyota and Honda's performance is also enhanced because they don't have the burden of legacy pension and health care costs that are such a burden to GM.

GM, in contrast, has more than seventy models in the U.S. market. Because many of its models lack the sophistication and consumer appeal of the Toyota and Honda offerings, GM cars are frequently offered with sizable discounts or rebates that wind up sapping the company's profitability and hurting the brand image.

To reach GM's goal of regaining market share Wagoner would have to make sure that GM is competitive in most of those more than seventy models, something that simply can't be done without huge amounts of cash and the general management, production, and design talent to overhaul the models to ensure they are what consumers want. It costs billions of dollars to redesign a car model from the ground up, and GM lacks the cash generation and operating margins to redesign all its models at the right frequency. Wagoner simply wasn't being realistic in setting a goal that his business didn't have the resources to accomplish. Toyota and Honda, on the other hand, have ample cash to continue to keep their models fresh, and they have the engineering and design talent to keep their cars on the cutting edge of technology and design. When the sharp spike in energy prices in 2005 took a heavy toll on GM's most profitable truck and SUV models, it was clear to everyone that there was no way GM could win the model-by-model hand-to-hand combat with Toyota and Honda.

What if Wagoner had chosen a different goal or even a different set of goals? For example, it would have been perfectly plausible for him to have announced a goal of survival to generate cash and improve margins. He would have been forced to decide how to proceed, say, by killing off some product lines that simply weren't sustainable in an intensely competitive market. Then he could have put a critical mass of money and talent to work on a select number of models that could gain market share in their segments as well as generate profits and cash. Focusing more narrowly on fewer models in fewer segments would also have made it easier for Wagoner to pick the best talent he could get to win in those segments. But he would have to accept the fact that by killing off some of the unprofitable lines he would likely see GM's overall market share decline even further rather than grow.

I happened to be meeting with a group of CEOs shortly after Wagoner announced his bold goal. None of them, observing GM from the outside, could understand why he would pursue market share rather than profits and sufficient cash generation from operations. In the summer of 2006, GM's overall market share continues to fall. In the five years since the CEO stated his goal of increasing market share, GM has actually lost nearly two points in the United States.

You have to be very clear in your thinking about what is really required to deliver the chosen goals. You need to assess whether the goals are do-able. When you assign goals to lower levels of the organization, you need to anticipate what decisions are likely to follow. At the same time you should not be impervious to real world difficulties lower levels will face. By saying "meet this goal—or else," you may be authorizing the systematic destruction of a perfectly good business.

One manager of a $1 billion division had consistently delivered on her goals, but as her boss congratulated her on her previous year's performance, he dropped a bombshell: in the coming year he wanted her to grow earnings before income taxes at least 10 percent over the previous year. The division manager knew she could do it, but only by doing things that would in her view severely compromise the future of the business. Her division had been under tremendous financial and competitive pressure. Raw materials costs were rising faster than anyone could have predicted. Energy alone was up nearly 30 percent since the beginning of the previous year. Currency swings were hurting demand in Europe, and the competition was being very aggressive with pricing to preserve their market share. China offered great opportunity. The timing to get a foothold was now. She was anxious to go forward to make investments and expand the business there.

She had already identified a technology company in China that would be an ideal acquisition and knew she could get it for about $10 million. But for accounting reasons, that would have to be expensed rather than capitalized, which would make it virtually impossible to hit the 10 percent growth goal her boss was demanding.

She explained the situation to her boss, stressing the importance of getting into China now and the ideal opportunity she'd uncovered. She knew that her competitors had to be thinking along the same lines and were also looking to get a foothold in China. If she couldn't establish a presence there by the end of the next year, the division might not be able to get another chance for a long time. Finding 10 percent more income while also doing the China deal would be the equivalent of hitting a 20 percent growth target compared to this year. It was just too aggressive.

Her boss only pretended to be concerned about her problems. He had been CEO of the company for a long time and had posted twenty-four consecutive quarters of double-digit growth in earnings per share. He wasn't about to let that end now. He expected her to find a way to do both. He reminded her that everybody in the company had problems of one sort or another, and that people were well paid to solve them.

As she continued to wrestle with the problem, none of the possibilities for generating the additional 20 percent income (including the China investment) seemed to make business sense. One possibility was to eliminate one of three products under development. The sales team had identified great opportunities for all three and the product development guys were working overtime to make them happen. Killing them would shatter the team's dream of launching a great product and her dream of gaining market share. Advertising and marketing expenses always seemed like a place to find more money, but the division manager had tried that gambit a year ago and, true to her marketing executive's predictions, the planned increase in sales didn't materialize and brand equity suffered. It almost cost her her bonus this year. She might find some extra money by increasing prices on the division's most popular products, but she knew marketing would object to that, too. The products could carry a premium price, but at some point customers would defect to the competition. Could she get some further productivity gains out of the division? She had toyed with the idea in the past of shutting down one of the three plants and consolidating production in the remaining two. But closing a plant would set off a firestorm. The union would go berserk and get the local politicians involved.

Unconvinced that her boss understood what would make her business competitive, the division manager couldn't help but wonder whether the company had much of a future. She added one more item to her list of options: find another job.

Many middle managers get caught between meeting the goals they've been given and doing what they know is best for the business. Of course, it's common for anyone at the receiving end of goals to feel some pressure. But when people are held accountable for goals that cannot be accomplished constructively, the emotional toll is very high, and the business suffers. A revolving door of managers is symptomatic. When you set the goals, you have to understand what actions and behaviors will follow as people try to achieve them.

Digging and Dialogue

Keeping the dialogue open with the people whose goals you assign helps ensure that you're not missing something, and that the goals you set are motivating rather than discouraging. Dialogue gets the assumptions behind the goals into the open and lets you be a coach who helps people think through how they might respond. While you may not have the same detailed knowledge of the business as the person who works for you, dialogue can help you steer through two concerns: that you're being sandbagged by goals that are too low, and that the goals are unattainably high.

Confronting the possibility that a goal is not right requires courage on the part of both the subordinate and the superior.

The courageous subordinate must be willing to initiate discussions with her superiors about a questionable goal. It may be she didn't fully grasp the logic on which the decision was based. But it may be equally true that the superiors didn't think through the unintended consequences of the decision. Sometimes the view from below is a wake-up call for high-level leaders.

A few years ago, a middle manager new to her position decided to cut $5 million from her budget by the end of the quarter because the division's revenue had unexpectedly dropped by that amount. A month later, she realized that the lost revenues would not come back next year; in fact, it looked like the division was headed for further declines, and she would have to again cut costs to hold margins steady.

The division made its money off of revenues from print advertising. With the advent of electronic media, that ad revenue was drying up. Quarter after quarter, as whole segments of customers began to defect to the new set of digital providers, the middle manager had to go to her direct reports with the bad news that they had to extract yet more cost savings. She and her team were constantly in catch-up mode, and senior management, refusing to face up to the revenue free fall, had made it her problem.

Finally, after several quarters of continued cutting and with no end to it in sight, the middle manager was at her wits' end. She and her team had racked their brains trying to figure out what to do. Her instincts kept telling her the same thing: the current path simply wasn't sustainable. She worried that her bosses would assume that she couldn't handle the job they had promoted her into, but she overcame her fear of response. She pushed back against the goals assigned to her and laid out her reasoned explanation.

Some leaders would have shot the messenger, but her bosses were psychologically open to new information and they trusted the young manager's analysis. They didn't immediately leap to the conclusion that the middle manager was at fault. Instead, they looked for cause and effect. They faced up to the stark issue that the business model wasn't working and set to work to fix it.

Dialogue prevents you from dodging another uncomfortable issue: the need to confront some leaders who are not performing. All too often, leaders ratchet up the financial goals of their high performers to make up for what the laggards fail to deliver. Instead of growing their businesses, the high performers are forced to make drastic cuts. Such situations are not sustainable over the long term and drive away the best leadership talent.

Some people are resistant to goals simply because they don't understand or agree with the logic of the goals. That's another reason why repetitive communication is so important. The natural tendency is for people to see things through their own prism. A sales manager, for example, might see a great opportunity to increase seasonal sales dramatically with a huge promotion requiring production to accumulate inventory. He's not concerned about cash requirements. But the company's CFO may be under immense pressure to preserve cash to prevent a downgrade that would have serious domino effects. Dialogue gives you the chance to show that the goals really do make sense given the pressures and constraints that exist elsewhere in the organization.

Setting Stretch Goals

Sometimes you might want to set goals that build the self-confidence of the organization. Usually that means goals that you are almost certain can be accomplished. When they are, the organization gets energized. Over time you can increase the goals as you simultaneously increase the self-confidence, and eventually you can begin setting stretch goals.

Stretch goals show people that they can accomplish more than they thought they could. The most common kind of stretch goal is tactical in nature. It seeks to achieve incremental improvements by encouraging the people who work for you to work harder, to become more vigilant and anticipatory and to be on the alert to achieve higher operational results in a shorter period than they thought they could. More rarely leaders employ stretch goals that are strategic. They require people to think about what they're doing in a radically different way, not just to work harder and be more alert. When Jeff Immelt set a goal of 8 percent organic growth for GE, the organization had to think and act in a different manner.

There is an art to setting those kinds of goals. Judgment, practice, and perceptual abilities come into play. What is it that will challenge and expand the organization's capabilities and what is it that will create a credibility gap? Stretch goals can fire up people's imaginations and bring energy to the organization, but only if they are do-able. The point is not to get people to work harder. Rather, it is to get people to do things differently and thus raise the capability of the organization. Such a goal carries with it higher risks. Unless you do the mental gymnastics necessary to figure out what has to radically change, setting a stretch goal won't be credible and the organization won't trust you. You have to be sure that people are prepared to think differently and have sufficient resources to accomplish the goals.

One company has a unique but very effective way of achieving ambitious goals by encouraging people to overshoot what they think they can comfortably achieve. The leaders of this company have consistently outgunned their much larger competitors for more than ten years in terms of market share gains, gross and net margins, and brand image. At the end of December these leaders announce a very realistic set of goals in terms of market share, gross margins, operating margins, revenue growth, and cash flow generation. The top team has no doubt that the company can achieve those goals barring a major unforeseen event, and they reserve significant funding for advertising, promotion, and sales force incentives so the company has the flexibility to do marketing, advertising, and promotions over the year. Then they test their capability to adapt to any new opportunities during the course of the year, moving quickly and with exquisite tactical coordination at all levels. People in the organization love having the flexibility to seize opportunities. The psychology is not "how am I going to meet my goals" but "how am I going to beat the competition and increase distance between us and them." Keeping it comfortable while aiming to beat what they did the previous year by executing a series of tactical moves has worked: the company has consistently achieved record results over ten years.

Setting Goals When the World Turns Upside Down

Goals are tied to how the business is positioned. In a complex and rapidly changing world, the nature of the goals as well as their magnitude may need to be radically different. Ann Moore, president of Time Inc., a unit of Time Warner, faced precisely that challenge as 2005 drew to a close. Ad pages for Time Warner's flagship magazines, *Fortune* and *Time,* were decreasing and it wasn't the typical cyclical decline. Many magazines and newspapers, as discussed earlier (pages 31–34) are facing a formidable new competitor: Google. Advertising revenue for business magazines like *Forbes, BusinessWeek,* and *Fortune* decreased significantly from their peaks. A gaping wound like that would require some dramatic cost cutting and downsizing, but would that be enough?

Within Moore's portfolio of magazines, there is a wide variety of publications that are positioned in different consumer segments. But almost all of them are experiencing shifts in how consumers consume media and how advertisers are adjusting to the new mix of media, including which devices—PDAs, laptops, or television—will carry what content over what carriers—broadband, cable, or wireless. Each of these uncertainties will affect how each magazine is positioned. Will it remain totally print or will it have to develop a Web presence? Should it be exclusively Web-based? Market research can tell her what the current reality is but can do little to tell her what the future will look like. She will have to assess which magazines should get more funding, which should get less. There is no question that she will have to reduce overall costs, but what key assumptions will she make about the speed and magnitude of revenue declines? Where will she find new sources of revenue and what investments will they require? What kind of talent and money will it take to fund new sources of online revenue? As she cuts costs, how can she be sure that she's not cutting potential sources of revenue growth?

The answers to those questions will have a critical influence on the choice of goals for Time Inc. Cost cutting as one goal is a foregone conclusion, although it has to be done in the right places, in the right way, and at the right time. But the more important goal, and the one that will be more difficult to set, is the growth of revenues, which means understanding the source of those revenues and the composition of them. It requires examining the new ways people are consuming media and working backward to find a way to increase revenues. Whatever goals Moore selects will carry risks, but failing to adjust the goals in the face of so much change is highly risky.

Not all change is so profound, but change is a fact of life, and leaders have to keep their eye on how it affects their goals. In January 2005, Dell was king of the PC hill, number one in worldwide market share. Dell's robust business model—selling direct to market and made to order—and unmatched execution had powered a 20 percent gain in revenue in 2004 and bested Compaq, which had been laboring under the strain of the 2002 merger with Hewlett-Packard.

But as the calendar turned from December 2005 to January 2006, conditions had changed. Competition had picked up steam, the market growth was slower, and Dell had missed the consensus estimates of Wall Street twice in the previous four quarters. The rate of revenue growth had not matched expectations. Would Dell need to adjust its mix of margin and revenue goals? Would it need to reposition?

Three major changes had occurred in the competitive landscape. First, IBM had sold its PC business to Lenovo, a Chinese company that was moving fast to grow the PC and laptop business it bought from IBM with a new cost structure and a focus on enhancing the products' aesthetics. Second, Lenovo had hired a key Dell executive who managed a critical part of Asia for Dell and who is an expert in supply chain management. Third, the conditions at archrival HP had changed radically. Mark Hurd had succeeded Carly Fiorina and had eliminated a major source of confusion by separating the PC business from the printer business. He had a clear focus about where his business was going. Equally important, he had hired a new leader with demonstrated skills in supply chain management and in the ability to rethink the landscape of consumers and resegment the market.

All those changes took place in the context of reduced rates of growth for PCs in different segments and in different ways. There was new uncertainty about consumer buying behavior as Apple continued to move ahead in aesthetics and innovation. Surely the goals for revenue growth, operating margin, and market share needed a closer look.

Even if the goals aren't adjusted quickly to fit with the changing realities, you can adjust the rewards that are linked to them. In 1996 even the famously tough-minded Jack Welch recognized that changing external circumstances could result in missed goals despite the best efforts of everyone concerned. He set ambitious goals, but he empowered his executives to do what they needed to do in the face of changing circumstances to achieve the best possible outcomes for the business, even if they fell short of the agreed-upon goals. That year Gene Murphy, president of GE Aircraft Engines, missed his goal, yet Welch didn't take him to task. Rather, he gave Murphy the largest bonus of any of the top executives and publicly praised him. The airline industry was going through an unexpected crisis and while it was true that Murphy missed his goal, he still beat the competition by a wide margin. It was unrealistic to think that in such a short time the goal could be restated and the compensation adjusted to reflect that. Instead, Welch dug into the cause and effect and took into account the changes in the external environment. He recognized that Murphy turned in a great performance amid the changing reality of the industry and that Murphy had earned his reward.

Keeping Goals Relevant

Having the right goals is inherently very demanding when customer demand shifts frequently and multiple silos have to continually coordinate to deliver on them. Keeping goals meaningful and the organization on track to achieve them under such conditions is challenging but very possible. Take, for instance, technology company RFMD, the North Carolina–based maker of components for wireless communications. Eric Creviston, the corporate vice president, cellular products, has a set of revenue, gross margin, and investment goals his business unit must meet. They are determined through an up-down, down-up process. Then it's up to him to set the goals for the divisions of his business unit and the functional line managers. In a technology business like his, doing so is a constant balancing and rebalancing act.

Each division has multiple technologies under development, and each of those has different requirements for human and financial resources over different time horizons, and each has different revenue potential also with different time horizons. To add a further complication, determining the resource requirements of technologies under development, particularly in whole new areas or technology platforms, is largely a guessing game. Most of the products involve invention, not just engineering, and it's impossible to predict exactly how much time and how many resources it will take to solve a problem. In the face of all that complexity and uncertainty, Creviston has to be sure that each of his division leaders has clear goals for his P&L center, and that the goals for the line managers who support the P&L centers are consistent with whatever marketing, engineering, fabrication, packaging, or testing they will need.

To focus people on the right projects and activities, he brings together his division and line managers to discuss the options several times leading up to annual goal setting and at least quarterly to rebalance during the course of the year. To ensure the discussion remains fact-based and doesn't get sidetracked by simple emotional appeals like "This technology could be huge!" he requires each participant to come armed with business plans, metrics, and data.

The group has intense discussions about each potential project and how they would work in combination to meet the overall goals for the business unit, with an eye toward balancing the timing and risk of pursuing various projects. They go through many iterations until Creviston is satisfied that the mix is right. Only then does he determine the specific goals for each of his direct reports, some of which are financial and some of which are tied to execution—for instance, for engineering to increase the reuse of some product design elements.

RFMD is heavily reliant on five large customers, whose

needs sometimes shift abruptly, requiring shifts in the projects RFMD is pursuing. Creviston has to be on constant alert, prepared in a moment to reconsider and readjust the goals for all of his direct reports. A leader who changes goals because he is indecisive creates confusion and loses credibility. But goals that start out right can end up being wrong simply because the world changes. Adjusting goals because reality has significantly changed is the sign of a leader's know-how. The goals of Creviston's business unit remain relatively stable for the year. It is the goals of his divisions and direct reports that go through frequent adjustments.

Setting the right goals means frequently rethinking every assumption about the market, the competition, and the business environment. You have to be cognizant that there are factors far beyond your ability to control, such as foreign exchange rates, commodity prices, and fiscal and monetary policy, that will impinge on the business. If you have an exceptional know-how you will take a broad look at what is on the horizon two or more years out, then work backward to visualize what you think the organization can achieve in that context, both over that longer term and in the interim. You also think about the quality of each goal. Can it be reached by doing things that strengthen the business, such as cutting costs through quality improvements? Or can it only be achieved through draconian measures that weaken the business, such as cutting mission-critical investment in R&D?

THE PSYCHOLOGY OF CHOOSING GOALS

Setting goals is never as objective and analytic as it sounds on paper. In real life, leaders have emotions and their own psychological quirks. Emotions and psychology can help you solve the goals puzzle and stick to goals you believe are right in the face of disbelievers. But emotions also can sometimes block clear thinking when it is needed most. If you are the leader of a public company and choose goals that are too modest, investors will take their money elsewhere in search of a bolder leader. But an unrealistically high goal that isn't met will hit the stock price even harder and damage the leader's credibility for a long time.

Different leaders faced with the same set of circumstances will make different decisions about which goals to pursue based on their psychology and cognitive abilities. You have to expand your observational lenses and weigh many factors, including your own psychology, personality, and cognitive skills before you can be sure your goals are right, or healthy, for the organization.

Ambition, pride, and in some cases excessive narcissism, often lead to setting a single goal that is bold, ambitious, captures the imagination, and is easy to communicate, but is ultimately bad for the business. Compensation schemes can exacerbate the problem by allowing leaders to declare and achieve a single goal that has devastating effects later.

For example, a CEO who had successfully executed a merger was growing the business at a healthy pace of 15 percent per annum earnings-per-share growth in an expanding industry. He set an ambitious goal to ratchet the company's growth rate up to 20 percent each year, and to accomplish that he devised a unique compensation scheme. His top team of twenty-five people would be required to devote the equivalent of two years' compensation to buying the company's stock. The team was to borrow money through interest-free loans. At that point the stock was trading at around $32 a share. They would not be allowed to sell the stock until the stock price hit $55 a share and stayed there for a minimum of ninety days, at which time they could cash out and repay the loans.

The team did as instructed. But within twelve months, industry growth began to slow, and one of the company's four divisions ran into the unexpected hurdle of a defective product that would take a long time to correct. Rather than rising, the stock price fell to $24. With so much of their compensation at risk, the top team began to lose faith in their leader. Eventually an astute board member got wind of the rising discontent and set in motion a ninety-day process that resulted in the CEO's departure. His team of direct reports had to repay the company loans out of their own pockets and suffered personal financial loss. The new CEO replaced the whole team. Two and a half years after the previous CEO's departure, the stock price remains below $35.

That goal—a specific price for the stock—was not under the company's control. Not only are investors very fickle, but in this industry, which is regulated, competitive or governmental actions could affect results and thus the stock price. In their effort to hit the 20 percent annual growth rate, the management had to set new and different priorities and take a new approach to resource allocation. When one division fumbled, they all suffered. The result was turmoil because the CEO had chosen a single goal. Further, it was the wrong goal, implemented poorly to boot.

People new in a job can be especially tempted to shoot for high, sometimes unattainable goals in order to impress others. An outrageous goal excites people and attracts a lot of attention. Many new CEOs have gone on the road to impress Wall Street, touting huge revenue growth five years out. Investors are seduced, the stock price rises, and the chief executive basks in the admiration until the lack of progress toward the goal becomes evident.

But this failure to deliver the touted goal results in devastating effects on the individual and the company. The same thing occurs at lower levels of the organization—people make big promises in hopes of being perceived as movers and shakers, then try to move on before the lack of results catches up with them.

The smarter approach is to underpromise and overdeliver.

People who use this approach are no less ambitious than their boastful competitors, but are more likely to have a longer-term set of goals that are continually evolving and being refined as external conditions change. Over time, of course, investors begin to calibrate the predictions of these seemingly modest leaders, adding a few pennies a share to their forecasts to account for that modesty. If they are seldom disappointed, investors come to admire these leaders because they can trust them not to overpromise and underdeliver.

Toyota has long been known as a company that consistently delivers slightly better results than it forecasts. Similarly, Southwest Airlines has an enviable reputation as one of the few airlines that can ride out surging fuel prices or low load factors with aplomb. It was one of the best shareholder returns over the past thirty years among companies that are in the S&P 500. Gillette under Jim Kilts paced the introduction of new products so that there wasn't either a feast or famine of product introductions.

You should do some self-assessment about why you are setting the goals you are. Leaders who are psychologically closed, for instance, might set modest goals because they have trouble seeing novel solutions, like forging partnerships with outsiders or leveraging other people's expertise. A fear of response can cause a leader to avoid tough choices, like killing off projects or products that have lost their promise or restructuring the business to reduce the number of people, things that should have been done anyway.

Perhaps the greatest psychological challenge associated with goals is dealing with the investment community. Finding the right balance between the short term and long term is a critical part of this know-how. After all, there is no shortage of predators looking for weak short-term performance that signals a floundering company. Your edge must be to find the balance, sacrificing short-term results only when doing so ensures greater benefits in the long term, and letting people know when their expectations are out of touch with reality. Doing so requires considerable courage in the face of constant pressures from powerful investors who seek instant gratification.

Bob Nardelli faced exactly that situation when he became CEO of Home Depot. Later he won some people over, but he had few supporters when he was mapping out the goals in the early years of his tenure. He had to make a lot of investments to create from scratch a technology and organizational infrastructure for the extremely internally decentralized company, and he had to increase margins and cash to pull it off. He had spent his early months walking the stores, soliciting input from sales associates and managers at every level as well as studying the dynamics of the industry and the economy overall. From that fact-gathering, he identified a huge opportunity for Home Depot to grow and formed a clear idea of what had to happen to go after it. All of that translated into clear, specific goals that established what the organization would accomplish in the near and longer term.

For Nardelli, however, determining the new goals was just part of the problem. The stock market wanted to see meaningful gains in sales at stores open more than a year. But that didn't happen right away. Nardelli's goals focused attention on cutting costs, putting the increased margins back into the company, and increasing inventory turnover to improve cash. The rate of new store openings was cut back in recognition of the fact that there simply weren't enough skilled store managers available. The stock market showed its disapproval of Nardelli's goals by cutting the stock price in half by early 2003 as investors defected to archrival Lowe's. But Nardelli's conviction didn't waver, even though he was new to the retailing business. He was sure he was doing the right things for the company, that the goals had internal consistency, and that they were grounded in the realities of what the organization could achieve in each time period. The changes he was undertaking had to occur in a certain sequence and be paced so that people could absorb them. Increased sales would come, but other things had to happen first. The board of directors, including Home Depot's founders, saw it too, and stood by him. Nardelli had both the know-how in setting the goals and the psychological fortitude to stick with them before the rest of the world could see that they were right. He came under increased pressure from investors when in May 2006 he discontinued the reporting of comp sales—a decision he later reversed—and for what some thought was an outlandish pay package, especially given Home Depot's stalled stock price. Undeterred, as of the summer of 2006, he continued to pursue his plan and was trying to get investors to focus on the measures he thinks matter most, summing it up for the *Atlanta Journal-Constitution* in July 2006: "I think the company and its associates are doing a great job, as evidenced in delivering 20 percent in earnings-per-share growth in each of the last four years. We've taken earnings from $1.10 per share to $2.72; we've taken return on invested capital from 19 percent to 24 percent. We've grown gross margin, we've grown operating margin, we've returned $15 billion back to shareholders in the last five years. We've taken the dividend from 16 cents, which was a 15 percent payout, to 60 cents, which is a 20 percent payout over that same period." In August 2006, director Bonnie Hill reaffirmed in the *Wall Street Journal* the board's full support.

Everybody knows the announcement of goals is not enough. Followers align emotionally with visions, mentally with the goals, and physically with priorities. Businesses have become so complex that leaders end up with too many priorities, or are overwhelmed when it comes to picking the right ones. It's choosing a few, and the right ones, and sticking with them that creates excellence in execution. That is what is shown in the next chapter.

What's the right goal for this European-based global company?

In 2003, the company, an equipment manufacturer and provider of professional services, appointed its third CEO in four years, the previous two having failed. The new leader came from a brand name global consulting firm. Earlier in his career he had been president of a division of another company that was one-third the size of his new employer.

During his first fifty days he visited customers across the globe. He also met with many people inside the company where he found incredible internal dissension, finger-pointing, and analysis-paralysis in decision making. His first steps involved finding ways to survive. The company had huge debt; the stock price had been cut 80 percent in the last four years; and the confidence of both managers and employees had been shaken.

There was the need to mobilize people, carve out a new vision and strategy, and set out goals, the delivery of which would re-build confidence. The CEO had in his mind an incredible number of actions regarding goals and priorities, but he knew that focusing and sequencing of goals absolutely matters.

Given the financial indicators he inherited (listed below), what set of internally consistent financial goals should he set for the next twelve months?

- Gross margin: 24 percent

- Selling expenses: 15 percent

- Other expenses: 7 percent

- Net operating profit: 3 percent

- Inventories: 30 percent

- Accounts receivable: 25 percent

- Accounts payable: 20 percent

- Capital investment: 6 percent

- Dividends: 1 percent

- Total revenue: 20 billion Euros, flat for the past three years

- Debt: 200 percent of equity

Many would rightly go to the issue of cash generation for survival, which in the short run will come from quick hits in reducing costs and from managing receivables and inventories and dealing with the underlying causes of poor performance. While these goals would certainly be helpful, *what will make the difference is setting the right goal for gross margin.* In this company, a higher goal for gross margin will prompt priorities and actions to deal with losing divisions or product lines, uncompetitive plants, or customers that are causing losses. In addition to improving gross margin, goals would include better focus, better recruitment of talent, and increased investment of resources in technology and marketing to differentiate offerings, thereby improving gross margin. It would be imprudent to set higher revenue and net profit goals for the next twelve months without the gross margin goal.

In this case the leader needs the psychological courage to set a higher gross margin goal and the tenacity to execute the right priorities and at the same time accept a lower revenue goal for the short term.

8

IT'S MONDAY MORNING—NOW WHAT?

Setting Laser-Sharp Dominant Priorities

Priorities are the pathway for accomplishing goals. They provide the road map that organizes and directs the business toward its goals. When the priorities are unmistakably clear and specific, people know what to focus on and, therefore, what should get their attention, resources, and follow-through. The right priorities, combined with appropriate follow-through, keep the truly important things from being driven off the radar screen in the day-to-day hurly-burly of life at work where everything can seem urgent and important. The right priorities help you rise above the constant demands that create stress and confusion. They enable you to provide clarity and focus for yourself and the other people in your organization. Without priorities people are apt to try to do everything, wasting precious time and energy on things that aren't important.

Goals are set at fifty-thousand feet. Priorities are set at ground level where you must have the tenacity, attitude, and willingness to probe the messy details to think through and define what the most important actions should be and what their second- and third-order consequences will be. Priorities determine how resources are allocated and thus have the potential for touching off clashes as resources are moved from one person to another. While the priorities must be absolutely clear, very specific, and, above all, doable, that isn't enough. Once set, you must repeat the priorities over and over again and follow through on them to be sure that people understand them, buy into them, and act on them so the organization executes them and doesn't deviate from the course the priorities set.

When Jeff Immelt determined that one of his primary goals would be to achieve an 8 percent rate of organic growth, he had to set the priorities that would ensure the business could achieve that ambitious goal. It was clear that the emerging nations, particularly China and India, would grow much faster than the developed world so he set as one priority that GE would derive 60 percent of its growth from the emerging markets. And since those countries would need infrastructure in the forms of turbines, water purification, railroads and airlines, all businesses in which GE had a stake, he set as another priority the reorganization of those infrastructure businesses to better tap those markets. Investing in technology—refurbishing existing GE research labs and opening labs in China and India—became a priority as did the realignment of GE's vaunted talent planning and succession process to define and incorporate the criteria for growth leaders of the future. Finally, he began making shifts in the social system by creating a new operating mechanism called the Commercial Council and changing the reviews of growth projects. He now has eighty projects of $100 million or more on his dashboard and he personally reviews ten a month.

When you select priorities you have to choose among four criteria: what is important, what is urgent, what is long-term versus short-term and what is realistic versus visionary. If you don't make choices among them because you want to do everything, the result will be muddled. You have to have the psychological conviction to choose the right balance among them, knowing that some may not be popular and will draw opposition. Others may change the balance of power among people. But if you have the inner conviction that your judgment is right and that you don't have to be liked by everyone you can make the right choices.

There is enormous energy generated inside the organization and among those who work with the organization, such as suppliers, by setting the right priorities. Conversely, enormous tolls are taken by the wrong priorities.

SETTING THE WRONG PRIORITIES

Some people set too many priorities in the mistaken belief that they must do everything. They fear that by selecting a few priorities and purposely not taking other possible steps they will be criticized by their peers, their employees, or the media. They dilute the entire effort by giving equal weight to everything and not determining which are the most important factors in reaching a goal. Others choose the wrong priorities because they don't have enough information. These people often obtain information through various filters that screen out important pieces of the puzzle, especially bad news. And certainly ego can play an important role in the selection of the wrong priorities. Some leaders don't want to face the conflicts or embarrassment that result when an emphasis on one priority necessarily reduces the resources allocated to someone else.

To avoid such conflicts, they may cede the decisions to finance people, who rely on financial tools instead of business judgment to determine where to invest. Some people don't do the mental work that goes into sifting, sorting, and selecting the right priorities out of a morass of complexity and possibility and reducing them to stark simplicity. And others, fearful of making a mistake, don't choose at all, preferring to procrastinate and make excuses, such as a lack of sufficient information.

You can have the right goals yet select the wrong priorities. But when you choose the wrong goals, your priorities will certainly be wrong and the business will be in danger.

As we discussed in the previous chapter, when Rick Wagoner focused on the goal of increasing overall U.S. market share, he set in motion priorities that would spread his limited resources—cash and management talent—over a wide variety of models. The result, of course, was that GM continued to lose market share, and its cash problems worsened. Given GM's situation in January 2005, what would appear to be realistic goals for the future and what priorities would be needed to achieve those goals?

The goals are fairly obvious. First and foremost is surviving, meaning conserving cash and watching the cash burn rate; second, converting company operations to breakeven or better and achieving positive cash flow from operations. This might mean gaining market share in some segments but overall market share in the U.S. market might have to decline. Third and finally, rebuilding the GM brand.

But what about the priorities to achieve those goals? There may be hundreds of action steps to take to meet those goals, but the leader has to determine which four or five are absolutely vital to the company's survival and then take them immediately. Different people will have different ideas about which priorities Wagoner should select. Looking at GM's situation as an outsider, one CEO I know listed the priorities he would set if he were in Wagoner's shoes. He would make the first priority to pick the most important market segments and ensure that the company was producing the right product with the right quality at the right cost. He would devote a disproportionate share of cash and the most talented people to make sure the effort succeeded. Selecting and delivering those products would increase market share in those segments, generate cash, improve morale among employees, convince dealers and suppliers to stay with the company, and might even convince investors and the media that GM can win. That would set the tone for everything else. GM has to give consumers the products they want. Unless it does, the situation will continue to deteriorate.

A second priority would be to raise cash to give the blood supply a boost while operational changes took hold. GM acknowledged the need to do that when early in 2006 it cut the dividend in half and senior executives also took substantial pay cuts. But those steps weren't enough. Is GM's insistence on trying to maintain more than seventy models realistic? It takes too much cash and engineering and design talent to keep that many models fresh and competitive and GM doesn't have enough of either. The company had talked sporadically about discontinuing its marginal Saab and Hummer brands, but eliminating them would still do little to save the amounts of cash necessary. Eliminating more lines would, of course, result in an overall decline in market share, something that as a goal is obviously painful for GM's leaders to contemplate.

A third priority would be to seek relief in some fashion from the crippling expense of pension and health care costs. If the company cannot reduce those costs, it will be hobbled in any efforts to compete long term against companies like Toyota and Honda that don't have these obligations. Both union and political support would be necessary to make such changes.

Fourth, he would close any plants that are deemed excess capacity as soon as possible. Revenues from the products those plants produce will continue to decline. The sooner they are shuttered and off the books, the better. Once again, such a drastic move would require consultation with both the union and politicians to ensure that the process goes smoothly.

Finally, he would examine the cadre of senior executives to determine if he had the quality, intensity, and depth of focus among them to direct the design, engineering, and marketing of the key products on which GM's future depends. And because GM's future hinges on its success or failure in the North American market, he would find someone to take over that job from Wagoner, who was then filling both that role and the role of CEO. If, as he suspects, he didn't have the right talent, he would begin immediately to find it. People, after all, are the single most important multiplier of a leader's abilities.

COMMUNICATING AND GETTING BUY-IN FOR YOUR PRIORITIES

It may be necessary for you to choose unpopular priorities that are nevertheless important for reaching your goals. Priorities hit people where they live on an everyday basis and are highly visible in terms of resource allocation and shifting power bases. If you are a leader who likes to be liked, you may not have the psychological courage to set the right priorities or the skills to convince the people in the organization that they are the right priorities. When people disagree with the priorities you set, it's one of the times when leadership becomes a performing art and you have to sell your ideas and get buy-in from those people who have to carry them out.

That was certainly the situation faced by Clive, who recently took over as editor of *Pacific,* a respected monthly magazine with a long history of doing excellent journalism. But as with almost all print media, *Pacific* is feeling the competitive pinch of the Internet with its blogs, online zines, and instant access to huge amounts of information. *Pacific*'s circulation has been declining and advertisers are telling the sales force that the magazine's readers are too old and the stories too long. Some of its best young writers have been lured away by weeklies and Web-based sites like *Slate*.

Clive's goals are to stabilize circulation and advertising at current levels and to cut costs to at least maintain the current levels of profitability. He explained those goals in an unusual mid-month staff meeting and then laid out his priorities for the editorial department to meet these goals. First, he said, *Pacific* will be eliminating coverage of some timely topics that the Internet and daily newspapers do much better than a monthly magazine. Subscribers didn't like paying money for a magazine that they thought simply rehashed material covered elsewhere. Second, because advertisers wanted younger readers, the magazine would begin covering topics of more interest to a younger audience, including personal finance and health and fitness. To cut costs many of those subjects would be outsourced to freelancers who were paid by the piece and weren't burdens on the magazine's health care and retirement benefit plans. Third, he told them that there was no longer a need for specialists on single topics and that everyone would be expected not only to develop stories on a broad array of subjects, but that they would also be required to do more than one story a month. The stories, of course, would be shorter than the lengthy "think pieces" the staffers were accustomed to doing. Finally, he said he had already hired a new designer to begin a wholesale overhaul of the magazine's appearance.

Not surprisingly, there was a lot of muttering and discontent among the editorial staffers. Many of them had worked hard earlier in their careers at newspapers and smaller magazines to establish the kind of credentials that got them hired here. They relished the easy pace of one story per month because it gave them time to probe deeply into whatever subject they were writing about. If their reporting required two weeks in California or Europe, so be it. The idea of doing two stories a month about things on which they had little or no expertise and doing much of their research online or by telephone couldn't possibly result in the same quality of journalism they were accustomed to producing. The new editor, many of them thought, was turning their cherished magazine into just another "news you can use" publication that would lack serious, in-depth investigations of crucial trends and events. A few of the senior staffers began to think about leaving. But when they looked around the magazine field, they discovered that they weren't alone. The same changes were taking place everywhere. There was no place else to go.

Clive heard some of the rumblings, of course. He began eating in the company cafeteria more often, sitting at a large table and making sure it was clear that staffers should feel free to join him. Since he knew what was on their minds, he was ready when they brought up their arguments that the magazine shouldn't be tampered with. "Given the trend lines I saw when I was talking about taking this job, we wouldn't have a viable magazine four years from now," he would tell the staffers. "As much as we would all like to do things the old way, the old way isn't working. We've got to change and we can't do it slowly or incrementally. The world is changing too fast and if we want to be a part of it, we have to change just as fast."

Clive stuck to his conviction and tried to personally sell the priorities to the staff using facts about circulation, costs, and revenue. It didn't work for everyone, but he didn't lose his entire staff either. A few months later some staff members had left, but the majority were still at *Pacific*. They missed their lengthy reporting trips, but they also found that it was fun to poke their noses into subjects they didn't know anything about. And it wasn't so bad having a couple of bylines in each edition instead of just one. The use of more freelancers created a need for more editors and some of the writers wound up getting a promotion to editor long before they had thought they would. When the magazine's circulation figures showed a slight gain at the end of the year, many of them acknowledged that Clive had been right.

PEOPLE AND PRIORITIES

It is people who must bring the priorites to life. Therefore, whenever you set new priorities, you have to ask, Do we have the right people to carry them out? The importance of having the right people is evident if you contrast GM's situation of declining market share and huge financial losses with its cross-town rival Chrysler, the U.S. subsidiary of Daimler Benz. Daimler decided years ago that it couldn't survive as a German-centered niche player in the automobile business and as a consequence bought Chrysler to gain a foothold both in the largest automobile market in the world as well as in a different market segment. But the merger seemed headed for disaster from the very beginning. Sold to investors as a "merger of equals" it quickly became apparent that Daimler was simply making Chrysler a subsidiary. The resentment among Chrysler managers was palpable. Worse, Chrysler's products weren't doing well in the marketplace and the American leaders in charge of Chrysler didn't seem to have the ability to create the kinds of innovative products that American consumers wanted. Exasperated and under mounting pressure from shareholders, Daimler CEO Jurgen Schremp sent one of Daimler's own product gurus, the soft-spoken Dieter Zetsche, to turn around Chrysler using the proven methods he had employed at Daimler's Mercedes Benz division.

Zetsche's first priority was to develop the right products, cars and trucks that struck a chord with consumers and rivaled offerings from Toyota, Honda, and Nissan. A second priority was to stabilize the dispirited and dysfunctional management team, where high turnover and squabbling had taken a huge toll following the merger. Zetsche imposed order on the chaos by carefully and methodically selecting the right people for the right jobs. Finally, he established close working relationships with suppliers that yielded cost and productivity gains in a regular and continuous manner that contrasted sharply with the sudden and unpredictable demands that other automakers made on suppliers. Chrysler's initial new products got rave reviews from the automotive press and consumers, an indication that Zetsche's approach was succeeding in getting the automaker on the path for survival. In the next few years Chrysler actually gained a few points of market share and was profitable. More recently, Chrysler has been fighting for its life. Despite their early success, it's unclear whether Zetsche and his team can fix the current problems.

Getting the right people—that is, finding and developing people who have the potential to become growth leaders—is a dominant priority of Jeff Immelt's at GE. In 2002 and 2003, having laid out the new positioning for GE and choosing, among other goals, to go from 5 percent to 8 percent organic growth, Immelt began to change the criteria of what it would take to be a leader at GE. The company had long emphasized productivity, but now growth became the mantra and Immelt carefully scrutinized and evaluated the roughly six hundred people who comprise the senior band of executives to determine who would be in charge of delivering goals. Through the regular operating mechanisms ("session C") at GE for talent planning and development, he and his senior HR executive assessed where each of the six hundred had flourished and how they met his criteria for growth leaders, and then decided where to position them next. A high priority was the development of a pipeline of growth leaders in China and other emerging markets and the assignment of budget and other resources to ensure that the pipeline was developed.

GETTING ON THE SAME PAGE

Maria Luisa Ferré Rangel is the CEO of the Ferré Rangel Group, a family-owned publishing company in San Juan, Puerto Rico, that owns two newspapers, *El Nueva Dia,* the largest in Puerto Rico, and *Primera Hora,* aimed at young adults. She knew that the Internet threatened the future of newspapers and she determined that the company had to make some major changes. She set two major goals: diversify the newspapers into multimedia properties and find ways to make money outside of Puerto Rico. With those two goals firmly in mind, she gathered the company's vice presidents, general managers, and newspaper editors to figure out what the priorities would be to achieve those goals. All had been given the company's financial statements for past years, so they were intimately familiar with the financial picture, a key to being able to bring clarity to the priority setting process.

"I explained the positioning and put it in the context of what is happening in the outside world because of the Internet. I asked them 'What are the things we need to do as a group to achieve these goals,' " she says. "I told them to be creative, to open their minds and to concentrate on the growth opportunities we might find and what are the blockers that might prevent us from achieving them. The process was very interesting. Everybody was talking, the room was energized."

The group broke up into smaller working panels to discuss ideas. When they reassembled, each of the groups presented its ideas to the full group. Surprisingly, different groups came up with some of the same ideas, such as leveraging the company's newspaper expertise to open a paper in a

U.S. city with a substantial Puerto Rican population. Yet at the same time some radical ideas also emerged, among them alliances with other Latin American news organizations to buy existing newspapers or chains in the United States. One group even suggested that the company add a completely different business to its portfolio to offset the exposure to the changing news business.

When everyone had spoken there were more than two dozen possible priorities. The discussion then centered on which ones were the most important and what might prevent them from being achieved. The emphasis was on specificity—drilling down into the small details of each idea—and the clarity with which each idea could be stated.

"We started eliminating ideas, looking for the three or four that would be the most important ones, the first ones that we needed to do," says Ferré Rangel. "We would keep many of the others, but we knew the important part was to end up with just three or four. You can't do everything at once."

At the end of the session, some clear priorities had emerged. Besides the two newspapers, the company also owned a small company, Virtual, that had been running the newspapers' Web sites separately from the newspapers' daily operations. The first priority was to grow that operation so that it could do two things: transform the newsrooms from traditional operations focused solely on producing a newspaper for the next day into multimedia newsrooms while at the same time developing a separate but parallel Web operation independent of the newspapers.

The restructuring of the newsrooms was no small task. It required a wide-ranging redesign to accommodate more sophisticated technology, including facilities to produce both audio and video Webcasts. At the same time the Internet operation required additional people to generate content separate from what the newspapers were producing. That content would be aimed mostly at mobile devices, such as cell phones and PDAs.

A second priority was to change the company's operating methods. Before undertaking the changes, the company's management was hierarchical and tended to be divided into separate silos. It was also, as newspapers tend to be, focused on the here-and-now of getting the product out every day. Little time was spent thinking carefully about the future. "We realized that if we wanted to accomplish our two goals we needed to transform ourselves, to create a space where we could begin looking at the future," says Ferré Rangel. "We were very good at the highest level at generating new ideas and being creative, but we realized we needed to push that deeper into the organization, to the group level."

The change is still in the early stages, but Ferré Rangel has drawn some important lessons from the process. The central one is that it takes time and effort to get everyone on the same page so that the priorities can be executed. "A very important part of this process is to be very specific and very clear," she says. "We learned that you have to repeat things a lot. You have to create communications channels that have consistency to keep the priorities from changing. At first, people understand them differently depending on their mindset. You have to be repetitive and consistent until they all understand exactly what they need to do."

Because the company's operating style changed from hierarchical to collaborative, the senior managers had to overcome a degree of suspicion among people in the ranks as well as reorient them to thinking beyond the next day's newspaper. "First you have to open up their minds and convince them you are listening. Too often in the past someone might say 'This is worrying me' and the leader would say 'We'll deal with that later.'" Now we have to know to stop and say instead 'Why are you worried?' and work it out right then."

Narrowing the number of priorities was an important

part of overcoming suspicion and refocusing people on the future. "We have to change the whole organization's mentality, but without creating too many distractions or worry," says Ferré Rangel. "That's why clear, specific priorities with a time frame are so useful. They help build confidence."

Ferré Rangel realized in the midst of the change process that her most important job was finding the right people to do the job. "We needed a different thinking structure," she says. "If everybody thinks the same way, then the new ideas and the questioning and the reframing of the questions don't happen."

She knew that first and foremost she wanted people who were both independent thinkers and team players. That quest took her to other industries—telecom and finance, for example—where she found people who, while they didn't necessarily know the news business, knew how to rethink and reframe questions about positioning, goals, and priorities.

She also sought much younger people. "They might not have the work experience, but their minds frame the way they look at things very differently. A twenty-two-year-old isn't looking at the world like a thirty-five-year-old does."

Candidates went through a rigorous interview process that included much probing into their willingness to work in a team environment. While it is still early in the process, the selection methodology seems to have worked well.

"This process is just getting started," Ferré Rangel says. "Some people will be able to embrace it and others will not. For those who do, this will be a central growth experience of their careers."

WITHOUT ASSIGNING RESOURCES, IT ISN'T A PRIORITY

Anyone can state a priority. It is only when resources are applied to it that it really becomes one. The flow of resources—

people and money—is a leading indicator of where the company is headed in the short and long term. Leaders who don't have a handle on the flow of resources aren't really holding the reins.

Anytime you shift priorities you have to assign accountability and resources to the new ones. That almost always requires reshuffling or reallocation of resources. It also implies that the power of some people may be shifted. In real life, people announce priorities but find it psychologically difficult to take resources from someone and give them to someone else. They hate conflict and avoid it. They often fall victim to the last-in, first-out syndrome we outlined in the chapter on molding a team of leaders (pages 172–173). You need to have a process to ensure that the necessary shifts take place. It isn't enough to just announce them. You also have to ensure that in the budgeting process the shift is in fact happening and then you have to monitor in your regular reviews that the shift is continuing to happen and that priorities are being executed.

It can be particularly difficult to shift human resources from the control of one business unit to another. Making sure that the shift is made is what Eric Creviston does as executive vice president of the wireless products business of RFMD. Creviston recently was faced with the need to develop a new platform of products beyond its core component. Yet the new undertaking couldn't disrupt the functioning of the existing product development, all of which takes place in a fast-paced and highly competitive business. The funds simply weren't available to hire a new set of engineers so the decision was made to share the existing engineering talent between the old product lines and the planned new platform. It was a major initiative, and everyone on the team understood its strategic importance, but the leader who ran the core component business found it hard to live with. He was getting calls every day from existing customers who were saying they needed more of this component or another version of that component, and the pressure to meet customer demands took all of his engineers' time—a critical resource in high tech. The engineers were supposed to be spending some of their time working with the sister division that was trying to build the new capability because the technologies overlapped, but day after day, it wasn't happening.

In some organizations, those kinds of problems go unrecognized and unaddressed, but Creviston created a short, focused Monday morning meeting of all his direct reports to root out such problems and get adjustments made in real time, transferring people and other resources in line with what was happening in the business that week to ensure the priorities were coming to life. Creviston says: "By getting everyone to understand everyone else's problems, goals, and priorities, we're able to get a much better rhythm for synchronization."

THE FRAMEWORK FOR RESOURCE ALLOCATION

Using the right priorities to drive resource allocation is critical to any business struggling in a shifting market or against strong competitors. But smart resource allocation is important for any company with multiple product lines even if it is performing exceptionally well. Thomson Corporation, a company with four major business divisions and more than sixty business segments, is moving aggressively to take the business to a higher level by extracting resources from some units to fund new priorities and enhance the focus on growth and returns in its business segments. It's a challenging process, but one made easier by Thomson's unique and sophisticated analytical approach. The implementation of the framework starts with the collection of precise historical financial data from each segment that shows its capital spending, revenue growth, and free cash flow (FCF) margin. Organic revenue growth is used as the growth indicator, while free cash flow margin is employed as the return indicator. Thomson's own research indicates that free cash flow margin captures both the profitability and capital intensity characteristics of the business and can be used as a proxy for improvement in return on invested capital. Each segment is then placed in the proper box of a four-box grid with organic revenue growth as the vertical axis and free cash flow margin as the horizontal axis.

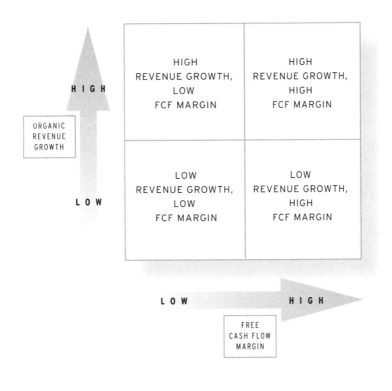

Figure 8.1: HISTORICAL ANALYSIS

Clearly business segments that fall into the high revenue, high FCF margin quadrant are among the most desirable while those that fall into the low revenue, low FCF margin box are the least desirable. But the analysis doesn't stop there.

Within each quadrant Thomson shows the capital spending that has been done on each segment, both in the last year and over its lifetime. That capital spending is further broken down into three categories—maintenance, growth, and efficiency— and captured at the individual project level. Ultimately, the process measures how much capital is being spent on each segment against its relative performance among all of Thomson's business segments.

This exercise is conducted annually. Each quarter, Thomson revisits this process to evaluate the performance of the business segments against annual plan expectations.

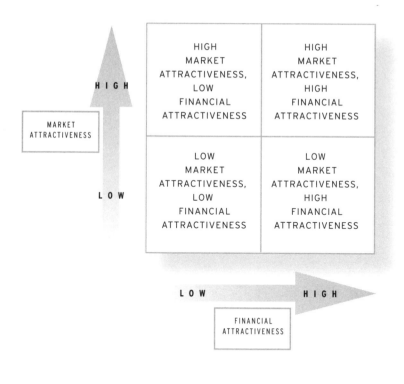

Figure 8.2: PROSPECTIVE ANALYSIS

The prospective analysis is done in much the same way but the business segments are placed in a grid that consists of market attractiveness (average market growth rates) as the vertical axis and financial attractiveness, which is defined as a blend of organic revenue growth and free cash flow margin, as the horizontal axis. The performers in the high market growth and high financial attractiveness quadrant operate in attractive markets and enjoy above-average revenue growth and FCF margins. By contrast, the business segments in the lowest quadrant operate in tougher markets and have below-average revenue growth and FCF margins. As this exercise is carried out regularly, it becomes evident where resources need to be applied and from where they should be withdrawn.

This approach is a systematic way to ensure resources are being assigned to maximize growth and returns simultaneously. In addition, Thomson evaluates the business segments in the lower left quadrant to see if they continue to fit the company's overall strategy or should be divested.

The Three-Day Priority Commitment and Resource Allocation Process

One of the best processes for setting priorities and allocations that I know of occurs at the DLP® division of Texas Instruments. It happens through the budget process, which the division has refined from a six-to-eight week, time-consuming back and forth negotiating process to a highly-efficient streamlined process that takes all of three days total. This is a consistent and effective process for reallocating resources on the basis of priorities.

Most companies do their annual budgeting from the top down. The process starts when divisions and other subordinate units are given their goals, usually growth targets for revenue, margins, cash generation, and capital spending, at a minimum. Each unit then goes through the budget to identify how it will reach its goals. Their analysis is sent back up to the top for modification and then goes back down again. Subsequent iterations are sent from up to down and down to up among the divisions themselves. The process can take as little as six weeks and as much as twenty weeks and involves the investment of huge amounts of time and energy by a lot of highly paid people.

DLP® is in a fast-paced industry. The division produces products based on a semi-conductor display solution that is built into the guts of some TVs, projectors, and digital cinema that receive electronic signals and convert them to pictures on a screen. The division, with its three sub units, faces tough competition from several Japanese and Korean companies. The technology moves fast and success depends on highly paid experts in specialized areas of technology. New product development is done on a project basis. In the past, the division's budgeting process mirrored the traditional up-and-down process described above.

Enter John Van Scoter, who took over as head of the division in 2000. To remain competitive, he had to radically rethink the process of resource allocation and the alignment of the people involved for carrying out the priorities the following year. The way to do that, he determined, was by compressing the six-week budgeting and resource allocation process into just three days. The purpose was not just to compress the time frame, but to use the process as the vehicle to get seventy leaders working as a team, simultaneously looking at the total picture in detail, debating options, and internalizing the reasons underlying trade-offs. The key is total immersion. Everyone gets on the same page on both the internal and external environment and understands and participates in the reasoning behind resource allocation and the commitment to goals. This process expands the cognitive bandwidth of the participants and is a great catalyst for collaboration across the silos.

The process begins with a statement by Van Scoter and the three sub-business managers about the details of the division goals and priorities for the next year. This is followed by intense discussions among the people about why these goals and priorities were chosen. This kind of discussion breaks the silo mentality. It's a process that requires the leader to have enormous patience, fielding skeptical questions from participants, most of whom are technical specialists.

Then all of the participants discuss and digest the intricacies of the sales forecast. They all get on the same page, laying the foundation for the priorities and resource allocation of each working unit of the division.

The participants work with a common set of spreadsheets and databases showing the total forecast and its components—revenue, cost of goods, R&D, and marketing. They then go through several iterations of simultaneous discussion until the leaders see the harmonization among the division's chosen goals and priorities and the priorities and resource assignments of each of the work units. Each iteration can take several hours and the work is intense.

The output of this process is a clear forecast with full commitment and everyone understanding what decisions were made, why they were made, and the assumptions and rationales that led to them. Knowing that reasoning allows them to make modifications later as external conditions change. In the process they discover things they would never have seen had the budget been done the old way. In their discussions about priorities and projects, they see that some are no longer high priorities. Van Scoter doesn't have to tell them why that is, they can see it for themselves in the cold, hard facts. They also find that one silo may be doing something that could be very useful to another silo and they combine forces to get it done with fewer resources than they would have needed to duplicate efforts. In one instance a product group discovered that it was devising a set of algorithms for its new offerings that could serve as the base for another group's products, a process that saved the second group a great deal of effort and cycle time. Disparate functions, such as engineering and sales, learn how the other sees the anatomy of the business.

The budget is done in three days and then is reviewed each quarter in a similar two-day meeting where adjustments are made. The budget becomes a living tool to adjust priorities and resource allocation as the external environment changes.

This process demands that the leader be driven to ensure transparency of information across silos and have the maturity to persuade people on the one hand and exercise power on the other to ensure decisiveness.

JUDGMENT AND STRENGTH OF A LEADER

The greatest psychological challenge in setting and acting on priorities has to do with resource allocation. Whether in a group meeting or through conventional budgeting and capital approval processes, you have to demonstrate judgment and courage in making resource allocation decisions that reflect your business priorities and in following through to ensure that the things that should be happening in fact are. You have to do the analytic work to separate out the facts and assess the opportunities and risks, but you also need to call upon your inner strength and judgment as John did as CEO of his company.

"You know I'm always behind you, John, but I think you're making a big mistake on this one," Art, one of the division presidents, told John during the usual bottom-up, top-down budgeting process. "My division contributes 65 percent of the company's profits and our brands need advertising support. If you think we're fighting for market share now, just watch what happens six months down the road when consumers forget who we are and we can't get on the shelves."

John listened intently to all that Art had to say. After all, Art was experienced, respected, and the strongest leader they had. It was true that Art's division brought in the lion's share of revenues and profits. The problem was that the division was not bringing in what the company needed most: profitable growth. All of the divisions had been hurt by soft markets and currency fluctuations, but Art's business was faced with especially intense competition that was pushing prices down, and it looked as if revenue and earnings would decline for the foreseeable future.

Cara's division, on the other hand, had good margins and was growing. John had combed through Cara's business plan and believed she had positioned the division well to grow faster than the market, but she would need ample resources to keep growing at the current rate.

Then there was Peter. He had already been to see John twice to try to impress on him the importance of continuing the development of the SAP initiative. The company had already spent some $50 million on it and Peter needed another $100 million spread over the next three years to bring it to fruition.

John knew that the decisions he made would seriously affect the future of the company and the lives of people who had put their hearts and souls into the business. But with earnings down and the price of the company's stock depressed and only limited capital available for investment, he knew that he was about to make some of those people very unhappy, so unhappy that they might even leave the company. Relying on the goals and priorities he had thoughtfully established to guide his decisions about where resources had to be deployed, how they might be generated, and where they had to be extracted, he prepared himself to withstand the fallout from those decisions.

Building a presence in growth markets was a top priority for the business so he increased Cara's budget. He made the business judgment that Art's division was on a downward slide that didn't look as if it would be reversed any time soon, and cut Art's budget. To free up more cash to pursue the opportunities in Cara's business, John pulled the plug on the SAP project, even though he knew it meant the loss of jobs for people who had been dedicated to it and a write-off of $50 million.

John's decisions were realistic, well reasoned, and anything but personal, but Art was deeply offended by what seemed to him a loss of power, and he began to consider his next career move. As hard as it was, John stood by his judgment to withdraw resources from places they had always gone. Six months later, the sales numbers for Cara's division came in weaker than expected, and John dug in to see what had caused the weakness. He realized that the numbers were low because of currency swings, that the business was on the right track, and that the growth prospects were as bright as ever. Even when the numbers went off track, his judgment told him that the priorities and resource allocations he had made were still correct, and he stuck with them.

The world of making money and running a business is complex and moneymaking is evaluated every month, every day, every hour, all the complexity notwithstanding. But your job does not end there. In this world of total transparency where business is a societal institution, like it or not, there are other special interest groups and stakeholders who have a say in how your business is run. It requires a special know-how to anticipate these cause-driven interest groups that can be contra to your company and industry. Next you'll learn the know-how of living with them.

The goals are set. What are the priorities?

The CEO of the company described at the end of the previous chapter set his primary goals as improving gross margin, recruiting better talent, and providing more resources for investment in technology and marketing. What should his priorities be? What 20 percent of actions will make 80 percent of the impact to deal with the problems facing the company, thereby building confidence that this leader is doing the right thing? Obviously he has to select the right people for teams, assign accountability, and set metrics. But strictly in the business analytic sense his priorities should be as follows:

- Set up a process for getting to the causes of lower gross margins, higher inventories, and higher receivables, then for making decisions about which divisions to keep, eliminate, or resize.

- Determine within each division the product lines and customer segments to emphasize more, deemphasize, or eliminate.

- Extract cash by selling assets that are not on the priority list.

- Determine immediately where to put more resources and a different caliber of resources (for example in technology and marketing) that will earn higher gross margins.

- Quickly install cross-functional teams that will deal with issues of customer satisfaction in chosen segments, reduce costs, and resize the organization for impending reduction of revenue.

- Set up "SWAT teams" for collecting receivables faster and improving inventory turns.

- Communicate the priorities. Then repeat. And repeat again.

When setting priorities do the right thing but avoid the temptation to do everything. Recognize that in such situations what is "urgent" often drives out what is important. Establishing the right priorities and communicating them provides the foundation to tell yourself and others what not to do—and the courage to stick with it. Kind in mind the following key points about priorities:

- Priorities are a road map that organizes and directs the business toward its goals. Without priorities people are apt to try to do everything, wasting precious time and energy on things that aren't important.

- Priorities are set at ground level where you must have the tenacity, attitude, and willingness to probe the messy details to think through and define what the priorities should be and what their second- and third-order consequences will be. Priorities must be absolutely clear, very specific and, above all, doable.

- Priorities are drawn from among four criteria: what is important, what is urgent, what is long term versus short term, and what is realistic versus visionary. If you don't make choices among them because you want everything, the organization will lack focus.

- Having too many priorities is the same as having no priorities.

- The wrong priorities often result from the lack of sufficient information, the avoidance of conflict, or the failure to do the mental work of sorting through the morass of complexity and possibility.

- Priorities aren't real until resources are applied to them.

- Because resource allocation can create conflicts, you must have psychological courage in setting the right priorities and the skills to convince people in the organization to make the necessary shifts.

- Executing priorities requires constant repetition and disciplined follow-through to ensure that everyone understands them, buys into them, and is following them without deviation.

9

IN THE COURT OF PUBLIC OPINION

Dealing with Societal Forces Beyond the Market

Moneymaking is your job. You spend most of your time and energy thinking about your business. Is it positioned correctly? Is your team of leaders synchronized in the pursuit of your goals? Are the priorities right? Is the social system healthy? But the job doesn't end there. Every business today operates in a complex societal and political milieu that demands more of it than just profits. Gone are the days when Milton Friedman could proclaim that "the business of business is business." It's a foregone conclusion that business leaders have to be able to deal with market forces, and over the years they've learned to live with them. In the twenty-first century, business leaders will be required to deal with issues that go beyond the market.

Special interest groups have of course long been with us. But today the stakeholders include a whole laundry list of groups and individuals, and it's not the mere number that's different. It's also the range of issues they're concerned about and their ability to impact the very heart of your business and industry. Consider a short list of topics that are generating controversy and threatening the very core of several businesses today:

- Obesity and its causes and consequences
- Stem cell research
- Environmental concerns about drilling for oil in Alaska
- The possible revival of nuclear power generation in the face of rising oil prices
- The rising cost of drugs to treat a wide array of diseases
- The high cost and lack of availability of health insurance
- Illegal immigration

Companies that are on the wrong side of an issue can suffer immense damage if it gains traction, which many special interest groups know how to accomplish. They know how to organize, get access to the media, form coalitions with groups with different causes, raise money, and influence customers and governments. They have unprecedented access to information through the Internet and can disseminate their views widely at low cost. Even an individual can exert influence through a blog. Special interest groups can be helpful if they share your business goals and philosophies, but more likely they don't. While you may be willing to do everything in your power to make the business flourish, they may be doing everything in their power to make sure it doesn't. Their agendas are logical to them but may seem illogical, even irrational, to a business person, and the interests of various groups may conflict with one another and pull your business in opposite directions. But avoiding such groups doesn't make them go away. If they choose to target your company or industry, there is no way to escape them. And don't count on first-rate lawyers. We live in an age of "moral liability" that imposes new responsibilities on companies to behave not just legally, but ethically as well.

The challenge is to keep abreast of changing societal expectations and adapt your business accordingly, while avoiding the landmines. Many special interest groups raise legitimate issues, and you need to understand and respond to them. Bear in mind that pressure from outside groups has led to many societal benefits, such as air and water pollution regulations, lower emissions and increased automobile safety, anti-discrimination laws, and workplace safety rules. Dealing with groups whose issues seem to be on the fringe is more delicate. You don't want to raise the stature of such groups by paying a lot of attention to them, but that doesn't mean you can ignore them just because they seem to lack power or their issues seem far-fetched. They can still do damage, and their status can change fast.

Dealing with external constituencies may not *create* shareholder value, but the failure to do so most certainly can *destroy* it and a leader who shies away from the challenge will often wind up looking for a job. A.G. Lafley, CEO of Procter & Gamble, captured the magnitude of the challenge when he said, "Honest to god, the responsibility is huge."[*]

Like all the other know-hows a leader must have, this one requires experience, yet it is the one know-how in which very few leaders get sufficient experience before reaching the CEO's office. Leaders reach the top accustomed to analyzing hard data and making decisions that are then carried out by subordinates. They simply aren't prepared for the psychological stress and frustration of dealing with the ambiguities and

[*] "The CEO as Global Corporate Ambassador," *Wall Street Journal*, March 29, 2006, page A2.

the lack of control that characterize the company's relations with such interest groups. For them, such tasks become time-consuming diversions from the real business of running the company. No matter how much you dislike dealing with special interest groups, you can't regard them as distractions from your day-to-day work of leading the company. You have to overcome any psychological aversion you might have to the ambiguities of such political and societal discourse and become, in Lafley's words, constructively engaged.

The know-how of dealing with forces outside your control is to identify new interest groups that are emerging and to discern which groups are gaining influence and have legitimate issues. You have to build relationships and understand the real motivations and attitudes of those groups and their leaders. You have to look for ways to communicate, knowing that if you bridge the gaps soon enough, you can help reshape the issues and outcome. If the issues are legitimate, you should respond, maybe by building coalitions among your peers so the industry doesn't continue to be attacked. While you have to be prepared to resort to legal channels and, frequently, negotiated settlements, you can't depend on them, because many battles take place in the court of public opinion and are won on the basis of emotional appeal rather than legal argument. Each move requires new analysis, like an evolving chess game where you have to see several moves ahead to predict the opponent's causes, power base, and passion. If you lack the will to get in the game, there's a high risk you could lose.

ADJUSTING YOUR ATTITUDE

You'll never master the know-how of managing external constituencies if you're not psychologically willing to deal with the inherent ambiguities and lack of control. It's a big mental adjustment for many business leaders accustomed to operating in an environment characterized by logic and relative control. Sitting across the table from a social activist who has little grasp of business realities yet is demanding the company take a certain action can be disconcerting or even painful for someone from a corporate environment. Most leaders get into trouble because they simply ignore advocates of change whose demands don't fit squarely with a business and economic rationale. If your company faces or may face challenges from outside—few companies will be able to avoid them in the future—and you don't like operating in that kind of environment you should at least question if you are the leader your company needs.

The most effective leader is psychologically open and willing to negotiate, adept at understanding that no matter how irrational the interest group's position may seem, it makes perfect sense to the opponent. The ability to listen with an open mind and determine what the group or its leaders are really after is essential, because listening itself can defuse an issue and because it helps you understand what "winning" and "losing" really mean to those parties. Outside groups often have goals that are idealistic and even admirable. But their leadership is often interested as well in personal aggrandizement or fame, and you develop those insights through observation and listening.

Imagining what an outside group is really after requires the ultimate in reframing, seeing things not just through a different lens but with a whole different logic and set of values. Robert Shapiro is one corporate leader who learned this lesson the hard way. Shapiro rose to the top of Monsanto Corp. with a powerful vision for transforming the company from a chemical manufacturer to a life sciences company using genetic engineering to produce "Food, Health and Hope." His logic seemed impeccable: use science, specifically genetics, to engineer plants that were resistant to disease, drought, and insects and that produced better yields per acre using less energy and pesticides. Monsanto spent millions of dollars developing the technology and several billion to acquire the seed companies and distributors it needed to make Shapiro's vision a reality. Wall Street applauded Monsanto's pioneering efforts. The stock price even rose after the company slashed its dividend to help cover its heavy spending.

Monsanto's genetically engineered products were a hit with big American agricultural companies. The soybean, corn, cotton, and other seeds, while more expensive to purchase than unmodified seeds, fulfilled Monsanto's promise of better yields. Cultivation of genetically modified crops in the United States soared from 18 million acres in 1997 to 58 million acres in 1998. By the end of that year Monsanto was on a path to generate $10 billion in annual revenue from a pipeline of new products to be introduced over the next few years.

Then the problems began. A farmer in Canada reported that some canola seeds, genetically modified to be pesticide resistant, had escaped and cross-pollinated with a related type of weed on the fringes of his field, creating, in effect, a "super weed" that couldn't be controlled by existing pesticides. A rival seed company introduced genes from a Brazil nut into a soybean to make it more nutritious as animal feed. But soybeans are a big source of protein for human consumption, too, and some people are fatally allergic to Brazil nuts. The product never made it to market, but news accounts speculating that modified soybeans could kill people allergic to Brazil nuts got plenty of attention. And then there was the Terminator gene. Monsanto bought a seed company that had patented the technology to insert a gene in crops that effectively sterilized new seeds when the crop was harvested. The idea was to prevent farmers from saving the seeds from a portion of their crop to plant the next year, in effect, protecting the seed company's proprietary genetic modification technology. Farmers would have to buy new seeds each year.

Everything came to a head when Monsanto applied to sell its genetically modified seed in Europe. Europeans were already reeling from a decade of health scares related to food, including Britain's terrifying encounter with "mad cow" disease. Although the European Union's regulators gave Monsanto permission to sell its modified products, consumer reaction on the Continent verged on hysteria. Environmental groups and the media led the charge against Monsanto, labeling its products "Frankenstein foods." Prince Charles weighed in with the opinion that "I happen to believe that this kind of genetic modification takes mankind into realms that belong to God, and to God alone." The German subsidiaries of both Nestlé and Unilever said they would not use Monsanto's genetically modified soybeans. Polls showed huge majorities of Europeans firmly against altered foods. Monsanto's efforts to counter the critics—a $5 million advertising campaign that told Europeans that while they were new to biotechnology, Monsanto had been researching the subject for twenty years—instead inflamed public opinion as being condescending.

Shapiro wasn't swayed by the furor. "This is the single most successful introduction of technology in the history of agriculture, including the plow," he proclaimed. He acknowledged the opposition, but contended that "eventually, scientific proof should win over reluctant and skeptical consumers."

But science had never been the real issue. Public opinion was what counted. A consultant whom Monsanto brought in to mediate with the company's growing number of critics gave up, claiming that Monsanto just didn't get it. "There is a barrier to really listening to what people are saying," he said of the company. In the United States, where small farmers were becoming increasingly incensed over Monsanto's efforts to collect fees and put restrictions on their use of modified seeds, Agriculture Secretary Dan Glickman got straight to the point, warning Shapiro to keep quiet because "every time he opens his mouth, U.S. agriculture loses millions more bushels of agriculture exports." Monsanto's stock price fell 35 percent even as the overall market rallied 30 percent in 1999.

The denouement came in October of that year when Shapiro made a stunning appearance, via a video address, at the annual meeting of the environmental group Greenpeace, which had become Monsanto's archenemy in the battle over genetically modified food. In his address he admitted that the company had underestimated public wariness about modified foods. "Our confidence in this technology and our enthusiasm for it has, I think, widely been seen, and understandably so, as condescension or indeed arrogance. Because we thought it was our job to persuade, too often we forgot to listen."

Shortly afterward Monsanto agreed to merge with the pharmaceutical maker Pharmacia & Upjohn. The terms of the merger reflected Pharmacia's desire to own Monsanto's Searle unit and effectively gave Shapiro's efforts to feed the world's growing population with scientifically designed high-yield crops a value of essentially zero.

For Shapiro and his team at Monsanto, the violent reaction against genetically modified food was an irrational response to what the company had intended to be a socially beneficial corporate initiative. But from the point of view of European consumers deeply concerned about the health effects of modern food processing technology—turning the brains of diseased cattle into cattle feed, for instance—Monsanto's aggressive efforts to push the modified foods into the market were profoundly troubling. One can argue that it was a failure of understanding on both sides, but in a pitched battle between a marketer and societal concerns, the societal concerns will almost always emerge triumphant. You have to be able to see your business through those eyes.

THE NEW FACTS OF LIFE

Before you can deal appropriately with interest groups and stakeholders, you have to understand their cause and analyze their power base. Their skillful use of the media can greatly affect public opinion, which in turn affects government and the actions of regulators and legislators and even juries. You should keep your lens open and periodically rethink basic assumptions about who the societal advocates are, what their causes are, what tools they might have available, and where the power to influence really lies.

Nothing Is Off-Limits

Every aspect of your business, including the very premise of your business model, is fair game for external constituencies. The long battle between natural resource companies and environmentalists over such issues as logging, mining, and drilling is by now a somewhat familiar battleground. Environmentalists have been particularly effective in generating support among the general population, although the behavior of some of the fringe elements of the movement—destruction of property and threatened violence—reduces their political effectiveness. And external constituencies aren't confined to the national stage. Wal-Mart deals constantly with community activists trying to prevent the company from building new stores. When they have the opportunity these local activists form networks or ally with other groups with different issues, such as organizations protesting Wal-Mart's labor practices.

The trend toward globalization ensures that more and more

companies will face the challenge of dealing with foreign constituencies. Even as savvy a global executive as Rupert Murdoch found himself repeatedly stymied when he tried to bring satellite television to China. Murdoch had infuriated China's top leadership in 1993 when in a London speech he said that advances in communications technology had "proved an unambiguous threat to totalitarian regimes everywhere." Russia was the regime Murdoch was talking about, but China took his warning as a dire threat. Unfortunately for Murdoch, his speech came only a few months after he had bought STAR TV in Hong Kong, a new satellite television network that reached every corner of China. China responded to his implied threat swiftly, banning private ownership of satellite dishes throughout China.

For four years Murdoch struggled to repair relations with China and have the ban on satellite dishes lifted. He hired consultants, donated money to foundations headed by Chinese leaders' relatives, and even gave one of the leaders' daughters a lucrative book contract, all to no avail. Only after Chinese President Jiang Zemin was scheduled to visit the United States did the Chinese meet with Murdoch, offering him access to the Chinese market in exchange for favorable treatment of Jiang Zemin's visit in Murdoch's many media properties.

Everything Is Transparent

Like it or not, "transparency" is a condition under which every company now operates. It wasn't that long ago that newspapers, magazines, radio, and television constituted "the media." For the most part only the national newspapers and magazines much mattered since they were the only ones with the financial muscle to deploy extensive reporting teams skilled in business topics. What's more, the media was choosy about the topics it covered. Hollywood studios got lots of play while stories about the steel industry were rare. But the growth of the Internet has made it possible for virtually anyone to become a media maven via personal blogs. While most of the millions of blogs get little or no readership, those that do attract an audience are often cause-related and often target a company or an industry. The reporting may not be as thorough, accurate, or unbiased as that done by national newspapers or magazines, but it can be more devastating, particularly when the blogger either works in a company or has sources in it. The company might control its own e-mail network, but nothing can stop a disgruntled employee from passing along information—rumors, conversations, or even purloined documents—via his or her own e-mail account at home.

Some external constituencies are highly skilled in using the media to promote their agendas. The plaintiffs bar has been especially effective in harnessing the power of the press. The railroad industry, for example, was the subject of a damning series of articles about deaths at highway rail crossings caused by the lack of adequate maintenance of crossing signals. Much of the information marshaled by the reporter came straight from the files of lawyers representing the families of those killed or injured. The reporter won a Pulitzer Prize, the lawyers won millions in settlements, and the railroad industry was forced by public opinion to correct its poor maintenance practices at an additional cost of millions and an inestimable loss of reputation.

Laws Come Too Late

Laws and the courts are a lagging indicator of society's evolving values and expectations, and a leader who focuses exclusively on parsing what is legal and illegal according to the law books is putting the company at risk. It is increasingly evident that juries are less than skilled at understanding complex business cases. In many foreign venues courts routinely succumb to societal pressures and expectations and reach decisions that clearly are not warranted by legal technicalities.

Societal trends tend to start in small ways that aren't readily noticed at the level of corporate leaders. Only when those trends have taken on a momentum all their own and are becoming popular topics in the media do they begin to become apparent. By that time it is often too late to do anything proactive and leaders are forced to go on the defensive. Rachel Carson's 1962 book *Silent Spring,* an indictment of the widespread use of pesticides, touched off the environmental movement and Ralph Nader's 1965 book *Unsafe at Any Speed* sparked a demand for safer automobiles. In retrospect it is very difficult to argue against protecting the environment or against seat belts and airbags, but at the time the industries under attack vilified both authors and resisted making changes until new laws forced them to do so.

Similar issues are brewing today, obesity being one of them. Many people doubtless got a chuckle when they heard news reports about two teenagers filing suit against McDonald's, claiming that eating at the Golden Arches twice a day was the root cause of their obesity. A judge rejected the suit. But reconsidered in the context of the Centers for Disease Control and Prevention's warning that obesity is the United States' most important health problem, that suit might best be seen as a warning shot. Already legislation has been introduced to require restaurant chains with more than twenty outlets to provide nutrition information on menus, a requirement that would be both burdensome and expensive. With an estimated 30 percent of American teenagers either overweight or obese, there are emerging campaigns in some communities to get soft-drink machines off school grounds and French fries out of school cafeterias. Any restaurant or food company that offers high-fat-content or high-sugar-content food and isn't already laying plans to ward off suits or legislation has its head in the sand.

Social advocacy organizations have become increasingly adept at both promoting new legislation for their causes and exploiting existing laws. In alliance with an increasingly active (and profitable) class-action legal fraternity, these organizations can mount sustained and sophisticated attacks on companies and even entire industries. There are now more than one hundred companies engaged in asbestos litigation. Johns Manville long ago entered into bankruptcy as a result of asbestos suits. It survived as a company by creating a trust to bear the brunt of liabilities and the company was eventually bought by Warren Buffett and operates today as a private entity. Other companies engaged in asbestos litigation include Ford and General Motors. Several companies have been forced into bankruptcy; examples include Federal-Mogul, Armstrong World Industries, and Owens Corning. They have been unsuccessful in trying to beat back the assault in the courts and resorted to seeking legislation to try to protect their assets.

Many companies employ skilled legal talent that might be able to fend off such attacks on strictly legal grounds. But in the wake of recent corporate scandals, most notably Enron and WorldCom, public opinion has shifted against the business community, creating a deepening sense that companies are obligated not just to follow the letter of the law, but its spirit as well.

Government Can Be An Ally

Such outside pressures don't all come from "do-gooder" organizations. Indeed, the two biggest sources of external interference are extremely apparent to any corporate leader: government and Wall Street. Government in its many manifestations—federal, state, or local, legislative or regulatory—acts in thousands of ways that affect companies and their leaders, from setting minimum wages to approving rezoning requests to protecting industries from import competition.

Governmental interference in business is so extensive and so important that it may come as a surprise that few leaders get enough exposure early in their careers to dealing with government agencies before they reach the CEO's office. Only when they reach the highest levels of the company are they suddenly thrust into the complex and confusing world of Congressional committees, intricate regulations, and bureaucratic inertia. Traditionally, lobbyists and governmental relation staffs did much of the day-to-day work gathering intelligence and ensuring that regulations are met. That has been particularly true in heavily regulated industries—utilities and pharmaceuticals are two obvious ones—that have cadres of experts to handle the rate-making and drug approval processes. But rising executives in those industries at least developed some experience working with important government relations crucial to the company's financial health and well-being. Today, however, the complexity of dealing with government at all levels—federal, state, and local—is increasing. Leaders need the know-how to deal with this complexity as it continues to evolve. This will be especially true of leaders in industries which to this point have had less government involvement in their affairs. Yet there is also a growing awareness in the executive suite that government intervention isn't always burdensome or unwelcome. More and more companies are seeking support in Congress and with the Administration to alleviate some of their most pressing financial concerns, including pension funding and health insurance costs.

Wall Street Is Different

Wall Street vies with government for the title of the most powerful—and time consuming—external constituency. Courting the securities analysts who cover a company was for many years a primary focus of most corporate leaders. Their relationships with analysts could be friendly or hostile, but the two sides knew one another well and the relationships were long-standing. But those days are long gone. Since then another, even more powerful, force has arisen on Wall Street: hedge funds. These huge pools of capital, using an array of sophisticated tools, including mathematical models, prowl the Street for arbitrage opportunities. Conservative managements that amass cash are vulnerable to attack by hedge funds, which move swiftly to buy shares and force changes in corporate strategy—a merger, the sale of assets or recapitalization— that quickly boost the company's stock price. A recent example is Knight Ridder being forced by a hedge fund to be sold to a smaller company against the wishes of the company's CEO and other top leaders.

Distinguishing What's Legitimate

Given the current realities of outside interest groups, you have to know how to identify issues long before they become a serious problem so your company can take a proactive approach to mitigating them. That requires an internal mechanism that brings budding issues to your attention as soon as possible. In many companies the general counsel, public relations, investor relations, and human relations departments are often the first corporate insiders to sense when an issue is becoming something more than a minor nuisance. They have the skills to analyze the issue, the players behind it, and the possible ways to neutralize it. To be proactive, you'll need to shape those departments into a cohesive issue-identification team that can provide early warning of potential problems when there is still time to act and not just react. Still, even those players can be caught up in the emotion of a developing issue or be reluctant to take bad news to the top. Thus it's wise to stay in touch with your own sources outside the company to help you pick up on new groups and issues that are on the rise. Employees who interact with people on the front lines can also help.

As basic as it may sound, something as simple as periodically "googling" the company's name will turn up negative information being spread on the Internet or through the media. Reviewing the bestseller lists for books that have even marginal impact on the company's business can also trigger an effort to learn more and to assess possible long-term risks. It isn't clear precisely what impact the book *Fast Food Nation* had on the growing emergence of the obesity issue, but its publication and rise to the bestseller list are at least symptomatic of growing public concern.

You'll benefit by spending a few hours each month with people who may not share your business acumen but have completely different views and agendas. Not only will you learn from other people, but those contacts can be extremely important in shaping a message if a crisis should erupt. At General Electric, local managers actively participate in the community, a great practice for helping develop relationships. Understanding the issues may require creative ways to engage in dialogue with leaders of special interest groups, such as using a neutral party to mediate discussions designed to hear each other out. Academics at Yale University helped fast food companies and social advocates engage in a dialogue about obesity. When an issue affects your whole industry, it's wise to build relationships with other leaders and engage in the dialogue together. You may not win the point or change other people's minds, but you will be sure you got your thinking—and your intentions—across. As Harvard professors Felix Oberholzer-Gee and Dennis Yao note, in the world of business, actions are largely evaluated on their outcomes, but in the realm of societal forces, intentions and how you approach a special interest group are just as important.

Having identified groups and issues, you have to separate which issues are truly important and which are superficial. Even superficial issues can erode your brand image and affect employee moral, and often the only way to deal with them is through legal remedies. But you can't assume that your business is beyond legitimate criticism, no matter how careful your decisions. A cause that is counter to your business might very well be in the best interest of society.

Global warming is one of the most contentious, pitting huge global industries against a growing number of scientists and environmentalists who contend that carbon-based emissions are setting the stage for profound shifts in the earth's climate. While many corporate leaders urged and support the Bush Administration's rejection of the Kyoto Treaty to regulate such emissions, some of the leading industrial companies in the United States nevertheless recognize the validity of the concerns and the need to find a solution. They are moving proactively to join the movement toward limiting emissions. Among them is General Electric, with its Ecomagination initiative to emphasize environmentally friendly products, from more efficient diesel locomotives to cleaner-burning jet engines and electrical power plants. GE CEO Jeff Immelt readily concedes that its Ecomagination initiative is essentially "a way to sell more products and services," but that doesn't change the fact that GE will be helping its clients avoid or mitigate future liabilities that will almost certainly become expensive issues in the future.

Flexibility in dealing with outside pressures is paramount.

When minor problems surfaced with Intel's new Pentium chip in 1994, Andrew Grove, Intel's president, concluded that the problem would only affect computer users undertaking heavy mathematical computation and even then the problem would be so rare that some other hardware failure would likely crop up first and cause the users to scrap their computers.

Despite demands from computer owners with "Intel Inside," Grove stood firmly on principle and refused to even consider replacing the chip. As the intensity of anti-Intel resentment soared, he then wavered and decided Intel would replace chips only after interviewing a computer owner to determine if the owner needed to do complex math calculations. A furious user base ultimately prevailed and Intel spent some $450 million replacing faulty chips. The money was no small thing, but it didn't compare to the damage done to Intel's reputation. Grove has since conceded that he didn't fully understand how important it was that Intel had established an identity inextricably imprinted on millions of computer owners.

CAUGHT IN THE CROSS FIRE

There is an emerging trend where two or more special interest groups have a deep passion for a societal issue affecting an industry or company in a way that their stands are directly opposite to each other. In such situations, the business leader is caught in a cross fire and may have extreme difficulty finding a win-win solution acceptable to all parties. That's exactly the dilemma Ford Motor Co. faced in 2005 as it sought to steer a safe path between two of the most powerful social forces at work in the United States: the gay community and the religious right. Ford was trapped squarely in the center of a cultural cross fire that is symptomatic of the polarized society in which we live.

In 2002 Ford approached advertising as if it were the straightforward issue it had always been: decide how you want to portray your product, prepare the ads and place them in media whose subscribers fit the overall profile you're targeting. The company undertook an unusually detailed analysis of the brand equity of its seven automobile brands—Ford, Lincoln, Mercury, Volvo, Jaguar, Land Rover, and Mazda—to determine where it might best apply advertising dollars in the increasingly influential gay-oriented media. Ford was no pioneer among automakers seeking to market directly to a gay audience. Subaru of America launched its first targeted gay advertising efforts in 1995 after market research revealed a large proportion of Subaru owners were lesbian. Volvo, the Swedish automaker, had long advertised in gay publications in Europe before it was acquired by Ford. But even before planning a gay-oriented ad strategy Ford had drawn plaudits from the gay community for its highly publicized decision to grant employee benefits to same-sex couples.

Soon after completing its research Ford began advertising its upscale Land Rover and Jaguar marques, along with Volvo, in gay media in the United States. Ford also made corporate contributions to gay organizations and events, often linking its advertising with its support for gay causes. Jaguar and Land Rover advertisements promised to donate one thousand dollars to the Gay and Lesbian Alliance Against Discrimination for every Jaguar sold to members of the group. The gay business community greeted Ford's new marketing effort enthusiastically, hoping it would encourage other large companies to launch their own gay-oriented advertising campaigns.

But the targeted ads, while successful in gaining market share among gays, and the company's policies toward gays drew the ire of anti-gay organizations. In May 2005 the American Family Association, a Christian activist group based in Tupelo, Mississippi, urged its members and other

Christians to boycott Ford products, labeling the automaker "the company which has done the most to affirm and promote a homosexual lifestyle." The AFA put up a website, boycottford.com, criticizing Ford for donating money to gay organizations and conducting diversity workshops for managers that included sexual orientation training. An executive of the AFA charged that Ford was "redefining the definition of the family to include homosexual marriage." The organization urged its members to pressure their local Ford dealers by phone, e-mail, and in person to lobby the company to stop advertising in gay publications and supporting gay organizations and events.

Shortly after the AFA launched the boycott, Ford and some of its dealers agreed to meet with representatives of the group. In exchange for Ford's agreement to meet, the AFA "suspended" the boycott until December 1, 2005. On November 30, following a meeting with Ford executives at its Tupelo headquarters, the AFA announced that the boycott would be canceled.

"They've heard our concerns; they are acting on our concerns," said the Reverend Donald Wildmon, chairman of the AFA. "We are pleased with where we are."

A few days later Ford disclosed that both Jaguar and Land Rover would cease advertising in gay-oriented media, although the company said Volvo would continue to run advertisement in gay publications. A Ford spokesman said the decision to halt the advertisements was made for business reasons and had nothing to do with the AFA boycott or its discontinuation.

The backlash was instant. Gay organizations took to the web, spreading the word of Ford's "capitulation" through countless blogs and barraging the company with e-mail complaints. Rumors of a "formal agreement" between Ford and the AFA were rampant. Some gay organizations threatened to launch their own impromptu boycotts of Ford products unless the company met with them. On December 12, representatives of nearly twenty gay organizations met in Washington with Ford executives, who again denied that the decision to halt advertising was related to the AFA's threatened boycott. After the meeting Ford Chairman William C. Ford Jr. issued a statement that said the company values all people, regardless of their race, religion, sexual orientation, and other differences. At the same time a representative of the gay organizations who attended the meeting said that as a group, "we were pretty united in our extreme disappointment at Ford's willingness to even take a meeting with this right-wing extremist group."

Unbeknownst at the time, Ford also was receiving some pressure from a powerful shareholder who supports gay rights. Alan Hevesi, New York State's Comptroller and the trustee of the New York State and Local Retirement System, which held 9.4 million shares of Ford stock, confirmed later that he had contacted William Ford to voice his displeasure after AFA claimed its victory. In a letter to Ford, Hevesi, a long-time advocate of gay rights, said "I am interested to know what cost/benefit analysis you performed in order to reach the conclusion that ending advertising to that particular customer base would be a positive strategic move for the company." Beyond pointing out the importance of diversity, Hevesi also noted that the gay market is worth an estimated $610 billion annually.

A few days after its meeting with the gay organizations Ford announced that while Jaguar and Land Rover would not resume advertising in gay publications, Ford would run corporate advertisements in the gay media extolling its entire product line with content "that will be appropriate and effective in connecting with the intended audience." Ford did not mention Hevesi's intervention and later denied that the trustee's inquiry had anything to do with the decision to run corporate ads in gay media.

The AFA, not surprisingly, soon reinstated its boycott. "We had an agreement with Ford, worked out in good faith," said Rev. Wildmon. "Unfortunately, some Ford Motor Company officials made the decision to violate the good faith agreement."

Societal pressures on business will continue to increase and so will interventions by governments. Leaders of the future have to like it or at least not resist it and build the know-how to deal with it. Otherwise their organizations may be put on the defensive. Leaders must be psychologically adept to anticipate such forces and deal with them effectively. They need to develop a framework, methodology, and tools and capability in the organization to anticipate them and develop effective solutions. Younger leaders may have something of an advantage in accepting societal pressures on business, but it's a challenge for every leader to develop a methodology and the judgment to handle it well. Clearly, being a business leader in today's world is not for the faint of heart.

How not to be between a rock and a hard place

- Get the management team psychologically prepared for the fact that societal issues will arise and can pick up steam fast given today's high transparency and the Internet.

- As you examine your company's positioning, you need to anticipate what societal issues might be raised and what kinds of advocacy groups might raise them.

- Develop a methodology for dealing with such issues, first in terms of your personal psychology, and second, for the organization. What are your methods for picking up early warning signals of issues that are just emerging or gaining traction? How will you assess the power of various causes?

- Be prepared to exchange information and build bridges with advocacy groups to help shape the issues and solutions. Go on the offensive.

LETTER TO A FUTURE LEADER

Dear Michael:

I was honored to be invited to your graduation from business school, and even more honored to be asked for my advice as you enter the corporate world. It doesn't seem that long ago when your father and I were roommates at business school. It was a different world back then, full of the toughest challenges imaginable, or so we thought. It seems every generation of leaders faces a distinct challenge. Your generation will have to bring clarity and a sense of direction to business in the face of the incredible complexity that characterizes the twenty-first century.

In every job you take, you'll face a dizzying array of factors and considerations. You'll need every ounce of ambition and tenacity to sort through it all. But ambition alone won't be enough to sustain your success. Ultimately, it's the content of your leadership that will count. Given the transparency of today's world, any shortcoming in your know-hows, personal traits, or character (I have no worries there) will be revealed very quickly.

I'm sure you'll have lots of resources available to you to help you develop, but don't put your fate in someone else's hands. Take charge of your development as a leader. I've explained to you the eight know-hows that are universally important. I've attached a summary of them to remind you. Pick one or two that you want to work on and improve, then as you reach a level of competence, continue to refine them as you take on one or two more. You'll find that some of them come more naturally than others. Those are the ones you should focus on and sharpen as you round out your leadership capabilities. Seek out situations that require those know-hows and put yourself to the test.

You could say that being a successful business leader comes down to judgment, that inner voice that tells you which way to go even though the analysis might point to a different path. Each know-how requires it. What you really need to do is improve your batting average in making those judgments so you can trust your instincts. The process of making judgments is largely unconscious, but that doesn't mean it's beyond your control. The more aware you become of your thought process and the more you reflect on it, the more quickly your judgments will improve.

Nobody knows exactly how the mind works, but everybody has some kind of mental model that is the unconscious basis for making judgments on people, the external environment, priorities, and other business issues. I'm sure there have been times when you've come to a conclusion but have had a hard time explaining how you got to it. That's your unconscious mind working. You've formed a mental model based on exposure to different situations. With every new situation, your unconscious mind contrasts what fits and doesn't fit with previous experiences, and your mental model gets updated and expanded.

If you pay attention to those inner thoughts and try to become aware of the adjustments to your mental model, you'll be less likely to repeat the same mistakes and better able to turn practice and experience into real learning. The key is to combine experience with honest self-reflection.

No two situations you encounter will be exactly the same. You should consciously search for the differences in each new situation. Go to work to figure out what's the same, what's different this time, and why. Then when you make a judgment, try to be aware of the key variables or factors that weighed more heavily in your mind and pushed you one way or the other. Later, when you've seen the results of your decision, reflect on whether you chose the right ones. What assumptions did you make? Why did you make those assumptions? What were the sources of information you relied on, and what's the track record of those sources?

Say you're the head of marketing for a business unit and you select someone to be the director of advertising. Three months, six months, a year down the road, take the time to reflect on how well you nailed that person's talents. If she surprised you in some way, what was it you didn't see? Why do you think you missed it? Maybe you were narrowly focused on a particular skill and weren't thinking broadly enough to see the whole person. If you noticed something she had to work on, did you pinpoint what it was and tell her right away, or did you fail to drill to the specifics and drag your feet because you were afraid of offending her? If you passed over someone else who later turned out to be successful in another department, think about what might have held you back. Is it possible that you felt threatened? This kind of self-reflection will make your judgment on people better next time, which in turn will build your self-confidence.

You can speed your progress by learning from other people's experiences too. Look for leaders who have particular strengths in areas you want to work on and watch them carefully. Don't get seduced by superficial things like stature or mental quickness. Take note of other leaders' actions, decisions, and behaviors and watch for the aftermath. They don't have to be your bosses or mentors; they could be your peers. Maybe a colleague of yours is particularly good at reframing issues or probing for specifics.

You seem to be psychologically open to new ideas and new people, and eager to tackle new problems and situations. Those personal attributes will work to your advantage to improve your decisions and allow your mental model and behavior to adjust more quickly. I've seen many bright young people whose inflexible attitudes and rigid thinking slowed their learning. Their mental models got locked in, and they tried to apply exactly the same thinking to every new situation, overlooking the critical differences. Some move up without the recognition that a simple personal trait, like being overly aggressive and shutting other people down, is a ticking time bomb.

As you exercise the know-hows, watch for psychological blockages. The stress of everyday life can take its toll and block your receptors, distort your thinking and behavior. While some young leaders are overconfident and overoptimistic, making snap decisions before they've looked at things from many angles, others hold back because of self-doubt or fear of response. You'll have to make decisions and act on them despite any psychological reservations. Don't be afraid to make mistakes; be more afraid that you won't take the time to learn from them. And don't let defensiveness block your learning. Leaders who continually learn and grow are willing to admit when they don't know something.

While I'm suggesting that you take charge of your own development, you shouldn't expect to do it alone. Design a way to get feedback on your know-hows and find people you can trust to give you legitimate, honest, timely input and who will help you be aware of any psychological distortions. You need a disciplined approach to be the best, like an athlete striving to be a champion.

Another part of taking charge of your development

is seeking out jobs where you'll expand. All the successful leaders I've known have had the benefit of multiple experiences in diverse situations. Some people got into those situations accidentally, but others aggressively sought those opportunities, some taking on jobs others refused to take because they were too difficult. All those experiences got etched in their unconscious minds, interacted with their psychology and emotions, reshaped their mental models, and got reflected in their judgments.

I urge you to seek out the experiences that will allow you to apply your know-how in diverse situations. Don't stay in the same job for ten years and don't do ticket punching, running through a series of positions that create a long resume but not much learning. Stay long enough in a job to test yourself, deepen your knowledge of that area, see the results of your decisions, and refine your instincts. I've always been intrigued by the fast growth of leaders like Jack Welch who became a successful CEO at age forty-five, and Michael Dell who was running a successful company at twenty-nine. Obviously, learning and changing your mental models can happen very fast.

There are times when you will be disappointed, you won't be recognized, or you'll be derailed. Such dark periods can provide great lessons. And don't be surprised if sometime after such an experience, you suddenly find yourself seeing the business in a different way. Everyone knows that human beings go through growth spurts when they're toddlers and adolescents. I see the same thing when it comes to mental growth. It, too, can come in spurts, when for instance you suddenly catch on to the notion of drilling down to the specifics of an issue, and your know-how of judging people, positioning the business, and setting goals and priorities simultaneously improve. Because they're interconnected, the improvement is exponential. It's exhilarating, and an impetus to continue to grow. That's how work can become a source of joy in your life.

It seems the longer I sit and think, the more advice springs to mind. Bear with me as I mention another point that seems worth making. There's no such thing as a renaissance leader, a leader for all seasons and every curve in the road. Every leader has a combination of know-hows and personal attributes that fits some situations better than others. A person who has honed the know-hows and personal traits in turnaround situations might not be prepared to spot the opportunities and handle the risks associated with organic growth. Again, you need to be honest with yourself about your fit in a leadership job. That will help you create your own good luck.

Remember that success is never final. That's a fact twenty-first-century leaders cannot escape. You will have to make a commitment to your ongoing personal growth. I urge you to do so as if the fate of the world depended on it, because in a way, it does. The country's economic standards are not made by economic theories or inventions or technologies. It is leaders, particularly leaders of businesses, that harness the expertise of various disciplines and fund the technologies and apply them, that take the risks in selecting inventions for commercial purposes, who ultimately drive a society's standard of living. You can be part of it by building the content of your personal leadership. Focus on the know-hows of business, become self-aware of how your personal traits affect them, and keep learning. I'm looking forward to sharing in your success.

Best regards,

Ram

THE EIGHT KNOW-HOWS

1. **Positioning and Repositioning:** Finding a central idea for business that meets customer demands and that makes money.
2. **Pinpointing External Change:** Detecting patterns in a complex world to put the business on the offensive.
3. **Leading the Social System:** Getting the right people together with the right behaviors and the right information to make better, faster decisions and achieve business results.
4. **Judging People:** Calibrating people based on their actions, decisions, and behaviors and matching them to the non-negotiables of the job.

5. **Molding a Team:** Getting highly competent, high-ego leaders to coordinate seamlessly.
6. **Setting Goals:** Determining the set of goals that balances what the business can become with what it can realistically achieve.
7. **Setting Laser-Sharp Priorities:** Defining the path and aligning resources, actions, and energy to accomplish the goals.
8. **Dealing with Forces Beyond the Market:** Anticipating and responding to societal pressures you don't control but that can affect your business.

PERSONAL TRAITS THAT CAN HELP OR INTERFERE WITH THE KNOW-HOWS

Ambition—to accomplish something noteworthy BUT NOT win at all costs.

Drive and Tenacity—to search, persist, and follow through BUT NOT hold on too long.

Self-confidence—to overcome the fear of failure, fear of response, or the need to be liked and use power judiciously BUT NOT become arrogant and narcissistic.

Psychological Openness—to be receptive to new and different ideas AND NOT shut other people down.

Realism—to see what can actually be accomplished AND NOT gloss over problems or assume the worst.

Appetite for Learning—to continue to grow and improve the know-hows AND NOT repeat the same mistakes.

COGNITIVE TRAITS THAT
IMPROVE THE KNOW-HOWS

A Wide Range of Altitudes—to transition from the
conceptual to the specific.
A Broad Cognitive Bandwidth—to take in a broad range of
input and see the big picture.
Ability to Reframe—to see things from different perspectives.

ACKNOWLEDGMENTS

This book is based on the talents and wisdom of many people I have been allowed to learn from and observe over the course of my life. I wish to thank my siblings, whose teaching got me started and gave me opportunities they didn't have, and the many brilliant business leaders who have shared their time and insights with me over several decades. I hope they will recognize themselves in the lessons and good examples in this book. Space does not allow me to mention them all by name, but I hope they know how truly grateful I am to them.

I would like to express my deep appreciation to a number of people who helped make this book possible by allowing me to probe and analyze their actions and decisions and the thinking behind them and/or by providing incredibly useful feedback on the book in its various stages: Pramod Bhasin, Frank Blake, Larry Bossidy, Todd Bradley, Ed Breen, Jack Breen, John Brennan, Dick Brown, Peter Cairo, Ben Cammarata, Governor Caperton, Dennis Carey, Richard Carrión, Paul Charron, Bill Conaty, Ian Cook, Dave Cote, Eric Creviston, Mike Critelli, Joe DeAngelo, Peter Dolan, Dennis Donovan, Tony Earley, Maria Luisa Ferré Rangel, Mark Fields, George Francis, Dennis Fritsche, Gordon Fyfe, Ron Gafford, Dick Harrington, Roberto Herencia, Jeff Immelt, Andrea Johnson, Cindy L. Johnson, Lois Juliber, Manfred Kets de Vries, Jack Krol, Roger A. Krone, Carl Liebert, Tom Loarie, Harsh Mariwala, Bill McComb, Ron Meeks, David Murphy, Bob Nardelli, David Novak, Dinesh Paliwal, Kathie Pringle, Paul Raines, Evelyn Rodstein, Dave Ropp, Peter Ross, Joe Ryan, Ivan Seidenberg, Brad Shaw, David A. Smith, Larry Steward, Tom Taylor, Carol Tomé, John Van Scoter, Patrick Wang, Mark Watson, Bob Whitman, Ed Woolard, and Dennis Zeleny.

Geri Willigan, who has worked with me since this book was just an idea and a cache of notes, took the lead in bringing it to fruition. Through discussions over many years, Geri helped me develop and sharpen many of the ideas and stories presented here. Having mastered the concepts and nuances, she used the editorial skills she polished at the *Harvard Business Review* to turn the ideas into a teaching document. I greatly appreciate the combination of analytic skill, writing ability, and high standards she brought to this project.

My editor at Crown, John Mahaney, went far beyond the confines of his job to become a true partner in shaping this book. He invested an incredible amount of mental energy, not to mention time, to ask the questions readers might ask, always searching for clarity and understanding to strike the right balance between a book readers can dig into and really learn from and one that is easy to read. His dedication, expertise, and professionalism are more than any author could hope for.

Doug Sease joined this project with many years of *Wall Street Journal* experience behind him and used his well-honed editorial skills to contribute to the book in many ways. His intelligence, knowledge of the business landscape, and keen editorial eye made the book better at every turn.

John Joyce, my former roommate at Harvard Business School, provided keen insight at key junctures in the book's progress, as he always does. Geoff Colvin, Paul Hemp, Rik Kirkland, Cait Murphy, and Larry Yu also made useful suggestions, all of which are greatly appreciated.

I must thank Cynthia Burr and Carol Davis, the magicians in my office who kept me and this project on track despite their dizzying array of responsibilities, and who seemed able to manufacture time when it was running short. Thanks, too, to Lindsay Orman, who did a great job of coordinating the project at Crown.

Last, thanks to the many up-and-coming leaders who ask me questions in their quest to solve the mystery of what good business leadership is all about. Their curiosity drives me to seek the answers on their behalf.

INDEX

ABOUT THE AUTHOR

RAM CHARAN is a highly sought after business adviser and speaker famous among senior executives for his uncanny ability to solve their toughest business problems. For more than thirty-five years, Dr. Charan has worked behind the scenes with top executives at some of the world's most successful companies, including GE, Verizon, Novartis, Dupont, Thomson, Honeywell, KLM, Bank of America, Home Depot, and MeadWestvaco. He has shared his insights with many others through teaching and writing.

Dr. Charan's introduction to business came early while working in the family shoe shop in the small Indian town where he was raised. He earned an engineering degree in India and soon after took a job in Australia and then in

Hawaii. When his talent for business was discovered, Dr. Charan was encouraged to pursue it. He earned an MBA and doctorate degrees from Harvard Business School, where he graduated with high distinction and was a Baker Scholar. After receiving his doctorate degree, he served on the Harvard Business School faculty.

Dr. Charan is well known for providing advice that is down-to-earth and relevant and that takes into account the real-world complexities of business. Among his recommendations for achieving profitable growth, for example, are to search for "singles and doubles" as well as home runs and to develop what he calls a "growth budget" to instill discipline on growth initiatives. Identified by *Fortune* as the leading expert in corporate governance, Dr. Charan is helping boards go beyond the requirements of Sarbanes-Oxley and the New York Stock Exchange by providing practical ways to improve their group dynamics. Boards, CEOs, and senior-most human resource executives often seek his advice on talent planning and key hires.

Many people have come to know Dr. Charan through in-house executive education programs. His energetic, interactive teaching style has won him several awards. He won the Bell Ringer Award at GE's famous Crotonville Institute and Best Teacher Award at Northwestern. He was among *Business-Week*'s top ten resources for in-house executive development programs.

Over the past decade, Dr. Charan has captured his business insights in numerous books and articles. In the past five years, Dr. Charan's books have sold more than two million copies. These include the bestseller *Execution: The Discipline of Getting Things Done* and *Confronting Reality*, both coauthored with Larry Bossidy, *What the CEO Wants You to Know, Boards at Work, Every Business Is a Growth Business, Profitable Growth*, and *Boards That Deliver*. A frequent contributor to *Fortune*, Dr. Charan has written two cover stories,

"Why CEOs Fail" and "Why Companies Fail." His other articles have appeared in *Financial Times, Harvard Business Review, Director's Monthly,* and *Strategy & Business.*

Dr. Charan has served on the Blue Ribbon Commission on Corporate Governance and was elected a Distinguished Fellow of the National Academy of Human Resources. He is on the board of Austin Industries and The Six Sigma Academy. He is a director designate of Tyco. Dr. Charan is based in Dallas, Texas.